The New Futures of Exclusion

Daniel Briggs · Luke Telford ·
Anthony Lloyd · Anthony Ellis

The New Futures of Exclusion

Life in the Covid-19 Aftermath

Daniel Briggs
School of Social Sciences
Northumbria University
Newcastle Upon Tyne, UK

Luke Telford
School for Business and Society
University of York
York, UK

Anthony Lloyd
School of Social Sciences
Humanities & Law
Teesside University
Middlesbrough, UK

Anthony Ellis
School of Social and Political Sciences
University of Lincoln
Lincoln, UK

ISBN 978-3-031-41865-5   ISBN 978-3-031-41866-2 (eBook)
https://doi.org/10.1007/978-3-031-41866-2

© The Editor(s) (if applicable) and The Author(s), under exclusive license to Springer Nature Switzerland AG 2023

This work is subject to copyright. All rights are solely and exclusively licensed by the Publisher, whether the whole or part of the material is concerned, specifically the rights of translation, reprinting, reuse of illustrations, recitation, broadcasting, reproduction on microfilms or in any other physical way, and transmission or information storage and retrieval, electronic adaptation, computer software, or by similar or dissimilar methodology now known or hereafter developed.
The use of general descriptive names, registered names, trademarks, service marks, etc. in this publication does not imply, even in the absence of a specific statement, that such names are exempt from the relevant protective laws and regulations and therefore free for general use.
The publisher, the authors, and the editors are safe to assume that the advice and information in this book are believed to be true and accurate at the date of publication. Neither the publisher nor the authors or the editors give a warranty, expressed or implied, with respect to the material contained herein or for any errors or omissions that may have been made. The publisher remains neutral with regard to jurisdictional claims in published maps and institutional affiliations.

This Palgrave Macmillan imprint is published by the registered company Springer Nature Switzerland AG
The registered company address is: Gewerbestrasse 11, 6330 Cham, Switzerland

Paper in this product is recyclable.

Foreword

As one of the architects of the ultra-realist research programme in social sciences, it's always a pleasure to see its recommended methods, theoretical framework, and principal aim employed to good effect. Seeing it expertly applied to a globally significant cluster of phenomena such as that associated with the recent Covid-19 pandemic is especially heartening. The multiple award-winning authors of this short and accessible text have an enviable track record in the production and dissemination of ultra-realist research, which demands that we confront reality square on and utilise our provisionally best methods and concepts in our efforts to understand its events, processes and human reactions. This book is another valuable addition to their list.

The pandemic came and at least partially departed, leaving behind haunting memories that tend to be a rather disconcerting mixture of trauma, relief, cynicism, and serenity. The bug was scary yet not unprecedented in its health risks, the lockdown juxtaposed trauma with comfort, the vaccine disturbed yet soothed us, the governmental measures were organised chaos pushing public incredulity close to the realm of nihilism, and the socioeconomic wreckage is dispiriting yet, for some, brimming with opportunities. In the midst of such confusion, the jury is still out on the management of the pandemic and shows little sign of returning an agreed majority verdict at any point in the foreseeable future. Heated arguments, some locked into dyads of unrelenting ferocity, are still ongoing.

Digging down as far as we can go for the moment, the pandemic and its reactions brought back into stark relief the ancient tension that exists between freedom and authority. The episode, some say, showed us who is in control of our lives—not just a self-organising 'system' in which we are all entrapped, but a system presided over by active agents who revealed their identities, we suspect, as the reaction took shape. A residue still remains of the temporary wholesale reorganisation of our lives imposed upon us by these agents—scientists, medics, corporate chiefs, and compliant politicians. Home life, education, work, consumption, and applied technology were all affected and are in important ways no longer what they were. New forms of social exclusion took shape to affirm the claim that it is indeed an inherent aspect of neoliberalism's world. People were not simply excluded from society, but also, as Simon Winlow and I have argued in the past (Winlow & Hall, 2013), society was excluded from many dimensions of human life. During the lockdowns and vaccination programmes, both forms assumed alarming proportions and appeared to mutate into new and intense variants. The pariah status dealt out to those who refused vaccination was a particularly stark example of divisive ideological attempts to dispense with rational debate and consign naysayers to the social margins.

While our disciplines still speak the tired postmodern narrative of fragmented culturalism and individualism, the global rollout of the lockdowns and vaccination programmes shouted out coordination and compliance on a scale we haven't seen since World War II. Committed liberals worry that as we examine this coordination we might enter the territory of 'conspiracy theory'. Despite the transparency of the programmes, some commentators suspected that strings were being pulled by corporate agents operating behind the scenes. As alarm bells rang, the managers of mass media and social media were quick to denounce such takes as dangerous fantasies set to falsely accuse and endanger specific social groups. However, the suppression was so hysterical, rapid, predictable, and coordinated it served only to further arouse suspicions. If we want to avoid disappearing down conspiracy theory's dark rabbit-hole, which is certainly not the place where thinking people should reside, we would be better off encouraging free, open, and rational debate. But this is not what the neoliberal elite want. Their fear of populism easily matches populist fear.

As this book emphasises, the pandemic and its reactions have renewed interest in the politics of fear. Examples of divisive rhetoric and coordinated fearmongering were periodically revealed by leaks of the sort of statements politicians seem unable to resist uttering. Principal among these was the demonisation of the 'anti-vaxxers' and anyone who complained too loudly about the deleterious effects of the lockdowns. Here the authors' application of ultra-realist principles proved especially useful—a mixed-methods approach of ethnography, interviews, and observation couched in a sophisticated and flexible theoretical framework helped to reveal both diverse and similar human experiences and perceptions during the lockdown. The ultra-realist aims of confronting inconvenient aspects of reality squarely in the face and moving beyond identitarian fragmentation while still acknowledging differential outcomes were met rather masterfully here. This constituted the empirical spine of the book. The research identified the 'anti-vaxxer' as the new scapegoat specific to the pandemic. In doing so, it showed neoliberalism to be a way of life that runs on the fostering of objectless anxiety sustained by socioeconomic insecurity, censorship, and disinformation, a permanently insecure climate in which new objects of fear can be constructed at will in ways that are politically convenient at any given time. The anti-vaxxer can now take its place in neoliberalism's rogues' gallery, along with populists, communists, conservatives, nationalists, and all the other usual suspects.

The anti-vaxxer is a pristine, clearly identifiable rogue who defies the new neoliberal scientific-political authority flexing its muscles on behalf of the corporations. In the wake of the now spent postmodernism that has done its job of helping neoliberalism destroy the political sovereignty that operated at national and international levels, the concentrated corporate and media power of the plutocratic elite can triumph.

Global coordination was there for all to see. As the chorus line of leading politicians all around the world mouthed the same platitudes on the path to the reparative slogan 'build back better', they acted as a fitting advertisement for neoliberalism's global credentials, which are comforting for believers but terrifying for all who dissent. The great risk was that such obvious coordination was a conspiracy theorist's wet dream. Indeed, the more outlandish conspiracy theories leapt into circulation, but the only impact they had was to assist neoliberal forces to submerge thoughtful analyses of the World Economic Forum and other organisations involved in neoliberalism's global coordination (see Green and Fazi 2023). Such analyses did not deny the deleterious health impact of the virus on vulnerable individuals, nor did they point the finger towards a singular conspiratorial group, but focused instead on a multipolar elite and the boost subsequent fearmongering gave to the authoritarian suppression of dissent and open debate.

This book is the latest in that line of thoughtful analyses. It begs a crucial question broader than the pandemic and its reaction—if this coordinated ideological power does indeed exist and is to varying degrees permanently active, which other debates are being stifled in other vital areas, such as political economy and geopolitics? Certainly, we can say, neoliberalism does not value freedom of debate and democratic political action. The form of freedom it champions is restricted to dispensing with the market regulations that hamper business activity and personal enrichment—the freedom of Tawney's pike rather than his minnows (see Tawney, 1952).

As the argument proceeds it becomes clear that ideology of 'capitalist realism'—that no feasible alternative to current forms of capitalism and liberal democracy can ever exist—has helped neoliberalism shunt us into a genuine plutocracy comprised of financiers, corporate chiefs, and successful entrepreneurs. As new and potentially virulent forms of populist or leftist dissent arose after the GFC, the pandemic gave the neoliberal elite the opportunity to construct appropriate forms of managing or, when necessary, crushing it. As rapidly advancing information technology now moves the technocratic elite through surveillance towards algorithmic governance (see Kuldova, 2022), there is no sign of the hopeful 'synopticon' giving us democratic balance. We have no means of looking back at the surveillance state in any revealing way beyond its symptoms, i.e. chronicling random incidents of hacking, police brutality, and suchlike as they occur. In a true democracy we would be snooping only on ourselves, but in a technocratically enhanced plutocracy surveillance takes its most sinister turn, even more sinister than previous dysfunctional, inept, and short-lived attempts at totalitarian governance. These older systems were clumsy, transparent forms of 'open closure', happy to warn people of the surveillance and punishment systems that bore down on them, thus on a daily basis revealing the basic shape of what they were up against and fueling clear-sighted resistance. Neoliberalism's constant suffocation of meaningful dissent and alternative thinking while it celebrates compliance, incorporated dissent, and impossible fantasised alternatives has led only to confusion, cynicism, democratic disengagement, and political homelessness.

The three great twenty-first century crises of financial crash, accelerated global warming, and pandemic—coming early in the century as crises often do—have together supplied grist to the mill of the 'Great Reset', the capitalists' open project of reorganising the global economy along the supposed lines of ecological care and social inclusion. But the non-negotiable caveat is that the project, which will require sweeping infrastructural renewal and is likely to be hugely profitable, must remain in the hands of private investors and corporations. However, the austerity, inflation, unemployment, and general insecurity experienced by western populations since 2008 are making the positive side of neoliberalism's ideological project increasingly difficult. Economic collapse after the lockdown, continued surveillance, and inflationary pressure have dealt neoliberalism quite serious body blows, fueling inarticulate populist dissent and cynical detachment in roughly equal measures. This has meant potential symbolic gains for the planned economies of the East, emboldening the BRICS bloc and boosting its impetus to expand its membership and move towards global decoupling.

Neoliberalism puts a lot of effort and expense into the ideological exercise of demonising the BRICS 'regimes' as totalitarian. However, whereas BRICS authoritarianism, where it exists, is open and managed, liberalism has always preferred to soft-pedal and conceal or even deny its own authoritarianism as it poses as the champion of freedom. The convergence of the three crises has compelled neoliberal authority to pedal as hard as any other regime, often in full public view. As the full collusion of neoliberalism's left and right mainstream wings in authoritarian measures became transparent—more so during the pandemic—cynicism and political homelessness, with strangled and inarticulate cries of dissent echoing in the background, have become more firmly embedded in western culture.

It is in this context that the book examines the human impact of the vaccine campaign and the ideological campaign that accompanied it. After first reminding us of the authors' previous research on the lockdown and its effects, it reveals the impact of big pharma, technocracy and digital surveillance, media complicity, vaccine mandates, and the ideological war waged against those reluctant to take the vaccines. Mental health, social life, educational outcomes, interpersonal violence, business, and jobs have all been badly affected. In the absence of a coherent left, dissent became skewed to the libertarian right, neoliberalism's political cousin, which further tarnished the left's already tattered reputation and ensured that dissent could find no political direction away from the current neoliberal order.

Following on from classic works such as Green and Fazi's *Covid Consensus* (2023), this book shows us how the neoliberal tail that has been wagging the political dog for over forty years has capitalised on a crisis to further establish itself as the governor of our lives. The corporate techno-pharma complex, supposedly replete with scientific evidence, can virtually compel governments to act on its behalf. Behind that, the immensely powerful global investment and asset management industry can lick its lips as it anticipates high returns in a world undergoing tectonic geopolitical shifts and moving towards an energy transition. Neoliberal governance can expect its arbitrary measures to be met with a combination of naïve compliance, cynical detachment, and marginalised dissent. As the authors stress, the left's simplistic response of "totalitarian lies declaring a state of emergency" simply does not aid our understanding. The virus, which is still around, is real, supplying experienced ideologues with a hugely convincing object of fear to draw upon neoliberalism's normalised climate of anxiety, steering the majority towards compliance and most of the rest towards domesticated forms of dissent. The liberal left, in its current condition of disarray and still fixated on older, obsolete forms of totalitarian power (see Winlow & Hall, 2023), is incapable of thinking through neoliberalism's uniquely effective form of power. Thus it cannot organise a coherent political opposition. The ultra-realist approach adopted in this book and others like it can help us to break out of liberalism's tunnel, clear our heads, and take a few steps towards that goal.

May 2023

Steve Hall
Teesside University
Middlesbrough, UK

References

Green, T., & Fazi, T. (2023). *The covid consensus: The global assault on democracy and the poor—A critique from the Left*. Hurst Publishers.

Kuldova, T. (2022). *The compliance-industrial complex: The operating system of a pre-crime society*. Palgrave Pivot.

Tawney, R. H. (1952[1931]). Equality. George Allen and Unwin.

Winlow, S., & Hall, S. (2013). *Rethinking social exclusion: The end of the social?* Sage.

Winlow, S., & Hall, S. (2023). *The death of the left: Why we must begin from the beginning again*. Policy Press.

Contents

1	A Brief Return to the Future	1
2	Crystal Ball Gazing: The Failure of Lockdowns, Restrictions, and the Pretext to the Covid-19 Vaccine	19
3	*Harmalogical Pharmacology* and the Covid-19 Vaccine	55
4	Technocratic Feudalism, Digital Apartheids, and the New Surveillance Governance	93
5	Asymptomatic Freedom, Resistance, and the 'Anti-vaxxers'	119
6	Heavy Hands and Iron Fists Against High Social Fevers	151
7	New Futures of Exclusion	183
Index		195

About the Authors

Dr. Daniel Briggs is Professor in Criminology and Sociology working in the School of Social Sciences at Northumbria University, Newcastle Upon Tyne, UK. As a researcher, writer, and interdisciplinary academic who studies social problems, he has undertaken ethnographic research into social issues from street drug users to terminally ill patients; from refugees to prostitutes; and from gypsies to gangs and deviant youth behaviours. His recent book *Dead End Lives: Drugs and Violence in the City Shadows* (2017, Policy Press), won the Division of International Criminology's Outstanding Book Award 2018 (selected by the American Society of Criminology). His most recent books are *Climate Changed: Refugee Border Stories and the Business of Misery* (2020, Routledge) and *Hotel Puta: A Hardcore Ethnography of a Luxury Brothel* (2023, RJ4All Publications). He is also co-author of *Researching the Covid-19 Pandemic* (2021, Bristol University Press) and *Lockdown: Social Harm in the Covid-19 Era* (2021, Palgrave).

Dr. Luke Telford is Lecturer in Criminal Justice and Social Policy working in the School for Business and Society at the University of York, York, UK. His main research interests are broad and include political economy, politics, uneven geographical development and 'left behind' places, qualitative research, and critical social theory. Luke has published widely on political dissatisfaction, deindustrialisation, left behind places, and the Covid-19 pandemic. He is the author of *English Nationalism and its Ghost Towns* (Routledge, 2022) and the lead author of *Levelling Up the UK Economy: The Need for Transformative Change* (Palgrave Pivot, 2022). He is also co-author of *Researching the COVID-19 Pandemic* (Bristol University Press, 2021) and *Lockdown: Social Harm in the COVID-19 Era* (Palgrave, 2021).

Dr. Anthony Lloyd is a Professor in Criminology at Teesside University, UK. He is an interdisciplinary academic who combines empirical research with the development of new theoretical frameworks. His main research interests combine workplace sociology, criminological theory and social harm. He is particularly interested in blending analysis of the workplace with emerging theoretical frameworks around 'harm' to understand experiences of work, initially in low-paid, insecure, and flexible forms of labour, but more generally across different experiences of work and labour market sector. He has published widely in this area, including *The Harms of Work: An Ultra-Realist Account of the Service Economy* (2018, Bristol University Press). He is also co-author of *Researching the Covid-19 Pandemic* (2021, Bristol University Press), *Lockdown: Social Harm in the Covid-19 Era* (2021, Palgrave), and *Making Sense of Ultra-Realism* (2022, Emerald).

Dr. Anthony Ellis is a critical, interdisciplinary scholar with interests in violence, criminological theory, and social harm. He was awarded the British Society of Criminology Critical Criminology book prize in 2016 for his monograph *Men, Masculinities and Violence: An Ethnographic Study* (Routledge). His monograph was based upon 2 years of ethnographic research with men in deprived communities in Northern England engaged in violence and crime. He was also awarded Best Blog of 2020 by the British Society of Criminology. He has written widely about violence, masculinity, trauma, social harm, and the Covid-19 pandemic. He is also co-author of *Researching the Covid-19 Pandemic* (2021, Bristol University Press) and *Lockdown: Social Harm in the Covid-19 Era* (2021, Palgrave).

List of Tables

Table 2.1 Population and Covid-19 'cases' in various African countries 31

Table 3.1 Constitutional symptoms reported to the VAERS (see Mushtaq et al., 2022: 5) 78

1

A Brief Return to the Future

The SARs-CoV-2 (hereafter Covid-19) pandemic represents the most significant and disruptive event of the twenty-first century so far (Briggs et al., 2021a; Hall, 2022). The consequences of this event were so far reaching that there are very few individuals alive today who lived through the pandemic that could say their life was not in some way, however small, affected by it. The core governmental response to the pandemic, what became commonly known as 'lockdown' policies, included a range of non-pharmaceutical interventions (NPIs) such as stay-at-home orders, social distancing, curfews, school closures, and the curtailing of sections of national economies. These control measures, which were rapidly implemented as the virus began to circulate, were prior to 2020 the kinds of interventions one reads about in dystopian fiction rather than structural conditions that could become a daily reality for most of the world's population (Briggs, 2022; Foster et al., 2021; Žižek, 2021).

Yet, as we write this in Spring 2023, amid the various crises that now engulf the globe in the post-pandemic era, practices that became part of people's daily routines—mask wearing, two-metre social distancing, working from home when possible, congregating in front of the television for the daily press conferences—feel like a distant memory. So distant, in fact, it feels like the pandemic, and the restricted social lives that most people experienced throughout that period (Green & Fazi, 2023), have now largely been eclipsed by new crises dominating news coverage and political debates, particularly following Russia's invasion of Ukraine in February 2022. Since the large-scale rollout of the vaccine programme, which started in December 2020 after the Pfizer-BioNTech vaccine was approved for usage in the United Kingdom (UK), alongside the cessation of social distancing and other measures, there seems to have been little time to pause and critically reflect upon what was a significant period in modern history. Attention has turned elsewhere, as new threats to the global economy and further geographical instability have emerged in the pandemic's aftermath. The global inflationary crisis and the escalation of tensions between Russia and the West have rapidly replaced concerns with the virus and the unprecedented measures that were enacted in response. Things have moved on very quickly. Authoritarian figures of the East are now, once again, regarded by the West as the enemies of freedom and civilisation, not the microscopic pathogen of Covid-19.

While these new crises demand attention, there is a pressing scholarly urge to pause and critically reflect on an event that, for a temporary period, fundamentally reordered social, cultural, economic, and political life globally (Briggs et al., 2021b; Green & Fazi, 2023; Hall, 2022). While some of the routine aspects of daily life and social organisation such as work and education have now returned, a residue remains. One in five children in the UK is now persistently absent from school (Adams, 2023). Patterns of remote or hybrid work have changed (Lloyd, 2022) and the knock-on effect for high streets and city centres is a noted feature of post-pandemic recovery (Hambleton, 2020). The disruption during the pandemic period possesses an indelible quality that leaves important questions to be answered, especially concerning pandemic governance and the political and economic future of nation states and the globe (Gerbaudo, 2021). Recent events in the UK, for example, provide an additional impetus to examine aspects of government action, or inaction, during the pandemic. Lockdown policies came under the spotlight in March 2023 following the release of what was termed the 'Lockdown Files', revealing the UK's former Health Secretary Matt Hancock's private

WhatsApp exchanges with other health officials (Lockdown Files, 2023). Messages indicating that the government needed to 'frighten the pants off everyone with the new strain' (Lockdown Files, 2023) have provided further justification to those commentators questioning the efficacy of many nation states' management of the pandemic and the use of fear to ensure greater compliance with the measures that were implemented (Dodsworth, 2021; Senger, 2023).

This dovetails neatly with circumspection concerning the efficacy of lockdowns that, at the time, were considered justifiable on the grounds of reducing Covid-19 transmission, hospitalisations, and saving lives. Gradually, evidence from a range of research studies points towards their potentially negligible impact upon transmission levels as well as their unintended social harms around the globe (for example, see: Bendavid et al., 2021; Briggs et al., 2021a; Chin et al., 2021; Foster et al., 2021; Green & Fazi, 2023; Woolhouse, 2022), something to which we will dedicate some of our attention in this book. In February 2023, the 5th US circuit court of appeals blocked the Biden administration's demand for all federal employees to be vaccinated against Covid-19 (McGill, 2023). Although the pandemic recedes into the background noise of daily life for most of us, in some ways we are still working through the legacy of the decisions that were made from early 2020 onwards.

Based upon a global multi-phase, mixed-methods research project which began in March 2020 (Briggs et al., 2021a), this book considers aspects of the latter stages of the Covid-19 pandemic. We consider the new forms of social exclusion and division that accompany policy directives such as vaccination mandates and vaccine passports. The aim of our global research study was to follow and understand the impact of the pandemic, particularly the lockdown policies.[1] From early into the pandemic, we tracked the public's attitudes, opinions, and the impacts of Covid-19 and governmental responses from across the globe and adapted our approach with each new phase of the pandemic. This involved online surveys, remote semi-structured interviews, digital ethnography, traditional ethnography, and a desk-based review of as much relevant literature as we could find. With such an organic methodology, we have

---

[1] For a more exhaustive explanation of our general research approach see (Briggs et al., 2021b).

been able to offer insight into consumer habits (Briggs et al, 2020), child abuse, and the future implications for violence (Ellis et al., 2021a; Ellis, 2022), working conditions and experiences of employees in care homes (Briggs et al., 2021c) and the UK National Health Service (Lloyd et al., 2023). We have addressed the impact on workers and service users in child protection and social work (Briggs et al., 2021d), considered implications for patterns of work more broadly (Lloyd, 2022), and conceptualised the idea of sacrifice during the pandemic (Ellis et al., 2021b). Finally, we have theorised the pandemic in the context of dystopia (Briggs, 2022) and considered the implications of vaccine passports (Telford et al., 2022).

In our previous book—*Lockdown: Social Harm in the Covid-19 Era* (2021)—we offered a detailed account that provided a balance of harm argument around the merits and flaws of lockdowns. That represents this book's natural point of departure: according to many, including Woolhouse (2022) and Green and Fazi (2023), lockdown was conceived to one degree or another as a temporary injunction to buy time until a vaccine was ready. Given our previous work has analysed the impact of that temporary injunction, our focus turns here to the vaccination programme, vaccine mandates and passports that characterised the latter stages of the pandemic.

We focus upon the Covid-19 vaccine and what many regarded as coercive and often aggressive efforts by some governments to vaccinate their populations (Green & Fazi, 2023; Telford et al., 2022). Data for this book was gathered from the beginning of 2021 until the summer of 2022 and is derived from several sources. This includes an anonymous online survey which generated 625 responses from 42 countries including the UK, Germany, Canada, South Africa, and New Zealand; 25 in-depth open-ended qualitative interviews on Zoom with individuals who had completed the survey and then consented to a more detailed discussion; 100 hours of research time in 10 Facebook forums dedicated to discussions on Covid-19 related issues; and our own ethnographic observations both within the UK and Spain. Our questioning revolved around the Covid-19 vaccine and the respective mandates put in place to encourage people into vaccination. We chose to focus on those who were critical of vaccine mandates or hesitant towards the vaccination as, at the time, they were the most publicly criticised group. We also wanted to understand the motivations to avoid vaccination and to think critically about narratives of 'anti-vaxxers', which were seemingly free from nuance and routinely applied pejoratively.

Perhaps unsurprisingly, then, almost all our participants in this book had refused to take the Covid-19 vaccine. Those who had been vaccinated were sceptical and often reported feeling a sense of regret for having done so. This book aims to understand how and why they were unconvinced about the vaccine, situating this scepticism within the wider context of policy initiatives that seemingly exacerbated forms of inequality and created new social divisions and exclusions. The book seeks to push beyond the rather simplistic analyses of some commentators on issues surrounding vaccination during the Covid-19 pandemic. Such commentators have often resorted to dismissing people who are critical of lockdown policies as 'Covid-deniers', 'Corona-clowns', 'Covid-sceptics', or 'anti-vaxxers' (Briggs et al., 2021b; Green & Fazi, 2023), stifling scholarly debate on important issues. There was also a crucial conflation of *anti-vaccination* and *anti-vaccine mandate* that was often overlooked in much media commentary, government rhetoric, and academic debate.

It is indicative of our fractured and atomised social climate (Raymen, 2022; Telford, 2022; Winlow & Hall, 2022) that we ought to point this out at the outset—however, we are not 'Covid-19 deniers' or 'anti-vaxxers'. Regardless of the policies enacted by politicians during the pandemic, we know that this infectious disease would have caused untold suffering to many people across the world. We have all previously been infected with the virus, and we know friends of friends who have died of/ with Covid-19. Our parents are elderly, indeed, we have family members who were categorised within the high-risk category during the pandemic. Equally, we know people who died abandoned in care homes as a consequence of lockdown and social distancing policies. We know people whose health conditions have deteriorated as a consequence of cancelled appointments, screening checks, and operations because post-pandemic, the ramifications of converting a health system around Covid-19 backfired. Finally, we also know people who have had medical confirmation that ongoing health issues are linked to their Covid-19 vaccination.

However, as critical interdisciplinary social scientists, we believe it is incumbent upon us to ask searching questions about government policies, especially the structural implications of mandatory Covid-19 vaccinations and vaccine passports particularly in terms of inequality, social exclusion, and division. As we entered the latter stages of the pandemic and began moving into a post-pandemic world, we were principally concerned with questions such as what new forms of social harm and exclusion have these policies created? How did these measures affect pre-existing social divisions? And what are the social, cultural, political, and economic implications, both in the present and for the future? These questions are the subject of this book. Before outlining the book's structure in more detail, and how it provides additional layers of analysis to our previous publications, a short detour is required to remind readers of the neoliberal context into which the virus emerged and signpost to the key theoretical ideas that will be presented in the forthcoming chapters.

Uneven Terrain: The Unequal Backdrop to the Pandemic

While remaining attuned to global geographical nuances, it is fair to say that the Covid-19 virus arrived as the structural tremors of the 2008 global financial crisis were still being felt across much of the world. Austerity, myriad economic inequality, and the rise of political dissatisfaction, particularly expressed through the Brexit vote and the election of Donald Trump as the President of the United States of America (USA) in 2016 (Telford, 2022), were just some examples of what had come to be regarded as the morbid symptoms of an interregnum in Western nations. Neoliberal capitalism was claimed to be nearing an end; but a new system had not emerged to replace it (Sassoon, 2021; Streeck, 2016). Drawing upon Margaret Thatcher's famous 1980s maxim that 'there is no alternative' to neoliberalism, Mark Fisher (2009) had deemed this period, and the several decades preceding it, the era of 'capitalist realism'.

Following the collapse of Social Democracy in the West in the 1970s and state-planned Communism in the East embodied by the Fall of the Berlin Wall in 1989, this was an epoch in which there was no other economic system considered politically practical or even socially imaginable (Fisher, 2009). The period of *capitalist realism* was accompanied by a growing apolitical culture of consumption, individualistic spectacle, and hedonistic pleasure (Raymen & Smith, 2019). Mainstream political parties converged upon the political centre-ground, while politics itself became largely akin to a neoliberal technocracy devoid of alternative visions of the future (Hochuli et al., 2021; Telford, 2022; Winlow & Hall, 2022). These trends in mainstream politics co-existed with the greater accumulation of wealth in Western nations, alongside increased economic inequality (Atkinson, 2020; Dorling, 2015). A significant proportion of wealth generated during this period was accumulated by a plutocratic elite, who were able to enhance their power and influence over political systems in a way that had not been witnessed for several centuries (Atkinson, 2020).

The 2008 financial crisis dealt a considerable blow to neoliberalism and its central ideological principles, not least given the considerable sums of state money provided to support banks. This damage, though, did not prove to be fatal. Despite large-scale riots and the emergence of political protest movements in various nations, epitomised by The Occupy Movement which spread from New York to countries around the world including Australia, France, Germany, Netherlands, New Zealand, and the UK, an alternative vision capable of attracting significant public support was neither conceived nor implemented (Winlow et al., 2015). Mainstream politics remained largely unmoved by the inadequacies and contradictions that the financial crisis had exposed, with parties in Britain and Europe generally agreeing that reduced state expenditure and wage suppression within the public sector were necessary responses (Mitchell & Fazi, 2017; Winlow & Winlow, 2022). Given that political and economic policy had not shifted substantially in response to the financial crisis, the question of how neoliberalism might end became increasingly subject to debate (Mitchell & Fazi, 2017; Peck, 2013; Streeck, 2016; Winlow & Hall, 2022). Following the work of French philosopher Alain Badiou (2007), Winlow and Hall (2013) settled on the transformative potential of a catastrophic global *Event* that they claimed might bring into even clearer view the inadequacies and injustices of neoliberal capitalism and stimulate its succession. As we know, in

2020 such a catastrophic and global *Event* did unfold. Covid-19 spread across the world's continents, from Eastern to Western nations, causing a chain reaction of governance measures to control it.

Yet, the significant transformation of our political economic system in the wake of the pandemic does not seem to have fully materialised (see Briggs et al, 2020). Not yet at least. This is despite the significant disruption caused by both the virus and lockdown policies (Foster et al., 2021; Green & Fazi, 2023). The inadequacies of the neoliberal state were further revealed as Covid-19 spread across national state borders, suspended lengthy global supply chains, and overwhelmed fragile and under-resourced healthcare systems (Jones & Hameiri, 2022a, 2022b; Lloyd et al., 2023). By contrast, state-planned, authoritarian regimes of the Far East seemed to fare better, arguably due in part to more recent experiences with viral epidemics that had negligible impacts upon Western nations and the presence of a well-resourced infrastructure for the production and manufacture of goods. Some speculated that the Covid-19 pandemic represented China's Sputnik moment (Hochuli et al., 2021); a symbolic victory in the new Cold War between state-planned capitalism of the East and its lightly regulated variant in the West. However, any symbolic gains in this respect were potentially damaged by China's, albeit short-lived, pursuit of a 'Zero Covid' policy that only temporarily suppressed the virus and further tainted the state's reputation on human rights.

Shortly after the pandemic was declared, the founder of the World Economic Forum (WEF), Klaus Schwab, with Thierry Malleret, published *The Great Reset*,[2] which outlined how the virus exposed various societal inequalities that had worsened during neoliberalism's reign. They argued that current systems of governance and infrastructure within many countries that, it had been presumed, would be best prepared to respond to a pandemic such as the UK and USA, fared badly

---

[2] This book ignited a range of 'conspiracy theories' about the pandemic, including how the pandemic was pre-orchestrated to fundamentally change the world especially in light of the ongoing environmental crisis (see: BBC, 2021). The book, though, outlines some important policy proposals for a more progressive world, while it is well trodden ground within the political economy literature that capitalist crises provide opportunities for epochal change (Harvey, 2023; Mitchell & Fazi, 2017; Streeck, 2016). As we will also see in Chapter 4, what was cast as a 'conspiracy theory' during the Covid-19 pandemic often quickly became a reality.

in terms of Covid-19 infections and mortalities. Schwab and Malleret (2020) argued that the pandemic provided an opportunity to '*reset*' the world by altering the organisation and management of economies to make them both economically and ecologically more just. Without question, the pandemic exposed governance structures in neoliberal states to be highly dysfunctional in times of crisis or acute stress, exemplified by failures to produce or procure enough personal protective equipment (PPE) for frontline healthcare workers (Jones & Hameiri, 2022a).

With hindsight, the dogma of free markets now very much resembles *"the rusty remains of a gullible era"* (Gerbaudo, 2021: 2) that oversaw the contraction and outsourcing of various health services during neoliberalism's austerity phase across 2010/20. This would prove problematic as the pandemic developed. Like the global 2008 financial crisis over a decade earlier, the Covid-19 pandemic signalled the distance between neoliberal rhetoric and neoliberalism in practice, specifically the apparent lack of reliance upon the state to support 'free' markets (Mitchell & Fazi, 2017; Winlow & Winlow, 2022). Under mounting pressure, many nation states had little choice but to authorise large-scale expenditure on furlough programmes, business support, and financial assistance to large sections of the public. Estimates suggest that in the UK, for instance, between £310 and £410 billion was spent principally upon public services, business support, and the furlough scheme (Brien & Keep, 2022). Such intervention, like the financial support provided to banks over a decade earlier, exposed the myths that had been used frequently by politicians to justify reduced expenditure and public sector cuts. This includes the hegemonic notion that there is no 'magic money tree', as well as household spending analogies that do not apply to a sovereign state with the ability to create currency reserves whenever required (see: Kelton, 2020; Mitchell & Fazi, 2017; Winlow & Hall, 2022).

All signs pointed towards neoliberalism's endpoint in the West, with the pandemic acting as the final nail in the coffin. Gerbaudo (2021) described the post-pandemic period in the West as '*The Great Recoil*', in which nations have begun to seek autonomy, retreat from globalisation, and dispense with the dogma of 'free market' neoliberal economics. For Gerbaudo, the recoil is not a process that has been driven solely by the pandemic; rather, it has been accelerated by it. Before the arrival of Covid-19 one can detect an embryonic neo-statism in the political rhetoric and policy direction of several states in the West, particularly the USA and UK (Martin et al., 2022; Muro, 2021). Donald Trump's protectionism has not been abandoned by the Biden administration, while the Conservatives in the UK indicated prior to the pandemic that increased state expenditure and intervention in the national economy, principally through 'Levelling Up', was required, even if this was laced with various problems (Fransham et al., 2023; Telford, 2023; Telford & Wistow, 2022).

Nevertheless, these developments appear to co-exist with the continuation of aspects of neoliberalism in what is an increasingly complex hybrid that does not indicate a clear break into a new system (Telford & Wistow, 2022; Winlow & Winlow, 2022). Neoliberal rhetoric, focused upon the limits of the state's fiscal capacity, has resurfaced recently in the UK in response to both the cost-of-living crisis and demands from various public sector trade unions demanding wage increases. Aspects of economic recovery plans post-pandemic contain many of the classic hallmarks of neoliberal ideology, such as the strategic importance placed upon lightly regulated freeports and Special Economic Zones (SEZs) in geographical locations in both the West and East (Hall et al., 2023). Early indications are that a complex and contradictory mix of shifts is underway in various national economies that do not signal the complete abandonment of the neoliberal variant of capitalism (Winlow & Winlow, 2022). This is an issue that we will return to towards the end of this book as a somewhat authoritarian variant of neoliberalism appears to be taking root across parts of the globe. Under various guises such as monopoly capitalism (Blakeley, 2020) or neo-feudalism (Kotkin, 2020), a more unequal form of capitalism, which combines concentrated wealth with stricter forms of social control, has been potentially forecast. For example, the Chinese Government's ability to seemingly uncouple democracy from market growth also offers an alternative form of authoritarian capitalism (Chin & Lin, 2022). These forms of authoritarianism or control were visible during the pandemic in numerous contexts, and it is important to analyse their manifestation in response to Covid-19 to understand what the new futures of exclusion may look like.

For decades, social scientists and political commentators provided stringent critique of neoliberalism and its role in growing and various forms of inequality (Dorling, 2015; Dumenil & Levy, 2013; Pemberton, 2016). Social exclusion also appeared to be consistent with neoliberalism—in fields such as criminal justice (Whitehead, 2015) and employment (Bauman, 2005) as well as in the context of youth transitions and educational achievement (MacDonald & Marsh, 2005). Winlow and Hall (2013) articulated an advanced notion of social exclusion as neoliberalism's successful separation of individuals from the very idea of the social, creating a *post-social* world of atomised and disaffected people. As neoliberalism faltered and stumbled on in the years following the 2008 financial crisis, these forms of inequality and exclusion have continued to plague advanced Western societies and continue to characterise the disparity between the West and the rest (Piketty, 2014; Streeck, 2016). The pandemic has undoubtedly created further forms of inequality but here we begin to consider new forms of social exclusion; from vaccine mandates to entrenched divides that exclude us from one another. These are key issues that we focus upon in this book. Before we deal with these matters, this is the order in which you can expect to find our arguments.

Book Structure

The rest of this book is organised as follows. Chapter 2, *Crystal ball gazing: The failure of lockdowns, restrictions and the pretext to the Covid-19 vaccine*, addresses the harms of lockdown policies throughout the Covid-19 pandemic, including neoliberalised healthcare's failure to protect the most vulnerable individuals—the elderly. It then explores how the blunt and universal policy of lockdowns glossed over how pre-existing social issues, particularly around social class, age, housing, health status, and locality of residence, shaped peoples' susceptibility of harm to Covid-19. Next, the chapter briefly looks at the impact of school closures on children, particularly the negative affects upon their educational and behavioural development and increases in poverty, child labour, and child abuse in many nations around the world. The chapter then outlines the aggravation of mental health issues such as depression and anxiety, alongside the rise in domestic violence and femicide in many countries across the globe. With attention drawn to the virus, these issues arose somewhat silently in the background.

Titled *Harmalogical pharmacology and the Covid-19 vaccine*, Chapter 3 offers a brief history of vaccines, both as sources of transformative public health interventions principally through saving countless lives and as generators of social divisions and controversy. It also explores the rise of the pharmaceutical industry, situating Big Pharma within the political economy of capitalism whereby perverse incentives weighted towards the financial bottom line have historically undermined health care outcomes. The chapter briefly outlines some examples of this history and details how these same companies were tasked with providing the keys to unlock lockdown. Chapters 2 and 3 provide the book's key contextual foundations, enabling a more detailed empirical exploration of the respondents' sentiments in the remaining chapters, especially Chapters 5 and 6.

Chapter 4, on *Technocratic feudalism, digital apartheids, and the new surveillance governance* introduces the role of technology in both pandemic management and our daily lives. Without digital and algorithmic technologies, certain aspects of pandemic management would be impossible, including digital vaccine certification and forms of track and trace. Data presented in this chapter shows scepticism towards the technological forms of control and management introduced during the pandemic and speaks to participants' concerns about freedom, control, and surveillance. Often dismissed as mere conspiracy, these worries require closer interrogation which we offer in this chapter.

The next chapter, *Asymptomatic freedom, resistance, and the 'anti-vaxxers'*, introduces the complex and nuanced motivations of individuals who refused the Covid-19 vaccines or regretted their decision after vaccination. As a necessary counter to the often simplistic and frequently individualistic analyses of those who displayed vaccine hesitancy or critique, this chapter utilises parts of Chapter 3 as a contextual frame that overlays the decisions and justifications of the participants who refused the vaccine or regretted having it. Here we also explore in empirical depth their resistance to the pressures that were applied from numerous sources and outline the structural fault lines that emerged between them and the vaccinated.

In the penultimate chapter entitled *Heavy Hands and Iron Fists against High Social Fevers,* the authoritarian response of states particularly Western liberal democracies, through hardened exclusionary discourse and vaccine mandates is discussed. The chapter explores these responses that were difficult to imagine before the pandemic given these states purported commitment to individual freedom and autonomy. We also empirically explore the rise of protest movements against vaccine mandates and passports during the pandemic, including the Canadian Government's authoritarian responses to the truckers/Freedom Convoy movement. The book's concluding chapter provides a summary of the key issues addressed in the preceding chapters. It closes by looking at the implications of these issues for the pandemics that inevitably await us in the future, as well as a discussion of the trade-off between freedom and security.

References

Adams, R. (2023). One in five pupils in England were persistently absent in past school year. *The Guardian.* https://www.theguardian.com/education/2023/mar/16/one-in-five-pupils-in-england-were-persistently-absent-in-past-school-year. Accessed on 5 April 2023.

Atkinson, R. (2020). *Alpha city: How London was captured by the super-rich.* Verso.

Badiou, A. (2007). *Being and event.* Bloomsbury.

Bauman, Z. (2005). *Work, consumerism and the new poor* (2nd ed.). Open University Press.

BBC. (2021). *What is the great reset—And how did it get hijacked by conspiracy theories?* BBC. https://www.bbc.co.uk/news/blogs-trending-57532368. Accessed on 23 March 2023.

Bendavid, E., Oh, C., Bhattacharya, J., & Ioannidis, J. (2021). Assessing mandatory stay-at-home and business closure effects on the spread of COVID-19. *European Journal of Clinical Investigation, 51,* 1–9.

Blakeley, G. (2020). *The Corona crash.* Verso.

Brien, P., & Keep, M. (2022). *Public spending during the Covid-19 pandemic* (Research Briefing. 09309). House of Commons.

Briggs, D. (2022). Hope, dystopian futures, and Covid-19 as the 'event' that changed the world (forever?). *Journal of Contemporary Crime, Harm, Ethics, 2*(1), 62–81.

Briggs, D., Ellis, A., Lloyd, A., & Telford, L. (2020). New hope or old futures in disguise? Neoliberalism, the COVID-19 pandemic and the possibility for social change. *International Journal of Sociology and Social Policy, 40*(9–10), 831–848.

Briggs, D., Telford, L., Lloyd, A., Ellis, A., & Kotze, J. (2021a). *Lockdown: Social harm in the Covid-19 era*. Palgrave Macmillan.

Briggs, D., Ellis, A., Lloyd, A., & Telford, L. (2021b). *Researching the Covid-19 pandemic: A critical blueprint for the social sciences*. Policy Press Rapid Response Series.

Briggs, D., Telford, L., Ellis, A., & Lloyd, A. (2021c). Working, living, and dying in COVID times: Perspectives from frontline residential adult social care workers in the UK. *Safer Communities, 20*(3), 208–222.

Briggs, D., Telford, L., Ellis, A., & Lloyd, A. (2021d). Closing the door on protection? Exploring the impact of lockdown upon children and young people's services in the UK. *Youth Voice Journal: Critical Youth Voices on the Covid 19 Pandemic: International Perspectives*, 114–126.

Chin, J., & Lin, L. (2022). *Surveillance state: Inside China's quest to launch a new era of social control*. St Martin's Press.

Chin, V., Ioannidis, J., Tanner, M., & Cripps, S. (2021). Effect estimates of COVID-19 non-pharmaceutical interventions are non-robust and highly model-dependent. *Journal of Clinical Epidemiology, 136*, 96–132.

Dodsworth, L. (2021). *A state of fear: How the UK government weaponised fear during the Covid-19 pandemic*. Pinter & Martin Ltd.

Dorling, D. (2015). *Injustice: Why social inequality still persists*. Policy Press.

Dumenil, G., & Levy, D. (2013). *The crisis of neoliberalism*. Harvard University Press.

Ellis, A., Briggs, D., Lloyd, A., & Telford, L. (2021a). A ticking time bomb of future harm: Lockdown, child abuse and future violence. *Abuse: An International Impact Journal, 2*(1), 37–48.

Ellis, A., Telford, L., Lloyd, A., & Briggs, D. (2021b). For the greater good: Sacrificial violence and the coronavirus pandemic. *Journal of Contemporary Crime, Harm, Ethics, 1*(1), 1–22.

Ellis, A. (2022). Tick, Tock, Boom! A critical forecast on interpersonal violence in post-pandemic UK. *Journal of Contemporary Crime, Harm, Ethics, 2*(1), 24–41.

Fisher, M. (2009). *Capitalist realism: Is there no alternative?* Zero Books.

Foster, G., Frijters, P., & Baker, M. (2021). *The great Covid panic: What happened, why, and what to do next*. Brownstone Institute.

Fransham, M., Herbertson, M., Pop, M., Morais, M., & Lee, N. (2023). Level best? The levelling up agenda and UK regional inequality. *Regional Studies*. Online First: https://doi.org/10.1080/00343404.2022.2159356

Gerbaudo, P. (2021). *The great recoil: Politics after populism and pandemic*. Verso.

Green, T., & Fazi, T. (2023). *The Covid consensus: The global assault on democracy and the poor—A critique from the Left*. Hurst Publishers.

Hall, A., Antonopoulos, G., Atkinson, R., & Wyatt, T. (2023) Duty free: Turning the criminological spotlight on special economic zones. *British Journal of Criminology, 63*, 265–282.

Hall, S. (2022). Neoliberalism and the opportunodemic: Covid-19, Furlough and why we missed the boat (again). *Journal of Extreme Anthropology, 6*(2), 44–62.

Hambleton, R. (2020). *Cities and communities beyond Covid-19*. Policy Press.

Harvey, D. (2023). *A companion to Marx's Grundrisse*. Verso.

Hochuli, A., Hoare, G., & Cunliffe, P. (2021). *The end of the end of history: Politics in the twenty-first century*. Zero Books.

Jones, L., & Hameiri, S. (2022a). Explaining the failure of global health governance during COVID-19. *International Affairs, 98*(6), 2057–2076.

Jones, L., & Hameiri, S. (2022b). COVID-19 and the failure of the neoliberal regulatory state. *Review of International Political Economy, 29*(4), 1027–1052.

Kelton, S. (2020). *The deficit myth: Modern monetary theory and how to build a better economy*. John Murray Publishers Ltd.

Kotkin, J. (2020). *The coming of neo-feudalism*. Encounter Books.

Lloyd, A. (2022). Covid-19 and the future of work: From emergency conditions to regimes of surveillance, governance and optimisation. *Journal of Extreme Anthropology, 6*(2), 1–20.

Lloyd, A., Briggs, D., Ellis, A., & Telford, L. (2023). Critical Reflections on the COVID-19 pandemic from the NHS frontline. *Sociological Research* Online, 1–18. Online First: https://doi.org/10.1177/13607804231156293

Lockdown Files. (2023). Lockdown files. *The Telegraph*. https://www.telegraph.co.uk/news/lockdown-files/. Accessed on 18 April 2023.

MacDonald, R., & Marsh, J. (2005). *Disconnected youth? Growing up in Britain's poor neighbourhoods*. Palgrave.

Martin, R., Martinelli, F., & Clifton, J. (2022). Rethinking spatial policy in an era of multiple crises. *Cambridge Journal of Regions, Economy and Society, 15*, 3–21.

McGill, K. (2023). *Court blocks Covid-19 vaccine mandate for US government workers*. ABC News. https://abcnews.go.com/US/wireStory/appeals-court-blocks-vaccine-mandate-us-govt-workers-98089140. Accessed on 2 March 2023.

Mitchell, B., & Fazi, T. (2017). *Reclaiming the state: A progressive vision of sovereignty for a post-neoliberal world*. Pluto Press.

Muro, M. (2021). Recognising the geography of discontent in the USA: "Building Back Better" by countering regional divergence. *Cambridge Journal of Regions, Economy and Society, 14*, 631–639.

Peck, J. (2013). Explaining (with) neoliberalism. *Territory, Politics, Governance, 1*(2), 132–157.

Pemberton, S. (2016). *Harmful societies: Understanding social harm*. Policy Press.

Piketty, T. (2014). *Capital in the twenty-first century*. Harvard University Press.

Raymen, T., & Smith, O. (2019). Deviant leisure: A critical criminological perspective for the twenty-first century. *Critical Criminology, 27*, 115–130.

Raymen, T. (2022). *The enigma of social harm: The problem of liberalism*. Routledge.

Sassoon, D. (2021). *Morbid symptoms: An anatomy of a world in crisis*. Verso.

Schwab, K., & Malleret, T. (2020). *Covid-19: The great reset*. World Economic Forum.

Senger, M. (2023). *The 'pure fear' excuse for lockdowns*. The Brownstone Institute. https://brownstone.org/articles/the-pure-fear-theory/. Accessed on 1 May 2023.

Streeck, W. G. (2016). *How will capitalism end?* Verso.

Telford, L. (2022). *English nationalism and its ghost towns*. Routledge.

Telford, L., & Wistow, J. (2022). *Levelling up the UK economy: The need for transformative change*. Palgrave Pivot.

Telford, L., Bushell, M., & Hodgkinson, O. (2022). Passport to neoliberal normality? A critical exploration of COVID-19 vaccine passports. *Journal of Contemporary Crime, Harm, Ethics, 2*(1), 42–61.

Telford, L. (2023). 'Levelling up? That's never going to happen': Perceptions on levelling up in a 'red wall' locality. *Contemporary Social Science*. Online First: https://doi.org/10.1080/21582041.2023.2207555

Whitehead, P. (2015). *Reconceptualising the moral economy of criminal justice*. Palgrave.

Winlow, S., & Hall, S. (2013). *Rethinking social exclusion: The end of the social?* SAGE.

Winlow, S., Hall, S., Briggs, D., & Treadwell, J. (2015). *Riots and political protest: Notes from the post-political present.* Routledge.

Winlow, S., & Hall, S. (2022). *The death of the left: Why we must begin from the beginning again.* Policy Press.

Winlow, S., & Winlow, E. (2022). Is the neoliberal era coming to an end? Ideology, history and macroeconomic change in the shadow of COVID-19. *Journal of Contemporary Crime, Harm, Ethics, 2*(1), 1–23.

Woolhouse, M. (2022). *The year the world went mad: A scientific memoir.* Sandstone Press.

Žižek, S. (2021). *Pandemic! 2: Chronicles of a time lost.* Polity.

2

Crystal Ball Gazing: The Failure of Lockdowns, Restrictions, and the Pretext to the Covid-19 Vaccine

Introduction

The Covid-19 pandemic, or perhaps more accurately the lockdown policies enacted to reduce Covid-19 transmission, hospitalisations, and mortalities, fundamentally reordered social life from 2020 to 2022. The rationale behind lockdown was relatively simple and pushed from several perspectives early into the pandemic: lockdown could buy time and save lives while a vaccine was manufactured (Green & Fazi, 2023; Woolhouse, 2022). This early consensus crystallised into a clear strategy that varied across countries, but it was largely in place for almost 18 months. Few citizens could have imagined the scale of change across the globe's continents, with scenes that had historically been reserved for dystopian fiction quickly becoming a reality (Briggs, 2022; Žižek, 2021). Adopting a global approach, this chapter considers the harms, inequalities, and exclusions that occurred during lockdown *while we waited for a vaccine*. Later chapters will explore the impact of *what we were waiting for*, but it's important to start with lockdown. Although the full extent of these harms is beyond the scope of this book (see: Briggs et al., 2021a)—partly because the consequences of lockdown are multi-faceted, ongoing, and likely to continue into the future (Green & Fazi, 2023)—it is useful to outline some of the core issues in this chapter (see: Bhattacharya et al., 2023; Briggs et al., 2021b; Green & Fazi, 2023).

Such social, economic, and cultural damage includes the intensification of poverty, deprivation, mental health problems like depression and anxiety, a rise in child abuse and domestic violence, the diminishment of children's behavioural and cognitive development and the failure to protect the most vulnerable citizens such as the elderly from Covid-19 (Datzberger et al., 2023; Green & Fazi, 2023; Jones & Hameiri, 2022a; Krupar & Sadural, 2022). Given this was a core rationale for lockdown, it is possible to say that, on its own terms, the policy failed. Such harms were particularly acute in Africa, since it contains the highest proportion of low-income nations whereby informal and insecure work constitutes a large proportion of the labour market (see, for example: Nechifor et al., 2021; Wegerif, 2020). Such nations are not as well developed as the West and experience issues of myriad poverty, economic uncertainty, civil unrest, war, and higher prevalence of endemic diseases like malaria and HIV and were therefore more vulnerable to the harms of lockdown policies (Alaran et al., 2022; Green & Fazi, 2023).

This chapter also shows how compliance with lockdown policies created further social divisions and exacerbated forms of exclusion. This included citizens who followed government rhetoric to criticise unvaccinated people (Telford et al., 2022). Social, political, and cultural fault lines existed prior to the pandemic; but new cleavages emerged around compliance with lockdown rules, face coverings, and vaccination status. While governmental 'emergency' legislation (Wagner, 2022) created new forms of social exclusion, so too did government announcements and behavioural psychology 'nudging' (Dodsworth, 2021) and public attitudes towards those who chose to avoid vaccination. Therefore, the chapter provides important context for the book's empirical exploration particularly of the social divisions generated by vaccine policies, including the political drive to vaccinate the entire world against Covid-19, lockdowns for the unvaccinated, and vaccine passports. In the second part of the chapter, we draw upon empirical data from our global, mixed-methods study of the pandemic to illuminate issues around compliance with lockdown policies.

The Days the Earth Stood Still

First discovered in Wuhan City in Hubei Province, China, in late 2019, humans infected with Covid-19 demonstrated symptoms akin to seasonal flu including a fever, bodily pains, loss of taste and smell, a runny nose, and a sore throat (Boni et al., 2020; Stokel-Walker, 2022). The first Covid-19 case appeared in China in December 2020, and the first reported case outside the country was in Thailand on 13 January 2020. The virus then spread around the world including to Japan, Republic of Korea, USA, and it was first recorded in Europe in France on 24 January 2020. Coverage of the initial outbreak in Wuhan depicted medical personnel wearing protective suits outdoors spraying the air. Media reports from the Lombardy region in Italy broadcasted images of overcrowded hospital corridors, people on ventilators, queues of coffins in churches amid funeral services unable to cope with demand, and deployment of the army to assist with burying the deceased (Reiss & Bhakdi, 2020). What was often overlooked was that Lombardy, and Italy in general, had seen health services dramatically reduced due to austerity measures in the preceding years (Bifulco & Neri, 2022). The country's struggle with Covid-19 was linked to broader political, economic, and social factors rather than just the severity of this novel virus (Usuelli, 2020).

In an age of 24/7 news and social media, Covid-19 inevitably became the first virus in history to receive round-the-clock media attention with morning, noon, and nightly updates on Covid infections, hospitalisations, and mortalities (Dodsworth, 2021; Stainback et al., 2020). With a global pandemic declared by the World Health Organization (WHO) on 11 March 2020, politicians put their nations on a war footing to elicit public support in opposition to a common enemy. However, by March 2020, many countries and the WHO were looking favourably on China's authoritarian response, despite China's history of human rights abuses which, by this point, included the arrest of medical whistle-blowers at the start of the pandemic (Jones & Hameiri, 2022a; Kheriaty, 2022). While traditional pandemic management had included interventions into social life and pandemic planning called for measures such as social distancing and, in extreme circumstances, workplace closures and curtailment of large events, the response in early 2020 now followed China's lead and included national lockdowns. While Italy implemented a lockdown on 21 February 2020, other countries followed in March 2020 including the UK, Australia, Argentina, Congo, Colombia, Croatia, Iraq, Lebanon, Netherlands, Panama, Romania, Serbia, Switzerland, and Zimbabwe. In the absence of a known cure or vaccine, this was an attempt to reduce transmission of Covid-19, prevent national health services from collapsing under the weight of excess patient demand, and reduce associated fatalities (Woolhouse, 2022). Such measures included the shutdown of significant sectors of the economy, restrictions upon leaving one's home, working from home where possible, wearing face masks, and social distancing. By 3 April 2020, over 3.9 billion citizens in more than ninety countries were in lockdown (Green & Fazi, 2023). This transformed social life as:

> whole industries collapsed, millions upon millions of people lost their jobs, and people living in poverty expanded as lockdowns, social distancing, self-isolation, curfews, and mask wearing became the uniform means of managing the transmission and spread of the new infectious virus. Public spaces and social life were symbolically redefined to generate 'compliance' to a 'new normal'. (Briggs, 2022: 63–64)

Curiously, the term 'lockdown' originated in the US prison system of the 1970s where inmates would be restricted to their cells for large periods of time (Briggs et al., 2021b; Green & Fazi, 2023; Jones & Hameiri, 2022a). For public health reasons, lockdowns had only been used in very limited ways. In 2014, a 72-hour lockdown was imposed in Freetown, Sierra Leone, and in Monrovia, Liberia to deal with the Ebola[1] outbreak in West Africa (Green & Fazi, 2023). However, they were absent in states' responses to dealing with previous global infectious disease outbreaks such as the 1918 Spanish Flu[2] and 1968 Hong

---

[1] It should be noted that Ebola poses a profoundly different risk to societies than Covid-19, since it possesses an approximate infection mortality rate (IMR) of 65% in African nations (Barry et al., 2015). As we will see, this is incomparable to Covid-19.

[2] While some commentators attempted to compare the severity of the Covid-19 pandemic to the Spanish Flu, again it is incomparable in terms of social harms as the latter killed around 50 million people and possessed a median IMR of age 28 (Ioannidis et al., 2022).

Kong Flu pandemic. The globalised and lengthy implementation of lockdowns during the Covid-19 pandemic was—to use overused phraseology in recent years—'unprecedented'.

Initially enacted on the premise of 'flattening the curve'[3] within several weeks, lockdowns were applied at varying indices of intensity for around two years. The UK's 2011 Influenza Pandemic Preparedness Strategy (Department of Health, 2011) outlined the need, among other recommendations, to identify individuals most at risk of harm from the virus, reduce transmission through handwashing and the use of PPE for frontline workers, and isolate the infected. It also questioned the efficacy of the public wearing of facemasks to curtail virus transmission. The WHO's (2019) document on *Non-Pharmaceutical Public Health Measures for Mitigating the Risk and Impact of Epidemic and Pandemic influenza* also generally mirrors the UK strategy. Lockdowns were absent in both pandemic preparedness plans. Yet, lockdowns were the key policy means used to control the spread of Covid-19, meaning *"the decades-long scientific consensus on how to handle epidemics and pandemics was thrown into the dustbin of history"* (Green & Fazi, 2023: 70). While we acknowledge the geographical nuances surrounding the *rollout* and *rollback* of lockdown policies (see: Briggs et al., 2021b), they were implemented across much of the world including in Australia, Cambodia, UK, Germany, Spain, France, Canada, India, Ireland, Philippines, Nigeria, Malaysia, New Zealand, Russia, Singapore, South Africa, and Thailand and caused profound social, cultural, economic, and political harms.

Perhaps the most obvious harm was the failure to protect the most vulnerable individuals (Bhattacharya et al., 2023). Jones and Hameiri (2022a, 2022b) link this failure with the neoliberalisation of societies over the past forty years particularly in the Western world. Often housing the frailest citizens who suffer from co-morbidities including Alzheimer's and dementia (Brown et al., 2020; Heneghan et al., 2021), the capacity of care homes particularly in the UK and USA was hollowed out in the austerity era across 2010/2020, not least as many were privatised and chronically underfunded (Power & Hall, 2018). As many hospitals

---

[3] This refers to an epidemic curve, indicating the amount of people infected with the disease over time.

lacked intensive care unit (ICU) beds and needed to create capacity for Covid-19 patients, care homes served as hospital overflows for elderly people (Krupar & Sadural, 2022). Unfortunately, care homes possessed a lack of resources such as PPE and had limited testing capacity, particularly at the start of the pandemic (Heneghan et al., 2021). The care sector had been chronically underfunded and workers were already underpaid, precarious, and over-worked (Briggs et al., 2021c). This created challenging conditions within which to discharge significant numbers of vulnerable patients at the outset of the pandemic. Perhaps unsurprisingly, the virus spread rapidly through this vulnerable population and transformed many nursing homes around the world into what Krupar and Sadural (2022: 1107) referred to as *"death pits"* during the pandemic. While deaths of elderly residents in care homes accounted for around 50% of all Covid-19-related deaths in Europe (Anand et al., 2022), estimates suggest around a third of all Covid-related deaths in the USA were from residents and workers in care homes (Krupar & Sadural, 2022).

Research in the UK indicated that lockdown restrictions had a detrimental impact upon the wellbeing of elderly people who were cut adrift from social support networks and unable to see loved ones, which accelerated physical and mental decline (Briggs et al., 2021c). Qualitative studies in the Netherlands involving both healthcare professionals and relatives of patients who died during the pandemic also found how staff shortages, increased workloads, and lockdown restrictions negatively affected end-of-life patient care (Becque et al., 2022; Zee et al., 2023). A lack of resources, reduced staff time to spend with patients, and restricted family visits meant *"some patients were completely alone in the last days of their life"* (Zee et al., 2023: 5). A similar study in Qatar found many patients were unable to see their family in their final days, intensifying their sadness and fear (Johnson et al., 2023). Research in Northern Italy similarly revealed how end-of-life patients were unable to see their loved ones, meaning they *"died without having family members present at the bedside, except by video call"* (Galazzi et al., 2022: 138).

Relatively early into the pandemic it became clear that the risk posed by Covid-19 was particularly determined by age, with elderly people possessing a thousand-fold increased risk of serious harm when compared to young children (Bhattacharya et al., 2023). This is, in part, because elderly people often possess co-morbidities which weaken their immune systems and increase vulnerability to infectious diseases. The average life expectancy in the UK, for instance, is 80.9 years, yet the average age of somebody dying with Covid-19 was 82 (ONS, 2021). While we do not downplay the loss of life, this highlights a key issue: lockdown policies were out of proportion with the potential risk and harm brought by the virus (Briggs et al., 2021a; Green & Fazi, 2023). The blunt instrument of lockdown was enacted universally on the premise that all individuals were at equal risk of serious harm. But this glossed over how individual risk is shaped by social class, race, disability, ethnicity, and the individual's place of residence (Bambra et al., 2023; McGowan & Bambra, 2022).

Indeed, the pandemic emerged into a context of myriad societal inequalities, particularly discrepancies in health outcomes (Bambra et al., 2023; Wistow, 2022). For instance, Global South countries with profound geographical health inequalities include, among others, India, Malawi, Zambia, South Africa, and Chile (McGowan & Bambra, 2022), while the USA possesses the worst health inequalities among more developed nations (Dobbs & Carson, 2022). In the UK, female life expectancy at birth in the most deprived places was 19.3 years lower than the least deprived localities (ONS, 2022). This is due to the concentration of structural problems in deprived places particularly poverty, low-income jobs, deprivation, unemployment, poor housing, overcrowding, mental ill health, crime, and a lack of welfare assistance (Patel et al., 2020; Wistow, 2022), engendering a higher prevalence of smoking, poor diets, obesity, and physical inactivity in these localities (Bambra et al., 2023; Dobbs & Carson, 2022). Inevitably the residents of deprived places tended to be at increased risk of serious harm to Covid-19, with evidence indicating that the UK's poverty-stricken locales tended to fare the worst regarding Covid-19 infections, hospitalisations, and mortalities (Dobbs & Carson, 2022; McGowan & Bambra, 2022; Munford et al., 2022). Therefore, as Patel et al. (2020: 110) outlined *"these policies have shown disregard towards those most economically disadvantaged"* who essentially formed *"the forgotten vulnerable"* during the pandemic.

Relatedly Bambra et al. (2023) intimated how Covid-19 morbidity and mortality are potentially determined by five interconnecting pathways. This includes *unequal exposure* largely shaped by where people live and work. Lower-income and poorly skilled employment tend to possess more hazardous conditions, with shift work and overtime negatively affecting one's health and wellbeing. Low-income citizens also tend to rely more upon public transport and often cannot work from home, which increased their risk of contracting Covid-19.

Unequal transmission symbolises inequalities in housing with marginalised neighbourhoods tending to be more overcrowded, possessing a higher prevalence of damp and mould that negatively affects individuals' respiratory systems. *Unequal vulnerability* denotes how citizens residing in impoverished localities, as mentioned, tend to possess worse health outcomes, while *unequal susceptibility* exposes how residents of marginalised places were more prone to contracting Covid-19 because of how their localised environment weakens their health, wellbeing, and immune systems. Lastly, *unequal treatment* symbolises the lack of access to comprehensive healthcare as well as lower vaccination uptake in deprived places. As we will see, there are various reasons for this including increased cynicism, mistrust, and suspicion of the government and the pharmaceutical industry (Chapter 3). Using traditional definitions of social exclusion, socially excluded groups were more at risk of the virus and more likely to be negatively affected by lockdown policies. Nevertheless, these important contextual conditions were generally absent from the political, policymaking, and mainstream media discourse on Covid-19. Instead, emphasis was placed upon a more reductionist *"no one is safe until everyone is safe"* approach, which became *"the mantra of the COVID-19 pandemic"* (Editorial, 2021: 1193) especially from 2021 onwards as the global mass vaccination programme was underway.

Despite the virus possessing negligible risk to school children (Townsend, 2020a), the disruption to their lives was significant. This was particularly through temporary school closures and remote learning (Bhattacharya et al., 2023), meaning they *"suffered immensely"* and *"sacrificed a lot"* (Townsend, 2020b: 1014). As Green and Fazi (2023) outlined, many schools closed for around a year in the Americas including in Brazil and Columbia while they closed for around two years in some nations like India. Confining children to their domestic residence impacted negatively upon their education, socialisation, behavioural and emotional development, and engagement in physical activities (Kawaoka et al., 2022), which detrimentally affected their health, wellbeing, and weakened their immune systems. In Japan, research ascertained children with neurodevelopmental disorders like attention deficit hyperactivity disorder (ADHD) endured an increase in aggressive behaviour as well as problematic thoughts (Kawaoka et al., 2022). While around 21% of children aged 5–17 were involved in child labour in Ghana before the pandemic, evidence indicates that this increased during school closures as they were often subjected to long and exhausting work on rural farms (Mohammed, 2022). As many Ghanian homes do not have electricity, children could not access digitalised platforms for their studies with negative consequences for reading and numeracy skills (Mohammed, 2022).

In Uganda, schools closed for 22 months which was the longest during the pandemic (Datzberger et al., 2023). Evidence indicates a significant decline in children enrolling in secondary school and increased school dropout rates, as well as a 17% increase in teenage pregnancies between March 2020 and June 2021 (Datzberger et al., 2023; UNICEF, 2021). UNICEF (2021) outlined how 15.2 million people in Uganda including 8.2 million children required humanitarian assistance to cope with lost livelihoods during the pandemic. In Hungary, research found school children's cognitive development declined particularly in numeracy skills, reading levels, and science, with educational inequalities widening further between children from the most deprived and affluent localities as the latter had more access to both resources and parental support (Molnar & Hermann, 2023). As many parents in Germany home-schooled their children during the lockdowns, they reported an increase in conflict, stress, demotivation, and concerns over their children's social skills (May et al., 2023). With the above in mind, it is not surprising that UNICEF (2022) reported how global learning poverty—where children cannot read a basic text by the age of 10—increased in low-middle income countries from 57% pre-pandemic to around 70% post-pandemic.

Perhaps one of the most disturbing consequences of lockdowns was the surge in reports of child abuse across the world. As contact time with social institutions such as schools declined and children spent more time in their residence, reports of child abuse increased in countries including Croatia, India, Uganda, UK, and South Africa where there was a 400% increase in calls to a national childcare helpline during the initial seven days of their first lockdown (Ellis et al., 2021a). Research in Ghana found sexual abuse of adolescent girls increased during the school closures, since safeguarding measures diminished including opportunities to report abuse to the authorities and a lack of supervision when parents could not work from home (Owusu-Addo et al., 2023). Evidence from the Netherlands also indicated a rise in abuse involving emotional neglect and witnessing domestic violence, with more households enduring increased stress, tension, and conflict during lockdown (Vermeulen et al., 2023). A study that explored increased violence against children in Cambodia, India, Indonesia, Sri Lanka, Laos, Myanmar, Nepal, and Vietnam found 41% of households reported violently disciplining their children, including hitting and verbal abuse. The study concluded that *"COVID-19 restrictions such as lockdowns and curfews, and pandemic-related stressors are linked with violent discipline of children"* (Kang et al., 2023: 11).

A significant increase in femicide and domestic violence was reported during lockdown periods in many countries. For example, during the first lockdown in Portugal there was a 95% increase in requests for help alongside a 53% rise in reports to the Portuguese Association of Victim Support of attempted femicide (Soeiro et al., 2023). In Chile, attempted femicide reached record levels in 2020, involving a 22% increase overall across the Covid-19 pandemic (Cantor et al., 2022). Reports of rape surged in Nigeria especially in Adamawa State, where rape reports were up by 173% in 2020 compared to 2019 (Owonikoko et al., 2023). In Greece, the rate of female victims of domestic homicide *"was four-fold higher on average"* in 2021 (Karakasi et al., 2022: 1), alongside a large increase in calls to helplines during 2020. In the Australian state of Victoria, which had some of the longest lockdowns in the world, violence against women during the first lockdown across March–May 2020 also increased significantly with a rise in women reporting violence to support services for the first time (Pfitzner et al., 2022). Quantitative research in the USA also found that domestic violence against women with no history of domestic violence victimisation increased (Scoglio et al., 2023). In Brazil, reports of domestic disturbances by neighbours on Twitter across February–April 2020 rose by 431%, while in Sao Paulo calls to the police reporting domestic violence rose by 44.9% in 2020 (Alloatti & Oliveira, 2023).

While mental ill health was already a significant issue in many parts of the world pre-pandemic, it is not surprising that this was exacerbated by lockdowns. As Townsend (2020a: 255) asserts, *"during lockdown, we have asked young people to live in conditions that have exacerbated key risk factors for self-harm and suicide ideation, including social isolation, loneliness, family problems and feeling trapped, defeated and hopeless"*. Mir et al. (2023) discerned that many Malaysian University students endured an increase in anxiety and depression particularly if the students were from a low-income family. Others highlight a reported increase in loneliness among school pupils, with 7% reporting self-harming during the first lockdown in England (Geulayov et al., 2022). Research by Owens et al. (2022) into UK University students and mental wellbeing gives weight to these findings, since they found increased stress and depression during lockdown, particularly among female students. Scholarship by Gaynor et al. (2023) also established that in the USA in 2021 around one-third of female students seriously considered attempting suicide, with about a quarter making a suicide plan. A recent meta-analysis of 53 longitudinal studies, involving over 40,000 children across 12 countries, also ascertained an increase in anxiety among children from high-income backgrounds during the pandemic (Madigan et al., 2023).

Low-income parents claiming welfare support during the pandemic also encountered increased anxieties, as they constantly worried about paying the bills and felt like a failure to their children (Patrick et al., 2022). Relatedly, the UK charity Rethink Mental Illness (2021) reported how across March 2020–March 2021 there had been a 703% rise in people seeking advice about anxiety, accompanied with a 459% rise in individuals seeking information about self-harm. Research on the European continent also found that most older adults endured a decline in their mental health during the pandemic, especially in nations that possessed high infection rates (Ludecke & Knesebeck, 2022).

The requirement to wear face coverings was occasionally related to these mental health difficulties. Research ascertained that face masks can aggravate a sense of social isolation, atomisation, and particularly anxiety for those who are already anxious (Saint & Moscovich, 2021). Scholarship in the USA also found that mask wearing among children can negatively impact their emotional development, with masked children demonstrating worse emotional recognition than unmasked individuals (Chester et al., 2023). Relatedly, a POLITICO-Harvard T.H. Chan School of Public Health poll (2022) found 40% of parents believed that mandating children to wear masks in school negatively affected their school experience, as well as their mental and emotional health (39%). Research in Japan outlined how wearing masks made it more difficult for children to read emotions, while prolonged usage was reported *"to cause headache and impaired cognition"* (Shobako, 2022: 9).

Such harms were felt most acutely in many African nations, since most of their economies are underpinned by the export of agricultural materials involving high proportions of informal work, while welfare support and social infrastructure are underdeveloped (Alaran et al., 2022; Green & Fazi, 2023; Munzhedzi & Uwizeyimana, 2022). As large amounts of people work in informal sectors characterised by unstable and insecure incomes, they were inevitably more susceptible to economic hardship during the lockdowns when business activity was significantly curtailed. Unemployment in Africa, for instance, reached 34.4% in the second quarter of 2021 (Munzhedzi & Uwizeyimana, 2022). A new precariat emerged in South Africa, constituting immigrant workers largely from Zimbabwe and Somalia who mainly worked casually in precarious industries such as retail and construction (Geyer, 2023). As they were made unemployed during the first lockdown, many were compelled to sell fruit and vegetables to try and survive often on an income of less than $100 a month (Geyer, 2023). Therefore, poverty and economic hardship increased across Sub-Saharan Africa with the food insecurity of Kenya and Uganda rising by 38% and 44% respectively (Mekonnen & Amede, 2022). A report by Oxfam (2022) outlines how, in Kenya, over 70% of employees lost some income during the pandemic with 64% eventually losing their jobs. The situation was similar in the Democratic Republic of Congo, with estimates indicating that 11 million more citizens will be pushed into poverty because of lockdown policies (Oxfam, 2022).

Research in Western Kenya highlights how a cohort of secondary school adolescent girls who had experienced lockdowns possessed twice the risk of falling pregnant and three times the risk of dropping out of school in comparison to the pre-Covid-19 cohort (Zulaika et al., 2022). Two weeks into the first lockdown in Nigeria, tensions between armed state personnel and citizens breaking lockdown rules resulted in 18 people being murdered by security forces (Alaran et al., 2022). Badran and Turnbull (2022: 264) suggest that North African states' responses to lockdown violations—many of whom were already authoritarian/undemocratic—embodied an 'Authoritarian upgrading'. Many states such as Egypt and Morocco used military force to crack down on dissenters such as public protests, consolidating their authoritarian power (Badran & Turnbull, 2022). Although, as will be discussed, this authoritarian crackdown was not unique to the Global South.

It is useful to highlight that the African continent has experienced very low Covid mortality in comparison to nations in Europe and North America, for example, as evidenced in Table 2.1 containing some of Africa's most prominent nations.

Scholars have highlighted various reasons for these, perhaps surprisingly low, numbers of deaths: the continent has a very young population

Table 2.1 Population and Covid-19 'cases' in various African countries

Country	Population (million)	'Covid-19 deaths'
Togo	8.6	290
Tanzania	63.5	845
Rwanda	13.5	1,467
Senegal	16.8	1,968
Zambia	19.5	4,017
Ethiopia	120	7,572
Egypt	109	24,613

Source Statista (2022)

with a median age of 19.8 which means large segments of the population are not at serious risk to the disease (Green & Fazi, 2023). Over half (59%) of African citizens live in rural localities with access to vast open space, reducing their likelihood of infection as the chances of transmitting Covid-19 outside are negligible (Bwire et al., 2022). While Africa did not test for Covid in the population as much as Europe (Bwire et al., 2022), Green and Fazi (2023) also highlight how many citizens already possessed pre-existing immunity built up through other viral infections.

The unintentional consequences of the pandemic response in many nations—the failure to protect the most vulnerable, reductionist public health messaging that glossed over structural inequalities, aggravation of unemployment, child abuse, domestic violence, femicide, mental ill health, and poverty—expose the relationship between lockdown policies and numerous harms (Bhattacharya et al., 2023; Dodsworth, 2021; Foster et al., 2021; Green & Fazi, 2023). The policy enacted while the world waited for suitable vaccines is implicated in significant damage, inequalities, and forms of exclusion. Given this social damage, it is somewhat of a conundrum that many citizenries across the world, including in the UK, largely supported these measures especially in the first half of the pandemic before lockdown fatigue became an embedded part of social life (Dodsworth, 2021; Foad et al., 2021). This is where the book now turns, occasionally drawing upon qualitative data from our global mixed-methods study to empirically illuminate compliance to lockdown policies.

The Compliance Narrative

A key aspect of the Covid-19 pandemic was the dismissal of dissent and any alternative approaches to managing the public health crisis. As governments coalesced under the singular ideal of 'following the science', other approaches such as *focussed protection* were dismissed. Such a strategy was central to the Great Barrington Declaration (GBD, 2020), which was signed in Barrington, USA, in October 2020 and pioneered by scientists Professor Jay Bhattacharya, Stanford University, USA, Professor Sunetra Gupta, Oxford University, UK, and Professor

Martin Kulldorff, Harvard University, USA. The GBD (2020) was designed as a middle ground between a 'let Covid rip' strategy and lockdowns, emphasising that resources should be principally directed towards the most vulnerable individuals while allowing people who are at minimal risk from the virus to live their lives (see: GBD, 2020). This would enable immunity to build up among the citizenry, which was vital since they argued *"herd immunity is the endpoint of this epidemic regardless of whether we choose lockdowns or focused protection to address it"* (GBD, 2020).

However, there was a coordinated campaign to discredit the GBD among the highest echelons of the political and scientific establishment. A Freedom of Information Request revealed an email exchange on 8 October 2020 between Professor Francis Collins, who was Director of the National Institutes of Health, USA, and Professor Anthony Fauci, the USA's Chief Medical Advisor and key figure behind the USA's lockdown policies. Essentially, the former claimed the GBD's three pioneers were *"fringe epidemiologists"* and that there needs to be a *"quick and devastating published take down of its premises"*, with Fauci then suggesting it is underway (Green & Fazi, 2023: 279). This would appear to indicate that the reality of messy scientific debate was less important than 'one version of the truth'.

At the time of writing, the GBD possessed over 937,000 signatories including from both members of the public and distinguished scholars from around the world. This includes the 2013 Nobel Prize in Chemistry winner Dr. Michael Levitt, Professor of Structural Biology, Stanford University, USA, Dr. Annie Janvier, Professor of Paediatrics and Clinical Ethics, University de Montreal, Canada, Dr. Karol Sikora, Professor of Medicine, University of Buckingham, UK, and Dr. Ariel Munitz, Professor of Clinical Microbiology and Immunology, Tel Aviv University, Israel (GBD, 2020). The notion that scholars supporting the GBD are marginal was challenged through research by Ioannidis (2022: 4), highlighting how some of the signatories are among the most cited scientists in the world meaning the *"GBD is clearly not a fringe minority report"*.

However, rather than engaging in dispassionate, rational, and stringent scientific discussion, opponents of the GBD often described the three world-leading scientists as *"crazy"*, *"mass murderers"*, *"exorcists"*, and

"*Trumpian*" (Kulldorff, 2021). Moreover, as Bhattacharya et al. (2023: 12) assert: it *"has been known since the Athenian plague of 430 BC that recovered individuals are protected when re-exposed to an infectious disease"* and that herd immunity is what brings an end to a pandemic. However, herd immunity was afforded little debate and often discredited in political, policymaking, and the mainstream media during the Covid-19 pandemic in favour of lockdowns and the drive to vaccinate the entire world. Professor Anthony Fauci went so far as to question if herd immunity was achievable with Covid-19 (Bhattacharya et al., 2023). It is less important to us, as social scientists, whether the GBD propose a better approach than lockdown or vice versa. What is important is to understand the ways in which debate was minimised and alternatives to the official approach were dismissed and undermined.

Government tactics also demonstrated an unwillingness to engage with opponents of official policy. In 2020, the UK Government launched a Counter Disinformation Unit to crack down on 'covid misinformation' online (Big Brother Watch, 2023). The Unit is underpinned by artificial intelligence to identify 'misinformation' particularly on Twitter, Facebook, and YouTube. However, the unit targeted people who were critical of lockdown policies. In effect, they *"secretly monitored, recorded and reported on mainstream political dissent under the guise of tackling "disinformation"* (Big Brother Watch, 2023: 17). Prominent individuals such as David Davis, a Conservative MP, who criticised the modelling used to justify lockdowns was continually monitored, alongside Peter Hitchens who was a leading lockdown critic (Big Brother Watch, 2023). Other scientists who were critical of lockdown policies were also monitored including Professor Carl Heneghan, University of Oxford, UK, and Professor Jon Deeks, University of Birmingham, UK (Big Brother Watch, 2023). As we will discuss (Chapter 4), this formed part of the widening of the state's authoritarian surveillance gaze throughout the pandemic.

As we mentioned in Chapter 1, the release of the Lockdown Files (2023) in *The Daily Telegraph* by journalist Isabel Oakeshott in March 2023 revealed over 100,000 WhatsApp messages between state officials and medical advisers acquired from Matt Hancock,[4] who was the UK's health secretary during the pandemic and played a key role in implementing lockdown policies. Among other issues, these messages expose how the UK Government regarded guilt and fear as vital tools to ensure compliance among the public. Matt Hancock sent WhatsApp messages about the need to *"frighten the pants off everyone with the new strain"*, while the Cabinet Secretary, Simon Case, laughed at how the state locked up people in quarantine hotels, or what he termed *"a Premier Inn shoe box"*, for breaking lockdown rules including flying abroad for holidays. In effect, these WhatsApp messages demonstrate how many state officials revelled in manufacturing fear and using authoritarian responses to obtain public compliance. This reveals much about approaches to governance and the impact on public debate. At the heart of the pandemic and this book are crucial questions about freedom, individual choice, social responsibility, rights, and obligations. These are ethical and moral questions that require debate and nuance. However, government policy and public discussion was often characterised by fearmongering and behavioural 'nudging' to comply with official policy, and the systematic exclusion of alternative ideas.

This occurred alongside the sensationalised reporting of Covid-19 through various media forums. Many internet companies, largely dependent on article views for their revenue through advertisements, used alarming and frightening words such as 'soaring' to describe Covid-19 infections alongside 'mutant' to describe the Covid variants (Dodsworth, 2021), especially Omicron which emerged in South Africa in November 2021 (Green & Fazi, 2023). However, Omicron was less virulent than prior strains of Covid-19 (Jefferson et al., 2023a). In South Africa itself, some of the media reporting on the virus was sensationalised and appealed to emotion particularly fear, anger, and sadness (Bosch & Wasserman, 2023). Relatedly, the Centre for Disease Control and Prevention is a key governmental agency in the USA, forming

---

[4] Isabel Oakeshott acquired the messages from Matt Hancock to help him write his (2022) book *Pandemic Diaries: The inside story of Britain's battle against Covid*. He resigned as Health Secretary on 7 May 2021, after photos and video footage emerged of an extramarital affair with his aide, Gina Coladangelo. However, at the time of writing in Spring 2023, Hancock is still an MP.

a core source of public information during the pandemic on Covid-19 infections and deaths that helped to guide lockdown policies and public behaviour. However, analysis by Krohnert et al. (2023) discerned 25 instances of statistical errors involving 80% where the severity of Covid-19 was exaggerated. Of these, 64% concerned children, where their perceived risk of harm from the virus was overstated (Krohnert et al., 2023). Nonetheless, public support for a second lockdown in the UK, which was initiated on 5 November 2020, was aided by scientific modelling presented through the media. This was premised on a 'do nothing death toll', which was unrealistic as it did not factor in behavioural change including people social distancing and socialising less to reduce their chances of Covid-19 infection (Lockdown Files, 2023). Green and Fazi (2023: 211) aptly observed how:

> Modellers over-predicted doomsday scenarios, the most extreme prediction was picked up by sections of the media to push for restrictions, and all sides then claimed that the actual outcome was entirely consistent with their predicted range. In the meantime these predictions were also used to push mass vaccination with the booster, even for people aged under forty or fifty, who were at very low risk from Covid.

While we explore the mass vaccination programme in Chapter 3, it is useful to highlight that such modelling provided the 'scientific' fuel to legitimate lockdown policies. Briggs et al. (2021b) and Green and Fazi (2023) outline how this can be traced back to Professor Neil Ferguson's Imperial College London research team publishing a non-peer-reviewed paper in March 2020, suggesting 500,000 UK citizens would die from Covid-19 if no restrictions were implemented. As such, it was essential that the government enacted a lockdown to prevent the health service from being overwhelmed. Professor Ferguson also distributed a copy of the article to the White House in the USA, purporting that 2.2 million American citizens may die in the pandemic's first 12 months unless a lockdown is initiated.

However, Professor Ferguson possesses an *"embarrassingly poor track record"* (Green & Fazi, 2023: 95) regarding infection and mortality projections brought by infectious diseases, which can only be described as *abject failure*. Considering the outbreak of avian flu in 2005, he claimed around 200 million people across the world could die; yet by 2010, 257 people had been killed (Green & Fazi, 2023). Secondly, in light of the UK's 2009 swine flu pandemic his modelling suggested up to 65,000 people may die; but the number of deaths equated to 457 (Green & Fazi, 2023). Ioannidis et al. (2022) suggest epidemic modelling more broadly has a poor track record as it struggles to account for the complexity of human societies, meaning it is rather surprising that it maintains credibility among politicians and policymakers.

Alongside worst-case modelling scenarios, governments used other means to instil fear in the population (Senger, 2023). The Scientific Pandemic Influenza Group which advises the UK Government, for instance, suggested that to get people to comply with the measures, *"the perceived level of personal threat needs to be increased among those who are complacent, using hard-hitting emotional messaging"* (Dodsworth, 2021). A coordinated fear campaign was launched, with advertisements on TV and posters in town centres depicting frightening images such as medical personnel wearing facemasks and visors set against a yellow and black background to denote danger and hazard (Dodsworth, 2021). Even electric road signs on motorways urged motorists to 'stay alert' and to 'stay home, essential travel only, save lives'. Similar approaches were adopted in many so-called liberal democracies, including in New Zealand where Jacinda Ardern, New Zealand's Prime Minister across 2017–2023, suggested people quarantined would be subjected to a *"two-week period of sustained propaganda"*, while in Germany the government displayed images of people choking to death in their homes as they regarded it as possessing the most shock and awe value (Dodsworth, 2021). For Dodsworth (2021: 70) this amounted to living under a *"psychocracy"*, whereby unelected behavioural insight advisors were a core part of the implementation of lockdown policies and ensuring compliance among the public.

Mask mandates were another means to elicit fear and compliance (Briggs et al., 2021b; Dodsworth, 2021). Although Professor Chris Whitty, the UK's Chief Medical Officer, and Professor Anthony Fauci, suggested in March 2020 that uninfected people wearing masks was not advisable as evidence of their efficacy in offering protection from Covid-19 is limited, like many other countries they u-turned shortly thereafter (Green & Fazi, 2023). Despite the most rigorous randomised control trial studies demonstrating a negligible/non-existent impact of wearing cloth masks on reducing the likelihood of Covid-19 infection (for example: Bundgaard et al., 2021; Jefferson et al., 2023b), governments across the world mandated wearing them in indoor or outdoor public space including in the UK, Spain, many states in the USA, Puerto Rico, South Korea, China, Zimbabwe, Bangladesh, Portugal, Syria, Germany, Poland, Turkey, and France. Masks served as a visible reminder of the threat posed by the virus and increased a social atmosphere of alertness and worry, while they also socially divided the compliant from the non-compliant (Briggs et al., 2021a, 2021b). This meant peoples' perception of the risk posed by the disease was out of sync with reality. For example, the UK citizenry believed the median IMR for Covid-19 was around 6%. However, global analysis found the IMR for age 7 was 0.0023%, for age 30 0.0573%, for age 60 1.0035%, and for age 90 20.31292% (Sorensen et al., 2022). This public misperception is perhaps understandable when we consider that the daily Covid-19 updates presented by governments and the scientific advisors were largely decontextualised; daily death rates from Covid-19 were never explained in the context of how many people die daily from all other illnesses or diseases.

If, as Green and Fazi (2023) suggest, that lockdown measures were designed to hold the virus at bay until a vaccine was ready, then sustained compliance would have required the mobilisation of political messages, mainstream media coverage, and the technology companies (see Chapter 4) filtering 'disinformation'. In this context of anxiety and worry, compliance with restrictions and a desire to be vaccinated is understandable—both in the context of wishing to protect others and due to fear. When the vaccines arrived largely at first in the developed world in late 2020, it was widely announced that this was the way to bring about the end of the pandemic. In one Facebook forum regarding discussions on Covid-19, Fred, a retired US army veteran, posted his pro-vaccine reflection in January 2021. He spoke about how:

The CDC recommends that everyone who is eligible for a vaccine should get one. All COVID-19 vaccines currently available in the United States have been shown to be highly effective at preventing COVID-19.

Getting vaccinated for Covid will help protect not only yourself, but everyone around you as well, from your family to your workplace to your whole community. We need as many people as possible to be vaccinated in order to end this pandemic.

Even after being vaccinated, it is still important to follow the CDC guidelines in regards to wearing a mask, keeping socially distant, and washing hands frequently. Each of these steps, and the vaccine, are individual tools that work together to minimize the spread of the virus.

As side effects present themselves (most common are soreness and headache), I will keep you all updated on the progress. These side-effects show that the body is responding to the vaccine and helps to show that I will be protected from Covid. I am in one of the first groups because I'm on a mission to help my community fight Covid, and I work closely with healthcare personnel on a daily basis.

As always, stay safe and stay hydrated everyone.

Such patriotic messaging embodies a call to arms, mirroring the warlike rhetoric politicians used to galvanise public support around the restrictions. Vaccines are available for many illnesses and diseases, and we are accustomed to the protection that they provide. In this sense, the arrival of vaccines taps into a long-standing trust of scientific development as well as a desire for the pandemic to be over. It also demonstrates the ideological potency of the singular narrative on the 'science' during the Covid-19 pandemic, whereby alternative strategies were never given any serious consideration in politics, policymaking, and the mainstream media (Bhattacharya et al., 2023). Instead, emphasis was placed upon vaccinating everybody regardless of one's risk to the disease (Telford et al., 2022). In the UK, a sizeable group of people were also active in the social media forums, reproducing governmental messaging to endorse vaccine take-up or, what they regarded as the 'cause'. Posting in November 2020, one of our participants Lena, wrote:

> I'm hopeful we can start vaccinating the most vulnerable next month.
>
> If those that are younger and healthier, or less worried about catching the virus, could keep up all the good work. Then we can prevent spread of the virus and hopefully we can get through with as few deaths and as little loss as possible and keep the NHS running as best we can.
>
> Masks please, all indoor spaces, even if you're not entirely convinced, err on the side of caution.
>
> Not much hardship and so much at risk.
>
> Regular ventilation to indoor spaces, socially distance, don't mix indoors, hand washing.
>
> Last push of holding up the efforts.

As prominent politicians and expert scientists outlined during the pandemic, individuals had to make *sacrifices* if the world was to overcome Covid-19 by honouring the restrictions and easing the burden on pressurised healthcare institutions (see: Ellis et al., 2021b). In November 2020, for instance, President Joe Biden spoke about the shared sacrifices made by Americans during the pandemic (Bredemeier, 2020), while in October 2022 Northern Ireland's outgoing Health Minister, Robin Swann, highlighted how he was forever grateful for the *sacrifices* made by the nation's healthcare staff (Department of Health, 2022). As we have noted previously (Ellis et al., 2021b), individual sacrifices reinforce the social fabric and in this sense compliance with the restrictions and vaccination programme served to uphold the neoliberalised social world. However, this narrative omits those who were sacrificed during the pandemic through the systemic violence of inequality, deprivation, precarity, and exclusion. Those 'shared sacrifices' are, perhaps, in the service of upholding a profoundly unequal and anti-social system. For some, such a sacrifice was not worth it, and we explore this later in the book. Notwithstanding, Facebook posts such as these from Alex, in the USA, November 2020, were commonplace:

> We are in a deadly Pandemic with a mortality rate of 3-4% globally. The rate of spread [R0 value] and mortality rate has increased exponentially over the last 30 days because not enough people are practically social distancing, wearing a facemask, washing their hands regularly or implementing the necessary preventive measures.
>
> I trust the Moderna and Pfizer COVID-19 vaccine.... because I believe in science, trust the data and trial success rate. This is our ultimate option since we cannot rely on the people in our community to be proactive and we can't resort to the herd immunity strategy. I will confidently take the COVID-19 vaccine from Moderna or Pfizer when it becomes available to the general public.

As the above reveals, the perception of risk posed by the virus did not match some peoples' experiences (Dodsworth, 2021). These admissions are also rather *hyper-conformist*, accepting government mandates and messaging and reproducing those arguments to others. Note how Alex places responsibility for a rising R rate on people he believes are not complying sufficiently with the rules and how science and the vaccine is the way out of the pandemic. Alex's sentiments demonstrate the hegemony of the singular narrative regarding lockdowns, involving no mention of any alternative approaches. As we noted previously (Briggs et al., 2021a), early sceptics of lockdown policies tended to be those who continued to work and had the primary experience of being exposed to the risk posed by the disease. Many of these individuals such as Mick, a UK construction worker, saw a disparity in what was said about the virus and what was happening in his daily life when he continued to work on home refurbishments. Nearly two years after the beginning of the lockdowns, in February 2022, he said:

> Takes something like this to realise how stupid humanity is, I mean sitting in your car with your mask on? 75% of people are already unmasked, people don't take notice, supermarkets don't ask, the problem with the UK is that the British people stand together in a crisis, like the war, we

are close, no one is putting up with it in the UK. Even the vaccinated people are saying to me now, they are done with it and no more vaccines.

Mick was critical regarding how *"there was no news about Covid protests"* (Chapter 6) and *"how we had false news all our lives, now all of a sudden, we believe precisely the thing which we didn't beforehand"*. He was in a situation where he was part of an identifiable minority who would be labelled as the 'anti-vaxxers' (Chapter 5):

> So tired of people telling me to get the vaccine and that I'm stupid when I go down the pub. I mean every country has done the same thing. I just don't want to be around people. Me own mates telling me to get the vaccine, 'Fuck off'! 'Fuck you', I say to em, 'fucking wake up and look at what is happening'. Fuck em.

As we will see, new forms of social division and antagonisms were generated by lockdown policies. This revealed an authoritarian cultural undercurrent in many Westernised liberal democracies, with many people content to police each other's behaviour and pressurise people to get vaccinated regardless of their risk of harm. In the above excerpt, Mick reflected how he wasn't sure *"what to believe"* since *"we don't live in a democracy anymore, we are slaves"* as *"Covid laws permitted emergency status which allowed all sorts of mischief"*. He also intimated how:

> I am drinking more, taking more drugs, mate it is a sad state of affairs. Society is really fucked. My problem is I really wished it never happened [covid restrictions]. It has and it has opened up so many rabbit holes, the corruption, the abuse, the…it is something which is never going to end. I don't want to go to work. I feel really distant from everything and everyone. I just don't have anything to look forward to anymore. It is a mindfuck.

Mick's admission of increased substance use and attendant feelings of despair are not isolated. Rather, it is part of a broader pattern discerned from research that indicates increased use of alcohol in the UK among some adults during the first lockdown (Sallie et al., 2020) and a rise in 'deaths of despair' such as from drug abuse in the USA (Petterson et al., 2020).

Those Standing in Line and Those Out of Order

Mick also describes an unbalanced and divided society whereby a large bulk of the population was supportive of lockdown policies. Such conformity to lockdowns formed the basis for compliant attitudes towards the Covid-19 vaccine. Josh, from Northern Ireland, correlates diminishing Covid-19 infections, and a low death rate with the 'vaccine' and 'successful science' in an international Covid-19 Facebook forum:

> It's the beginning of the end for covid 19!! Thousands upon thousands are being vaccinated every day!! Science won in the end!! Can't wait until we are all free to wine and dance, go clubbing and go to concerts!! I look forward to seeing all your beautiful smiles out there (without the mask!!!!).

The responses—many of which break off into mini conversations—are a mix of agreement and scepticism:

> *Michael*: Ah, this pandemic is just getting underway. Hate to mess up your Friday (Canada).
> *Josh*: Life goes on folks!!! Some vaccines are proving to be over 90% effective! Soon this will all be a distant memory! Make sure to get your vaccines! (South Africa).
> *Sasha*: If you really believe everything they tell u I am so excited for u but the flu vaccine has been out since 1944 and still nowhere close to 90% effective and you really believe covid vaccine is I am glad some believe this but if that was the case you'd think a reg flu vaccine would be 90% effective after all these years wouldn't you and nope I have never had a flu vaccine I am 41 years old and can't really ever recall having the flu and I sure will not take this vaccine (USA).

Rudiger: It is remarkable how now deaths following vaccinations are commented in the way that they most likely were caused by pre-existing illnesses. Before, Covid-related deaths were regularly put under Corona, where from the circumstances it was evident that a huge percentage was and is in fact caused by other factors (Germany).

Another participant, Ben, was supportive of the initial lockdowns in Germany but developed doubts when he: *"started to research Mexico's response and Sweden's refusal to put in lockdowns"*. Ben was a student when we first talked to him over the summer of 2020 just after many countries had experienced a lockdown. When he explored the few other countries which had not locked down, he claimed perhaps they were not necessary in the first place:

> We had lockdowns, everything closed, summer 2020 things started to open and you could go to shops and everything but in October 2020 the government made another lockdown, 6 months but in December 2020, the vaccinations started and it got worse here, more infections and this created more fear.

Ben became more critical that his country's scientific experts and politicians overemphasised the medical context of Covid-19, with almost no attention paid to *"the social or psychological impact"*. As discussed in this chapter, the unintentional consequences of lockdown policies are considerable and profound. This corresponds with Mark Woolhouse (2022), an epidemiologist, who stated that perhaps the management of the pandemic should not have been left to epidemiologists, such was their focus on health at the expense of everything else. Such harms fed into Ben's reservations about the vaccine and doubts about the severity of the virus, which led Ben to break the rules surrounding lockdown restrictions:

> Most of my friends are compliant with everything: the rules, the vaccine, then things changed with Delta and Omicron because the virus became much less harmful but most followed the advice to get the vaccine, the booster and they are willing to take a fourth, fifth or sixth vaccination and we are talking about people like me, mid 20s, no risk group, young,

healthy. I started to ignore rules and met in secret places, like forests and we could be together for the weekend. Then I heard different stories like from Spain and Portugal with the curfews and people couldn't go outside for months and so in comparison it wasn't that tough but you just couldn't meet people. We got caught a few times and the police asked us to leave, they were ok about it. We were just four of us drinking in a flat.

In this chapter, we explored some of the unintentional consequences of lockdown policies including an intensification of mental ill health such as anxiety and depression, domestic abuse, femicide, unemployment, child abuse, and social divisions. While this chapter also outlined the suppression of alternative scientific policies in addressing the Covid-19 pandemic, it explicated some of the empirical data surrounding compliance with the lockdown measures and sentiments on the vaccination programme. In the next chapter, we more closely examine issues surrounding vaccinations including how they became an essential public health tool in human societies' fight against infectious diseases, the rise of Big Pharma, and some of the respondents' nuanced sentiments surrounding the Covid-19 vaccine.

References

Alaran, A., Badmos, A., Bouaddi, O., Adebisi, Y., Umeh, K., Idris, U., & Lucero-Prisno, D. (2022) Decisive or impulsive? Re-examining Africa's lockdown response to Covid-19. *Tropical Medicine and Health, 50*(22), 1–6.

Alloatti, M., & Oliveira, A. (2023). Deepening and widening the gap: The impacts of the COVID-19 pandemic on gender and racial inequalities in Brazil. *Gender, Work & Organization, 30*(1), 329–344.

Anand, J., Donnelly, S., Milne, A., Nelson-Becker, H., Vingare, E., Deusdad, B., Cellini, G., Kinni, R., & Pregno, C. (2022). The Covid-19 pandemic and care homes for older people in Europe—Deaths, damage and violations of human rights. *European Journal of Social Work, 25*(5), 804–815.

Badran, S., & Turnbull, B. (2022). The COVID-19 pandemic and authoritarian consolidation in North Africa. *Journal of Human Rights., 21*(3), 263–282.

Bambra, C., Munford, L., Khavandi, S., & Bennett, N. (2023). *Northern exposure: COVID-19 and regional inequalities in health and wealth.* Policy Press.

Barry, M., Toure, A., Traore, F., Sako, F., Sylla, D., Kpamy, D., Bah, E., Bangoura, M., Poncin, M., Keita, S., Tounkara, T., Cisse, M., & Vanhems, P. (2015). Clinical predictors of mortality in patients with Ebola virus disease. *Clinical Infectious Diseases, 60*(12), 1821–1824.

Becque, Y., Geugten, W., Heide, A., Korfage, I., Pasman, H., Philipsen, B., Zee, M., Witkamp, E., & Goossensen, A. (2022). Dignity reflections based on experiences of end-of-life care during the first wave of the COVID-19 pandemic: A qualitative inquiry among bereaved relatives in the Netherlands (the CO-LIVE study). *Scandinavian Journal of Caring Sciences, 36*, 769–781.

Bhattacharya, J., Bienen, L., Duriseti, R., Hoeg, T., Kulldorff, M., Makary, M., Smelkinson, M. & Templeton, S. (2023). *Questions for COVID-19 commission.* The Norfolk Group.

Bifulco, L., & Neri, S. (2022). The Italian National Health Service: Universalism, marketization and the fading of territorialization. *Forum for Social Economics, 51*(2), 192–206.

Big Brother Watch. (2023). *Ministry of truth: The secretive government units spying on your speech.* Big Brother Watch.

Boni, M., Lemey, P., Jiang, X., Tsan-Yuk, T., Perry, B., Castoe, T., Rambaut, A., & Robertson, D. (2020). Evolutionary origins of the SARS-CoV-2 sarbecovirus lineage responsible for the COVID-19 pandemic. *Nature Microbiology, 5*, 1408–1417.

Bosch, T., & Wasserman, H. (2023). South African tabloid coverage of Covid19: The Daily Sun. *Media, Culture & Society.* Online First. https://doi.org/10.1177/01634437221140514

Bredemeier, K. (2020). *Biden discusses 'shared sacrifices' as coronavirus looms over thanksgiving.* Voice of America news. https://www.voanews.com/a/usa_biden-discusses-shared-sacrifices-coronavirus-looms-over-thanksgiving/6198788.html. Accessed on 21 March 2023.

Briggs, D., Telford, L., Lloyd, A., Ellis, A., & Kotzé, J. (2021a). *Lockdown: Social harm in the Covid-19 era.* Palgrave.

Briggs, D., Ellis, A., Lloyd, A., & Telford, L. (2021b). *Researching the Covid-19 pandemic: A critical blueprint for the social sciences*. Policy Press Rapid Response Series.

Briggs, D., Telford, L., Lloyd, A., & Ellis, A. (2021c). Working, living, and dying in COVID times: Perspectives from frontline adult social care workers in the UK. *Safer Communities, 20*(3), 208–222.

Briggs, D. (2022). Hope, dystopian futures, and Covid-19 as the 'event' that changed the world (forever?). *Journal of Contemporary Crime, Harm, Ethics, 2*(1), 62–81.

Brown, E., Kumar, S., Rajjio, T., Pollock, B., & Mulsant, B. (2020). Anticipating and mitigating the impact of the COVID-19 pandemic on Alzheimer's disease and related dementias. *The American Journal of Geriatric Psychiatry, 28*(7), 712–721.

Bundgaard, H., Bundgaard, J., Pedersen, D., Buchwald, C., Todsen, T., Norsk, J., Heje, M., Vissing, C., Nielsen, P., Winslow, U., Fogh, K., Hasselbalch, R., Kristensen, J., Ringgaard, A., Andersen, M., Goecke, N., Tribbien, R., Skovgaard, K., Benfield, T., Ullum, H., Pedersen, C., & Iversen, K. (2021). Effectiveness of adding a mask recommendation to other public health measures to prevent SARS-CoV-2 infection in Danish mask wearers: A randomized controlled trial. *Annals of Internal Medicine, 174*(3), 335–344.

Bwire, G., Ario, A., Eyu, P., Ocom, F., Wamala, J., Kusi, K., Latif, N., Kondwani, J., Wanyenze, R., & Talisuna, A. (2022). The COVID-19 pandemic in the African continent. *BMC Medicine, 167*(20), 1–23.

Cantor, E., Salas, R., & Torres, R. (2022). Femicide and attempted femicide before and during the COVID-19 pandemic in Chile. *International Journal of Environmental Research and Public Health, 19*(3), 1–13.

Chester, M., Plate, R., Powell, T., Rodriguez, Y., Wagner, N., & Waller, R. (2023). The COVID-19 pandemic, mask-wearing, and emotion recognition during late-childhood. *Social Development, 32*, 315–328.

Datzberger, S., Parkes, J., Bhatia, A., Nagawa, R., Kasidi, J., Musenze, B., Naker, D., & Devries, K. (2023). Intensified inequities: Young people's experiences of Covid-19 and school closures in Uganda. *Children & Society, 37*(1), 71–90.

Department of Health. (2011). *UK influenza pandemic preparedness strategy 2011*. Department of Health.

Department of Health. (2022). *Departing minister thanks health and care staff*. Department of Health. https://www.health-ni.gov.uk/news/departing-minister-thanks-health-and-care-staff. Accessed on 21 March 2023.

Dobbs, T., & Carson, A. (2022). The hidden factors associated with poor health outcomes. *Jama Network Open, 5*(10), 1–3.

Dodsworth, L. (2021). *A state of fear: How the UK government weaponised fear during the Covid-19 pandemic.* Pinter & Martin Ltd.

Editorial. (2021). COVID-19 vaccine equity and booster doses. *The Lancet Infectious Diseases, 21*(9), 1193.

Ellis, A., Briggs, D., Lloyd, A., & Telford, L. (2021a). A ticking time bomb of future harm: Lockdown, child abuse and future violence. *Abuse: An International Impact Journal, 2*(1), 37–48.

Ellis, A., Telford, L., Lloyd, A., & Briggs, D. (2021b). For the greater good: Sacrificial violence and the coronavirus pandemic. *Journal of Contemporary Crime, Harm, Ethics, 1*(1), 1–22.

Foad, C., Whitmarsh, L., Hanep, P., & Haddock, G. (2021) The limitations of polling data in understanding public support for COVID-19 lockdown policies. *Royal Society Open Science, 8*, 1–11.

Foster, G., Frijters, P., & Baker, M. (2021). *The great Covid panic: What happened, why, and what to do next.* Brownstone Institute.

Galazzi, A., Binda, F., Gambazza, S., Cantu, F., Colombo, E., Adamini, I., Grasselli, G., Lusignani, M., Laquintana, D., & Rasero, L. (2022) The end-of-life patients with COVID-19 in intensive care unit and the stress level on their family members: A cross-sectional study. *Nursing in Critical Care, 28*, 133–140.

Gaynor, E., Krause, K., Welder, L., Cooper, A., Ashley, C., Mack, K., Crosby, A., Trinh, E., Ivey-Stephenson, A., & Whittle, L. (2023). Suicidal thoughts and behaviours among high school students—Youth risk behaviour study, United States, 2021. *Centre for Disease Control and Prevention: Morbidity and Mortality Weekly Report, 72*(1), 45–54.

Geulayov, G., Mansfield, K., Jindra, C., Hawton, K., & Fazel, M. (2022). Loneliness and self-harm in adolescents during the first national COVID-19 lockdown: Results from a survey of 10,000 secondary school pupils in England. *Current Psychology.* Online First. https://doi.org/10.1007/s12144-022-03651-5

Geyer, H. (2023). Precarious and non-precarious work in the informal sector: Evidence from South Africa. *Urban Studies.* Online First. https://doi.org/10.1177/00420980221138315

Great Barrington Declaration [GBD]. (2020). *Great Barrington Declaration.* Massachusetts. https://gbdeclaration.org/why-was-the-declaration-written/. Accessed on 16 March 2023.

Green, T., & Fazi, T. (2023). *The Covid consensus: The global assault on democracy and the poor—A critique from the Left*. Hurst Publishers.

Heneghan, C., Dietrich, M., Brassey, J., & Jefferson, T. (2021) *Effects of Covid-19 in care homes—A mixed methods review*. Collateral Global.

Ioannidis, J. (2022). Citation impact and social media visibility of Great Barrington and John Snow signatories for COVID-19 strategy. *British Medical Journal Open, 12*, 1–8.

Ioannidis, J., Cripps, S., & Tanner, M. (2022). Forecasting for COVID-19 has failed. *International Journal of Forecasting, 38*, 423–438.

Jefferson, S., Kohl, A., Pena, L., & Pardee, K. (2023a). Recent insights into SARS-CoV-2 omicron variant. *Reviews in Medical Virology, 33*(1), 1–14.

Jefferson, T., Dooley, L., Ferroni, E., Al-Ansary, L., Driel, M., Bawazeer, G., Jones, M., Hoffmann, T., Clark, J., Beller, E., Glasziou, P., & Conly, J. (2023b). Physical interventions to interrupt or reduce the spread of respiratory viruses. *Cochrane Database of Systematic Reviews, 1*, 1–326.

Johnson, J., Bulushi, A., Idris, Z., Essa, Z., & Hassan, A. (2023). The experience of palliative care nurses in Qatar during the time of COVID-19: A qualitative study. *Journal of Nursing Research, 31*(1), 1–6.

Jones, L., & Hameiri, S. (2022a). Explaining the failure of global health governance during COVID-19. *International Affairs, 98*(6), 2057–2076.

Jones, L., & Hameiri, S. (2022b). COVID-19 and the failure of the neoliberal regulatory state. *Review of International Political Economy, 29*(4), 1027–1052.

Kang, Y., Colson-Fearon, D., Kim, M., Park, S., Stephens, M., Kim, Y., & Wetzler, E. (2023). Socio-economic and psychosocial determinants of violent discipline among parents in Asia Pacific countries during COVID-19: Focus on disadvantaged populations. *Child Abuse & Neglect, 139*, 1–14.

Karakasi, M., Voultsos, P., Fotou, E., Nikolaidis, I., Kyriakou, M., Markopoulou, M., Douzenis, A., & Pavlidis, P. (2022). Emerging trends in domestic homicide/femicide in Greece over the period 2010–2021. *Medicine, Science and the Law*, 1–12.

Kawaoka, N., Ohashi, K., Fukuhara, S., Miyachi, T., Asai, T., Imaeda, M., & Saitoh, S. (2022). Impact of school closures due to COVID-19 on children with neurodevelopmental disorders in Japan. *Journal of Autism and Developmental Disorders, 52*, 2149–2155.

Kheriaty, A. (2022). *The new abnormal: The rise of the biomedical security state*. Regnery Publishing.

Krohnert, K., Haslam, A., Hoeg, T., & Prasad, V. (2023). Statistical and numerical errors made by the US Centers for Disease Control and Prevention During the COVID-19 pandemic. PrePrint. https://papers.ssrn.com/sol3/papers.cfm?abstract_id=4381627

Krupar, S., & Sadural, A. (2022). COVID "death pits": US nursing homes, racial capitalism, and the urgency of antiracist eldercare. *Environment and Planning C: Politics and Space, 40*(5), 1106–1129.

Kulldorff, M. (2021). *Why I spoke out against lockdowns*. Spiked. https://www.spiked-online.com/2021/06/04/why-i-spoke-out-against-lockdowns/. Accessed on 20 March 2023.

Lockdown Files. (2023). Lockdown Files. *The Telegraph*. https://www.telegraph.co.uk/news/lockdown-files/. Accessed on 15 June 2023.

Ludecke, D., & Knesebeck, O. (2022). Decline in mental health in the beginning of the COVID-19 outbreak among European older adults—Associations with social factors, infection rates, and government response. *Frontiers in Public Health, 10*, 1–10.

Madigan, S., Racine, N., Vaillancourt, T., Korczak, D., Hewitt, J., Pador, P., Park, J., McArthur, B., Holy, C., & Neville, R. (2023). Changes in depression and anxiety among children and adolescents from before to during the COVID-19 pandemic. *JAMA Paediatrics*, 1–15.

May, I., Awad, S., May, M., & Ziegler, A. (2023). Parental stress provoked by short-term school closures during the second COVID-19 lockdown. *Journal of Family Issues, 44*(1), 25–45.

McGowan, V., & Bambra, C. (2022). COVID-19 mortality and deprivation: Pandemic, syndemic, and endemic health inequalities. *Lancet Public Health, 7*, 966–975.

MeKonnen, E., & Amede, A. (2022). Food insecurity and unemployment crisis under COVID-19: Evidence from sub-Saharan Africa. *Cogent Social Sciences, 8*, 1–17.

Mir, I., Ng, S., Jamali, M., Jabbar, M., & Humayra, S. (2023). Determinants and predictors of mental health during and after COVID-19 lockdown among university students in Malaysia. *PLoS ONE, 18*(1), 1–16.

Mohammed, A. (2022). Children's lives in an era of school closures: Exploring the implications of COVID-19 for child labour in Ghana. *Children & Society, 37*, 91–106.

Molnar, G., & Hermann, Z. (2023). Short and long-term effects of COVID-related kindergarten and school closures on first to eighth grade students' school readiness skills and mathematics, reading and science learning. *Learning and Instruction, 83*, 1–13.

Munford, L., Khavandi, S., & Bambra, C. (2022). COVID-19 and deprivation amplification: An ecological study of geographical inequalities in mortality in England. *Health & Place, 78*, 1–9.

Munzhedzi, P., & Uwizeyimana, D. (2022). Editorial: COVID-19 in Africa: The good, the bad and the ugly. *African Journal of Governance and Development, 11*(1), 1–6.

Nechifor, V., Ramos, M., Ferrari, E., Laichena, J., Kihiu, E., Omanyo, D., Musamali, R., & Kiriga, B. (2021). Food security and welfare changes under COVID-19 in sub-Saharan Africa: Impacts and responses in Kenya. *Global Food Security, 28*, 1–9.

Office for National Statistics [ONS]. (2021). *Average age of those who had died with COVID-19.* ONS. https://www.ons.gov.uk/aboutus/transparencyand governance/freedomofinformationfoi/averageageofthosewhohaddiedwithco vid19. Accessed on 11 March 2023.

Office for National Statistics [ONS]. (2022). *Health state life expectancies by national deprivation deciles, England: 2018 to 2020.* ONS. https://www.ons. gov.uk/peoplepopulationandcommunity/healthandsocialcare/healthinequa lities/bulletins/healthstatelifeexpectanciesbyindexofmultipledeprivationimd/ 2018to2020. Accessed on 12 March 2023.

Owens, M., Townsend, E., Hall, E., Bhatia, T., Fitzgibbon, R., & Miller-Lakin, F. (2022). Mental health and wellbeing in young people in the UK during lockdown (COVID-19). *International Journal of Environmental Research and Public Health, 19*, 1–15.

Owonikoko, S., Momodu, J., & Suleiman, J. (2023). Trend and pattern analysis of incidents of rape during the period of Covid-19 pandemic in Adamawa state, North-eastern Nigeria. *African Security Review.* Online First: https://doi.org/10.1080/10246029.2022.2159464

Owusu-Addo, E., Owusu-Addo, S., Bennor, D., Mensah-Odum, N., Deliege, A., Bansal, A., Yoshikawa, M., & Odame, J. (2023). Prevalence and determinants of sexual abuse among adolescent girls during the COVID-19 lockdown and school closures in Ghana: A mixed method study. *Child Abuse & Neglect, 135*, 1–12.

Oxfam. (2022). *The inequality crisis in East Africa: Fighting austerity and the pandemic.* Oxfam.

Patel, J., Nielsen, F., Badiani, A., Unadkat, S., Patel, B., & Wardle, R. (2020). Poverty, inequality and COVID-19: The forgotten vulnerable. *Public Health, 183*, 110–111.

Patrick, R., Power, M., Garthwaite, K., Kaufman, J., Page, G., & Pybus, K. (2022). *A year like no other: Life on a low income during COVID-19*. Policy Press.

Pfitzner, N., Fitz-Gibbon, K., & True, J. (2022). When staying home isn't safe: Australian practitioner experiences of responding to intimate partner violence during COVID-19 restrictions. *Journal of Gender-Based Violence, 6*(2), 297–314.

Petterson, S., Westfall, J., & Miller, B. (2020). *Projected deaths of despair from Covid-19*. Robert Graham Center.

POLITICO Harvard T.H Chan School of Public Health. (2022). *Conflicting views among parents about the impact on their children of continuing mask mandates in schools*. Harvard University.

Power, A., & Hall, E. (2018). Placing care in times of austerity. *Social & Cultural Geography, 19*(3), 303–313.

Reiss, K., & Bhakdi, S. (2020). *Corona, false alarm?* Chelsea Green Publishing.

Rethink Mental Illness. (2021). *Demand for mental health advice soars in year after lockdown*. Rethink Mental Illness. https://www.rethink.org/news-and-stories/news/2021/03/demand-for-mental-health-advice-soars-in-year-after-first-lockdown/. Accessed on 23 March 2023.

Saint, S., & Moscovich, D. (2021). Effects of mask-wearing on social anxiety: An exploratory review. *Anxiety, Stress & Coping, 34*(5), 487–502.

Sallie, S., Ritou, V., Bowden-Jones, H., & Voon, V. (2020). Assessing international alcohol consumption patterns during isolation from the COVID-19 pandemic using an online survey: Highlighting negative emotionality mechanisms. *British Medical Journal Open, 10*, 1–10.

Scoglio, A., Zhu, Y., Lawn, R., Murchland, A., Sampson, L., Rich-Edwards, J., Kha, S., Kang, J., & Koenen, K. (2023). Intimate partner violence, mental health symptoms, and modifiable health factors in women during the COVID-19 pandemic in the US. *Jama Network Open, 6*(3), 1–14.

Senger, M. (2023). *The 'pure fear' excuse for lockdowns*. Brownstone Institute. https://brownstone.org/articles/the-pure-fear-theory/. Accessed on 1 May 2023.

Shobako, N. (2022). Lessons from the health policies for children during the pandemic in Japan. *Frontiers in Public Health*, 1–14.

Soeiro, C., Ribeiro, R., Almeida, I., Saavedra, R., Caridade, S., Oliveira, A., & Santos, M. (2023). Violence against women during the COVID-19 pandemic: From children to the elderly. *Social Sciences, 12*(2), 1–10.

Sorensen, R., Barber, R., Pigott, D., Carter, A., Spencer, C., Ostroff, S., Reiner, R., Abbafati, C., Adolph, C., Allorant, D., Amlag, J., Aravkin, A., Bachmeier, S., Jensen, B., Bisignano, C., Bloom, S., Castellano, R., Castro, E., Collins, J., Comfort, H., Dai, X., Dangel, W., Dapper, C., Deen, A., Earl, L., Erickson, M., Ewald, S., Ferrari, A., Flaxman, V., Frostad, J., & Fullman, N., et al., (2022) Variation in the COVID-19 infection-fatality ratio by age, time, and geography during the pre-vaccine era: A systematic analysis. *The Lancet, 399*, 1469–1488.

Stainback, K., Hearne, B., & Trieu, M. (2020). COVID-19 and the 24/7 news cycle: Does COVID-19 news exposure affect mental health. *Socius: Sociological Research for a Dynamic World, 6*, 1–15.

Statista. (2022). *Number of coronavirus (COVID-19) deaths in the African continent as of November 18, 2022, by country*. Statista. https://www.statista.com/statistics/1170530/coronavirus-deaths-in-africa/. Accessed on 23 March 2023.

Stokel-Walker, C. (2022). How similar is covid-19 to the flu? *British Medical Journal., 379*, 1–3.

Telford, L., Bushell, M., & Hodgkinson, O. (2022). Passport to neoliberal normality? A critical exploration of COVID-19 vaccine passports. *Journal of Contemporary Crime, Harm, Ethics, 2*(1), 42–61.

Townsend, E. (2020a). Debate: The impact of school closures and lockdown on mental health in young people. *Child and Adolescent Mental Health, 25*(4), 265–266.

Townsend, E. (2020b). COVID-19 policies in the UK and consequences for mental health. *The Lancet Psychiatry, 7*(12), 1014–1015.

UNICEF. (2021). *Uganda Annual Report*. UNICEF, Uganda Country Office: Kampala.

UNICEF. (2022). *The state of global learning poverty*. UNICEF.

Usuelli, M. (2020). The Lombardy region of Italy launches the first investigative COVID-19 commission. *The Lancet, 396*(10262), 86–87.

Vermeulen, S., Alink, L., & Berkel, S. (2023). Child maltreatment during school and childcare closure due to the COVID-19 pandemic. *Child Maltreatment, 28*(1), 13–23.

Wagner, A. (2022). *Emergency state: How we lost our freedoms in the pandemic and why it matters*. The Bodley Head.

Wegerif, M. (2020). 'Informal' food traders and food security: Experiences from the Covid-19 response in South Africa. *Food Security, 12*(4), 797–800.

WHO. (2019). *Global Influenza Programme: Non-pharmaceutical public health measures for mitigating the risk and impact of epidemic and pandemic influenza*. WHO.

Wistow, J. (2022). *Social policy, political economy, and the social contract*. Policy Press.

Woolhouse, M. (2022). *The year the world went mad: A scientific memoir*. Sandstone Press.

Zee, M., Bagchus, L., Becque, Y., Witkamp, E., Heide, A., Lent, L., Goossensen, A., Korfage, I., Philipsen, B., & Pasman, H. (2023). Impact of COVID-19 on care at the end of life during the first months of the pandemic from the perspective of healthcare professionals from different settings: A qualitative interview study (the CO-LIVE study). *British Medical Journal Open, 13*, 1–9.

Žižek, S. (2021). *Pandemic! 2: Chronicles of a time lost*. Polity.

Zulaika, G., Bulbarelli, M., Nyothach, E., Eijk, A., Mason, L., Fwaya, E., Obor, D., Kwaro, D., Wang, D., Mehta, S., & Phillips-Howard, P. (2022). Impact of COVID-19 lockdowns on adolescent pregnancy and school dropout amongst secondary schoolgirls in Kenya. *British Medical Journal Global Health, 7*, 1–9.

3

Harmalogical Pharmacology and the Covid-19 Vaccine

Ben: "The German health minister, who is triple vaccinated, got the virus. They say to us how they are protecting us but look how anyone can get this virus. It is not about science anymore, it is about political goals. I am also sceptical how fast they invented it *[the vaccine]*. On one hand, it is quite a scientific achievement but the AstraZeneca - which was hailed as one of the best - then the problems with the blood clots and it was withdrawn. Same with Johnson & Johnson. They just say wait a year. Then there is BioNtech but Moderna is not recommended for under 30 year olds. But everyone was saying they are safe and nothing can happen. Even scientists now say we made a mistake with those vaccines. The companies have not been clear about the side effect reactions as well. Before the pandemic, I never doubted these things like vaccines. But it is true, they *[the vaccines]* don't really do much as you can still get infected".

Ben told us this halfway through 2021 when the vaccination campaign was well under way in Germany. He had doubts about the vaccine, particularly how quickly it was conceived, made available, and distributed which was why he refused it. Eight months later, in March

2022 when Covid-19 infections were at their highest in Germany and one of the highest in Europe at 262,593 cases (Oltermann, 2022), he gave us an update as the German government began the relaxation of their Covid-19 restrictions, after having prevented unvaccinated people from undertaking various activities or denying them entry to certain places:

> *Ben*: Well time is running so fast nowadays… there are no more restrictions, except for masks in public transportation and in health facilities. But there are certain people who already plan new restrictions for winter… it is pretty much like some people really need restrictions like last winter. I don't know if you heard about this but there was a commission that evaluated the effects of the *[Covid-19]* measures and they concluded for example that policies like restricting unvaccinated from going to restaurants had no effect. What was the point of the vaccine or even of the measures they *[the government]* took to prevent Covid-19?

Green and Fazi (2023) outline how the global quest to develop Covid-19 vaccines was nationalistic, following pre-existing geographical schisms. Many countries worked on producing their own vaccine including the UK, Turkey, Russia, and the USA. The Bill and Melinda Gates Foundation initially invested $125 million to speed up the development and delivery of these vaccines, in collaboration with a range of pharmaceutical companies such as Bayer, Johnson & Johnson, and Pfizer. Given the huge profits that were to be made by the pharmaceutical industry—or what is more commonly known as Big Pharma—it was arguably the "*twenty-first century equivalent of the Californian gold rush*" (Green & Fazi, 2023: 177). As we will see, vaccination was cast as the only means to escape the restrictions, with not getting vaccinated regarded by many commentators as immoral and unethical; only something an irresponsible citizen would do (Telford et al., 2022).

Although safe vaccinations generally take between 5 and 10 years to create (Briggs et al., 2021b), and on average 16 years to be commercially available (Tahamtan et al., 2017), governments commissioned pharmaceutical companies to devise a vaccine for Covid-19 within weeks of its outbreak. By the summer of 2020, Big Pharma companies like Moderna and Pfizer were already undertaking phase II clinical trials, and by the end of the year governments around the world had started to receive millions of approved doses. Much political, mainstream media, and public emphasis was placed upon the vaccine being the 'miracle cure' for Covid-19, with the idea that "*nobody is safe until everyone is safe*" embodying a drive to vaccinate the entire world against the disease regardless of individual risk (Editorial, 2021). Its arrival, as we indicated in earlier work, symbolised the *impending end* of the pandemic (Briggs et al., 2021b). This retired man from the UK observed how:

> The UK has used fear as a weapon to cow a population into accepting controlling and coercive measures introduced undemocratically by an abuse of Parliament. Lockdowns have not controlled the virus and have been a catastrophe in all other respects. The suppression of science and of debate by government and media has resulted in ignorance and a pursuit of damaging agendas including a belief that we are powerless before this virus other than by the magic of a vaccine. The latter, by the way, is also a failure.

These testimonies from 'anti-vaxxers'—as they were often referred (Roberts et al., 2022)—go beyond a critique of lockdown and are directed at the vaccine. In this chapter, we take a closer look at how the Covid-19 vaccine was conceived, deployed, and administered. To begin with, we provide some brief historical context, which considers the pre-pandemic established science around vaccinations and their evaluative process as remedies for infectious diseases. Much of this 'established science' was based upon decades of scientific advancements which, as we will see, was disregarded in the case of Covid-19. Other scientific knowledge related to virology and immunology was similarly ignored. Lockdowns and curfews limited the transmission of other viruses thus weakening immune systems, while advice relating to healthy eating, physical exercise, and Vitamin D exposure, which all help to reduce the risk of viral infection and the severity of illness, were ignored too (Bhattacharya et al., 2023). It speaks to a disjointed public health response where vaccine-acquired immunity was valued over public health. We weren't encouraged or incentivised to live healthier lifestyles; but we were strongly encouraged to get vaccinated. We also introduce the term *harmalogical pharmacology* to explain how pharmacological business interests trumped public health needs during the Covid-19 pandemic. Throughout the chapter, we deploy data from our global mixed-methods study to expose peoples' complex sentiments surrounding the Covid-19 vaccine.

Vaccines: The Established Science

Historically pandemics involving infectious diseases such as influenza or coronavirus strains have infected and killed millions of people, not only because of rapid infection but also because effective scientific medications and vaccines did not exist until the latter stages of the nineteenth century (Tahamtan et al., 2017). While societies and cultures had specific traditions and practices regarding curing illnesses, the evolution of vaccines occupies only a short period of time in our recent history and is set within a context of advances in scientific knowledge (Khan et al., 2021). Undoubtedly, vaccines have achieved incredible societal feats including boosting immunity, curbing potential infection, diminishing the severity of certain ailments, eradicating entire diseases, and saving countless lives. For example, it has been estimated that current vaccination interventions for all diseases around the globe save the lives of five people per minute (Tahamtan et al., 2017), preventing around 2.5 million deaths annually (Stevens et al., 2017).

Derived from the breakthroughs of scientists such as Edward Jenner in the eighteenth century and Louis Pasteur, Robert Koch, and Paul Ehrlich in the nineteenth century, vaccines emerged from pioneering scientific studies of immunisation (Plotkin, 2014). Early efforts to introduce the idea of vaccination, however, were not dissimilar to some attitudes and reactions we have seen to the Covid-19 inoculation (Chapters 5 and 6). In eighteenth-century Europe smallpox possessed an IMR of 20–60% and killed around 400,000 people annually, while about a third of survivors suffered blindness (Riedel, 2005). The long story of eradicating what Riedel (2005: 24) termed *"the scourge of mankind"* was initiated by the physician Edward Jenner. Riedel (2005) described how after hearing stories that dairymaids were afforded immunity from smallpox after previously being infected with cowpox, in 1796 Jenner inoculated an 8-year-old boy with cowpox and ten days later with smallpox lesion. No infection developed. As the Latin terminology for cowpox is vaccinia, Jenner labelled the inoculation procedure *vaccination* (Riedel, 2005).

Social hostilities emerged after smallpox vaccination for infants was made mandatory in England and Wales through The Vaccination Act 1853 (Millward, 2019). Representing one of the first main governmental public health interventions into peoples' personal lives, the obligation to vaccinate in Britain became a source of division and "*created the first 'anti-vax movement*" (Bardosh et al., 2022: 5). This was particularly among working-class groups who saw its imposition as another example of class oppression in a broader structural climate of profound economic inequality, widespread poverty, and malnutrition (Hobsbawm, 1987). Public resentment manifested in demonstrations in 1885, whereby protestors often held up anti-vaccine banners. Shortly after, many middle-class groups joined the protests, enabling the issue to advance to parliament. This was bolstered by the support of high-ranking physicians, most notably Dr Charles Creighton and Dr Edgar Crookshank, who started to support anti-vaccination organisations (Baker, 2003). As the country gradually built up immunity through vaccination and the disease was largely eradicated, mandatory vaccination was dropped in 1971 (Millward, 2019).

At the turn of the twentieth century, diseases such as Rabies, a virus that is transmitted through animals, Typhoid, a gut and bloodstream infection, as well as other diseases like Diphtheria, Tuberculosis, and Pertussis were prevalent (Rappuoli, 2007). While Louis Pasteur and colleagues had pioneered the use of infectious agents as components of early vaccines, Emil Von Behring and Kitasato Shibasaburo advanced the scientific knowledge of antibodies in 1890 particularly through working on diphtheria and tetanus immunity in animal experiments (Kaufmann, 2017). As they pioneered the first successful therapy for diphtheria and tetanus, Emil Von Behring was the first person to be awarded the Nobel Prize for Medicine in 1901 (Kaufmann, 2017). Emile Roux and Alexandre Yersin discovered the soluble toxins for Diphtheria and Tetanus, which led to the development of the first active immunisation against those diseases respectively (Butler, 2014; Kaufmann, 2017).

By the 1940s, science had advanced sufficiently to enable the mass production of vaccines. The arrival of vaccines for Polio and Influenza in the post-war period (1945–1979) marked a new era of investment in science by global organisations such as the WHO (Hoyt, 2006). In the aftermath of the Second World War specific vaccination programmes became central to a general trend towards supporting and sustaining collective public health (Clem, 2011). Such agencies led the way in global public health initiatives. For example, in 1959 the WHO launched an ambitious campaign to eradicate smallpox. Although these efforts were mired by a lack of resources and commitment from various nations, in 1971 the disease was eradicated from South America, then Asia (1975) and Africa (1977). Indeed, the WHO declared that smallpox had ceased to exist in 1980 (Fenner et al., 1988). As global disease-related mortality rates reduced, due to vaccines and the eradication of smallpox and Polio, the early period of the second half of the twentieth century became known as the "*golden age of vaccines*" (Saleh et al., 2021: 1). By the late 1960s, vaccines had been created and licensed against Measles, Mumps, and Rubella (Plotkin & Plotkin, 2011). These inoculations remain the cornerstone of paediatric immunisation.

Also known as 'whooping cough', pertussis is a highly transmissible infectious disease that blighted many countries and caused significant illness and death, especially among children in the early twentieth century (Black, 1997). For example, in the USA pre-pertussis-vaccination records highlight around 270,000 pertussis cases and 10,000 deaths annually (Decker & Edwards, 2021). Across the 1940s in the UK pertussis afflicted between 60 and 70% of school age children and led to 9000 deaths (Baker, 2003), which far outweighed the impact of other diseases. A combined vaccine named diphtheria-tetanus-pertussis (DTP) was licensed in the USA in 1949, recommended for universal usage by the American Academy of Paediatrics and distributed in most developed nations (Guiso et al., 2020). Up until the early 1970s, this combined vaccine had significantly reduced disease-related infections and mortalities (Black, 1997). Although there were isolated case reports that the vaccine could ignite fever that resulted in seizure and more serious complications such as encephalopathy,[1] permanent neurological injury, and potential death in the late 1940s and 1950s (Guiso et al., 2020), few questions were raised about the vaccine since the British Medical Research Council had not reported any of these issues in their initial clinical trials with around 36,000 children in 1957 (Baker, 2003; Millward, 2017).

However, further doubts about the DTP vaccine's effectiveness and potential neurological harms were raised in the 1970s and 1980s. Baker (2003: 4003) outlines how the release of an article in 1974 from the *Hospital for Sick Children at Great Ormond Street*, UK, highlighted how 36 children had endured myriad neurological problems following DTP inoculation, engendering "*the most significant setback for the cause of immunization since the smallpox vaccine debates of the previous century*". A significant reduction in vaccine uptake followed, and infection rates rose considerably (Millward, 2019). The subsequent media storm left parents convinced their child's disabilities were a direct result of the vaccine. Baker (2003: 4007) claims a core problem at the time was how:

> Popular media responds to drama, whether in the form of victims of vaccines or epidemics. It serves to reduce the complex kinds of arguments made in medical journals to the level of human-interest stories.

Consequently, the UK Government investigated through two advisory panels and found the vaccine was associated with a very low risk of developing acute neurological illness (Baker, 2003). The Joint Committee of Vaccination and Immunisation's (JCVI) national study evaluated and reported that the absolute risk of acute neurological illness presented was 1 in 111,000 while permanent neurological damage represented a lower risk at 1 in 310,000 (Miller et al., 1981). Attempts to hold the medical authorities to account and bring justice to some of the alleged vaccine victims failed, mainly due to contradictions and disparities in the parents' testimonies and discrepancies in hospital records. As a consensus gradually emerged that the vaccination was safe for most people, coupled with

---

[1] Encephalopathy refers to any disease of the brain that alters brain function or structure. It may be caused by an infection, metabolic or mitochondrial dysfunction, brain tumour, or increased pressure in the skull. In general, it is now a treatable brain disease.

ever diminishing outbreaks of pertussis, immunisation rates recovered to their pre-1974 levels by the end of the 1980s (Millward, 2019).[2]

Stern and Markel (2005) explain how both safety concerns and deep-seated public fears of inoculation frequently reappear throughout history. Other high-profile cases demonstrate public mistrust. In the USA, mistrust of authorities and public health interventions is common in minority communities with the Tuskegee experiment a common example. The US Government's 1932 Tuskegee Syphilis Study included 400 black sharecroppers who were not told they had syphilis and were not treated as part of the study (Corbie-Smith, 1999). The study aimed to observe the infection's natural progression without intervention but violated the men's informed consent (Telford et al., 2022). Despite the emergence of antibiotics to treat syphilis in the 1940s, the trial continued until 1972. This example demonstrates that trust in public health can be broken through misrepresentation, and communities often do not forget long after the injustice has occurred. This, as we will see, is evident in some of our data on Covid-19 vaccination.

The second example, from the UK, is the MMR vaccine scandal that emerged in 1998. In a paper published in *The Lancet* by British gastroenterologist Dr Andrew Wakefield and twelve of his colleagues, they presented apparent evidence of a link between the MMR vaccine and autism in children (Wakefield et al., 1998). Although the study was subsequently discredited as fraudulent and ethically dubious, with *The Lancet* retracting the paper and Wakefield taken off the medical register by the General Medical Council, the public hysteria around MMR and autism created significant concern with vaccination rates dropping from 91% in 1998 to below 80% in 2003 (Flaherty, 2011). Although vaccination rates increased eventually, Brown et al. (2012) noted that MMR hesitancy remained which was linked to parents with strong anti-immunisation views.

Evidently, concerns around vaccines and faith in public health were strongly connected before the advent of the Covid-19 pandemic, though these worries manifested again across 2020–22. Such concerns were

---

[2] Similar occurrences were observed in other countries. For example, in 1975 in Japan, the vaccine was suspended when two child deaths became widely publicised leading to a major outbreak of pertussis (see: Kanai, 1980).

also informed by the reputation and behaviour of the pharmaceutical industry who had, historically, followed capitalism's injunction to profit at the expense of public health (Meier, 2020), embodied in numerous high-profile scandals that further eroded faith and trust. Our data exposes how this was evident in the participants' responses particularly regarding how established processes around vaccine development diminished with the onset of Covid-19:

> It is virtually impossible to control spread of a respiratory virus so all 'efforts' have been hard to swallow. (Female, 40, Geophysicist, UK)

> The whole thing has felt like a totalitarian regime. 'Laws' don't follow scientific data and instead are based on "THE Science" of government preferences from cherry-picked data. (Male, 50, Teacher, New Zealand)

> The UK had a long-standing protocol for a pandemic, particularly pertinent to vaccine development, which was based on peer-reviewed scientific research: this was completely ignored at beginning of Covid, leading to unnecessary measures. (Male, 47, Police officer, UK)

Having outlined a very brief history of the development of vaccines with a particular focus on the UK, the next section explores the rise of Big Pharma alongside some of the industry's controversies. This particularly involves morally and ethically dubious practices for the purposes of expanding markets and maximising profitability.

The Evolution of Big Pharma

Malerba and Orsenigo (2015) outline how the modern pharmaceutical industry has its origins in the late nineteenth century, largely involving European companies in Germany, England, and France who manufactured chemicals. Pfizer, founded in 1849, was initially a chemicals business which expanded during the American Civil War (1861–1865) as the demand for painkillers and antiseptic increased. After the war, one surviving Colonel, Eli Lilly, set up a pharmaceutical business in 1876— Eli Lilly and Company—pioneering new methods in the industry, particularly the idea of research and development alongside manufacturing (Payette & Davis, 2001). It was not until the advent of World War Two, though, that the industry undertook pervasive research and development, increasing medical knowledge, innovation, growth, and the potential for new products (Malerba & Orsenigo, 2015).

Although penicillin was first discovered in 1928 in London by Alexander Fleming (Gaynes, 2017), the emergence of new products particularly in the 1950s including antibiotics for clinical usage was cast as "*arguably the greatest medical breakthrough of the 20th century*" (Hutchings et al., 2019: 72), which gave rise to a considerable growth of the industry. The momentous rise of Pfizer in the USA and Hoechst, Schering, and Bayer in Germany meant the "*industry took on a prominent new international and transnational character*" (Liebenau, 1990: 727). Unprecedented amounts of money were poured into sales and marketing, with growth levels generally above 10% from the 1950s to 1980s (Malerba & Orsenigo, 2015). As the industry grew wealthy thanks to its growing portfolio of products, the potential ethical conflicts of profiteering from the sale of healthcare products became increasingly apparent. Purdue Pharma epitomised this contradiction. Purdue created painkilling drugs such as Oxycontin which were aggressively marketed as addiction-free pain relief (Meier, 2020). Despite increasing evidence to the contrary, Purdue's sales representatives continued to push Oxycontin as the answer to America's pain problem, convincing, incentivising, and corrupting doctors to continue prescribing its product (Keefe, 2021). By 2017, sales of Oxycontin alone exceeded $31 billion with the three main wholesalers of prescription drugs in the USA—McKessen, Cardinal, and AmerisourceBergen—shipping 780,000,000 pills between 2007 and 2012 alone (Meier, 2020). Alongside these phenomenal sums, by 2019 70,000 Americans were dying annually from opioid overdoses (Ghose et al., 2022). Undoubtedly pain relief is a positive development in medicine, but the combined factors of light regulation, marketing, and unrestrained profit under neoliberal capitalism combined to create a public health crisis rather than a solution.

The neoliberal turn in the 1970s reconfigured the relationship between the state and the market with the government's role to foster conditions conducive to market opportunity; yet ready to intervene in the event of a market crash (Mitchell & Fazi, 2017). Rather than intervene directly in the economy, the state's role was to regulate in favour of corporate expansion and 'free markets'. In terms of regulation, pharmaceutical companies are ostensibly policed by state bodies (in the UK, National Institute for Health and Care Excellence, in the USA, the National Institutes of Health). However, as Harvey (2010) notes, a symbiotic relationship between the institutions and actors of state and market exist whereby rules and laws are written by the industries themselves and a 'revolving door' exists between the public and private sector. In Big Pharma, the development of Tagamet, an ulcer medication, became the first 'blockbuster drug' to earn its manufacturers more than $1 billion in sales in 1986 (Li, 2014). This paved the way for companies to compete for the next big pharmaceutical remedy, either through research and development, often with government subsidies and support or through the more entrepreneurial acquisition of other drug companies or price gouging (McLean, 2016).

Stevens et al. (2017) outline three key phases attached to developing a commercial vaccine—preclinical, clinical, and post-licensure. Accordingly, compliance policies and ethical frameworks should govern such companies to ensure the safe production, storage, and distribution of these drugs, and manufacturers must monitor the vaccine's efficacy to avoid any adverse events ('AE' hereafter). As we have noted, it can take well over a decade to conceive and safely mass manufacture a commercial vaccine. But such potentially long processes are both costly and challenging for pharmaceutical companies who must attract investment, develop research, and generate new treatments before making any profit. This is otherwise known as an 'incentive structure', and it works well.

Hawksbee et al. (2022) demonstrate that the largest pharmaceutical companies make profits significantly higher than other sectors without their products necessarily being of public benefit. The incentive structure of for-profit pharmaceutical companies has resulted in major threats to public safety and the neglect of public health. Companies will invest in the products that can generate profit; but not necessarily those that will be of the biggest benefit to the public. There is little financial incentive for a for-profit pharmaceutical company to invest in product development if there is no market. As such, profit inevitably goes into the development of products most likely to yield future profitability and shareholder dividends. The bottom-line imperative of Big Pharma therefore creates conflicts of interest that we explore next.

The Cure Worse Than the Disease?

In the 30 years prior to the Covid-19 pandemic, some of the world's largest and most powerful pharmaceutical companies—including those incentivised to create Covid-19 vaccines—were guilty of a range of misdemeanours and faced criminal and libel charges. As we have suggested, however, such corporate transgressions should be framed within a wider neoliberal context of maximising efficiency and ensuring profitability at the expense of ethical practice and social harm (Raymen, 2022).

According to their website, Amgen (n.d.) is a company "*committed to unlocking the potential of biology for patients suffering from serious illnesses by discovering, developing, manufacturing and delivering innovative human therapeutics*". However, they were prosecuted for $762 million in 2012 for misbranding an anaemia drug called Aranesp to gain a competitive edge in the market (Senior, 2013). Their drug was in direct competition with Johnson & Johnson's *Procrit*—both of which were intended to treat anaemia in cancer patients. However, the American Food and Drug Administration (FDA) found instead that the drug heightened the risk of death in patients (Brower, 2010). In 2019, Bayer and Johnson & Johnson settled over 25,000 lawsuits from people who reported how their anticoagulant drug, *Xarelto*, led to internal bleeding, stroke, and even death (Dyer, 2019a). Prosecuting judges said that patients were not informed of the major risks of the drug since many people developed life-threatening conditions after taking it. Without assuming liability, the companies jointly settled the cases by simply paying off the claimants to the tune of $775 million (Dyer, 2019a; Pollack, 2012).

Prior to the pandemic both Johnson & Johnson and Pfizer, two corporations which were involved significantly in the development and rollout of the Covid-19 vaccine, were found guilty of downplaying risks associated with their medicines. In 2013, Johnson & Johnson were found guilty of unlawfully promoting two antipsychotic drugs called *Risperdal* and *Invega* and the heart failure drug *Natrecor*. They were fined $2.2 billion to settle the allegations, which is *"one of the largest in US history"* (Kmietowicz, 2013: 1). In 2009, Pfizer were forced to pay $2.3 billion after it was found that *Bextra*—an anti-inflammatory drug—had to be withdrawn from the market because of safety concerns, with the fine amounting to *"the largest ever imposed in the United States for any matter"* (Ratner, 2009: 961). Pfizer also illegally promoted three other drugs, including the antipsychotic drug *Geodon*, antibiotic *Zyvox*, and anti-epileptic drug *Lyrica*. Healthcare providers had also been receiving payments for prescribing these drugs to patients without prescription (Harris, 2009).

Very often, the consequences of these offences impacted disproportionately upon the poor and vulnerable and had generational ramifications for public health in the decades that followed. A good example of this is the 1996 meningitis outbreak in Northern Nigeria, which particularly affected children and saw recorded cases reach 109,580 and 11,717 deaths (Mohammed et al., 2000). Pfizer had sought to launch its new antibiotic, *Trovan*, but had not conducted clinical trials with children (Lenzer, 2006). The drug was approved for various usages among adults in 1997, though it did show serious side effects including liver problems (Malakoff, 2001). Pfizer used the meningitis outbreak to test *Trovan* in a paediatric setting and out of 100–200 children involved in a two-week trial, 11 died (Malakoff, 2001). Parents also reported that children developed disabilities including liver failure and paralysis (Lenzer, 2006).

Pfizer denied misconduct and unlawful activity, and instead declared that the children had died of meningitis rather than their drug. Yet an independent investigation by a panel of experts hired by the Nigerian Government found Pfizer to be at fault for the children's deaths and guilty of conducting human trials without informed consent (Lenzer, 2006). Despite a court settlement for some of the families and the Nigerian Government, distrust of Western-associated agencies including the WHO increased. This culminated in a Polio vaccination boycott in Nigeria in 2003 which considerably set back global Polio eradication efforts (Yahya, 2007); by 2006 five Northern Nigerian states including Katsina, Kano, Jigawa, Kaduna and Bauchi accounted for 51% of all global Polio cases (Jegede, 2007). Accordingly, analysing past medical injustices reveals how "*there is an underlying logic to public anxieties often dismissed as 'anti-vaccination rumours*" (Yahya, 2007: 185) in Northern Nigeria.

Mendoza et al. (2021) outlines how public mistrust in vaccines remains low in the Philippines following the 2016 rollout of French drug *Dengvaxia*—the world's first vaccine for the mosquito-borne disease, dengue fever (Tully & Griffiths, 2021). Sanofi Pasteur's (pharmaceutical company) drug passed clinical trials that demonstrated effectiveness in reducing the severity of dengue fever; but within a year guidance changed to warn that the vaccine could cause more severe illness in children who had previously not contracted the disease (Lasco & Yu, 2021). Despite warnings, the vaccine was still deployed but was withdrawn in 2017 after it had been linked to the deaths of several children. Although no link was established between the vaccine and the children's deaths (Lasco & Yu, 2021), distrust remains strong among Filipinos (Mendoza et al., 2021). This was most recently seen during a 2019 measles outbreak where both cases and deaths were significantly higher than expected, with measles vaccination rates dropping from a high of 88% in 2014 to 55% in 2018 (Dyer, 2019b).

Among the numerous vaccine scandals in China over the last 30 years, the most recent pre-pandemic example involved Chinese vaccine maker Changsheng Bio-Technology. They were found to have produced fake data on its rabies vaccines and administered 215,184 'ineffective' Diphtheria, Tetanus, and pertussis (DTP) vaccines to Chinese children (Editorial, 2018; Philips, 2018). The Chinese Government imposed an unprecedented fine of $1.7 million on Changsheng Bio-Technology, removed its permit to produce the rabies vaccines and arrested several of the company's executives (Cyranoski, 2018). However, it also censored online and media criticism, detained any activism associated with the scandal, and threatened parents who publicly reported vaccine injuries among their children (Dyer, 2018).

Introduced in 2006, *Gardasil* is a vaccine developed by Merck & Co that is recommended to females as it provides some protection against various cancer-causing strains of human papillomavirus (HPV), a sexually transmitted virus linked to cervical cancer (Burd, 2003). This vaccine, though, has been mired in controversy and inoculation rates have been poor (Grimes, 2016). For instance, the FDA's Vaccine Adverse Event Reporting System (VAERS) reported AEs linked to the vaccine include paralysis, blindness, speech problems, seizures, and short-term memory loss as well as 26 deaths between 2010 and 2011 (Lind, 2014). As a result, US courts have awarded almost $6 million to 49 victims of *Gardasil* (Lind, 2014). However, studies have consistently found that the vaccine is safe, and AEs are extremely rare (Vichnin et al., 2015). Yet, evidence from countries like the USA demonstrates that parents consenting to HPV vaccinations for their children continues to be relatively low (Chen et al., 2021), based upon the grounds of 'safety'. For example, HPV vaccination rate among males and females under the age of 21 in the USA in 2018 was 68.1% (Chen et al., 2021).

Interestingly, Merck had initially fast-tracked its approval from the FDA in 2006 to recoup profit in the wake of the company's *Vioxx* disaster which had previously cost Merck billions in losses. Merck had developed *Vioxx* in 1999 as an effective, safer alternative to non-steroidal, anti-inflammatory drugs for the treatment of pain associated with osteoarthritis (Krumholz et al., 2007). Despite this, it was found that the drug significantly increased the risk of cardiovascular disease (Biddle, 2007; Krumholz et al., 2007). Research in the aftermath found in America alone 55,000 people may have died due to taking Vioxx (Biddle, 2007). The drug was withdrawn in 2004 and in 2007 the company was ordered to pay $4.85 billion to end around 27,000 lawsuits (Wadman, 2007). Evidently, the moral and ethical quagmire created by Big Pharma's pursuit of expanding markets and maximising profitability often trumps public safety and creates unsafe products that cause profound harm.

The New Covid-19 Vaccine

Big Pharma have a long and problematic history with clinical trials, misrepresentation, and an apparent preoccupation with profit over safety. This is not to say that there are not dedicated and high-minded individuals working in pharmaceutical companies, driven by the best of intentions. However, like all industries characterised by the neoliberal dogma of efficiency, profitability, and productivity (Lloyd, 2018), the practices and motives of corporations should be questioned. With lockdown designed to buy time for a vaccine, this was the industry we collectively turned towards to provide the keys to freedom. There was suddenly another research and development race for the next 'blockbuster' solution. By 8 April 2020, there were 115 vaccine candidates. Of these, 78 were considered active possibilities, with 73 either already at exploratory or clinical stages of development (Thanh Le et al., 2020). Experts such as Cohen (2021) and Graham et al. (2013), who had previously suggested that suitable vaccines against betacoronavirus[3] could have been developed which would have reduced the chances of evolving variants including Covid-19 and potentially prevented future betacoronavirus pandemics, were dismissed.

Government-initiated emergency laws (Rahmani et al., 2022) allowed million-dollar lobbying donations to court the business of pharmaceutical companies—often without transparent procurement procedures. In one of the few high-profile public challenges throughout the pandemic, Mislav Kolakusic (cited in Roscoe, 2022) of the European Parliament said in late 2022 that *"the purchase of 4.5 billion doses of the Covid-19 vaccine for 450 million EU residents is the biggest corruption scandal in the history of mankind"*, before pressing the President of the European Commission, Mrs von der Leyen, for evidence of *"the communication she had with Pfizer during the procurement of 4.5 billion doses of vaccines at a time when there was absolutely no proof of the effectiveness, and especially not of the harmfulness of that product"*. In a scathing critique, he added: *"based on that calculation, each child, newly born, should receive ten doses of something that no one in the world except maybe two or three people, knows what it contains"*.

The quick and seemingly unlimited availability of public money bolstered by emergency legal conditions was inevitably going to attract business interest, which in the context of health has often produced problematic procurement procedures mired by corruption (Rhodes et al., 2021; Schultz & Soreide, 2008). Like the lack of clarity around

---

[3] Defined as any or one of four genera (Alpha-, Beta-, Gamma-, and Delta-) of coronaviruses.

procurement of government contracts for PPE equipment (Jones & Hameiri, 2022), the contracts for Covid-19 vaccines were equally unclear (Green & Fazi, 2023). Rhodes et al. (2021) indicate that 182 agreements were drawn up for the purchase of 12 different Covid-19 vaccines; yet only 6% of the vaccine contracts between developers and public buyers had been published through formal channels and only 1 contract had been published without redaction by the buyer. Along with the lack of transparency around vaccine pricing, this has been an endemic issue linked to corrupt practices centred upon maximising profitability and avoiding accountability for any subsequent harm (Arguedas-Ramírez, 2022).

Relatedly, one of the main reasons why there was such a race between numerous pharmaceutical giants to develop a vaccine was that it was not paid for by them, their investors, or stakeholders, it was primarily funded by governments. While the European Commission (2020) pledged €350 million for vaccine development, the US Government invested $18 billion for vaccine development and capacity to Moderna, AstraZeneca/Oxford, Johnson & Johnson, and Sanofi/GSK (Lalani et al., 2022). The speculation of investment excited global markets (Chan et al., 2022) as the blank cheques issued by governments attracted increased investment in pharmaceutical companies and their potential Covid-19 vaccines. Such companies tend to conserve their intellectual property rights (IPR) as research and development is directed towards what is 'potentially profitable' (Hawksbee et al., 2022). This framework tends to only benefit shareholders, while neglecting diseases which blight poor communities and countries.

This was evident during the 1990s as antiretrovirals required to combat HIV/AIDS were very slow to reach developing countries (Ford et al., 2011). While pharmaceutical companies retained IPR and relatively expensive pricing, there was inadequate international aid for the necessary investment in infrastructure—hospitals, clinics, physicians—to administer the drugs in the worst afflicted nations (Attaran & Gillespie-White, 2001). This proved to also be the case during the Covid-19 vaccine rollout, where Africa was once again neglected (Green & Fazi, 2023). Not only did such nations struggle to fund initial orders but the prevalence of increased variants, particularly Omicron, increased the demand for more vaccines. Accordingly, richer countries engaged in *vaccine nationalism* and both stockpiled vaccines and administered them to low-risk groups, while many developing nations waited longer for their first batches which jeopardised the lives of many high-risk individuals (Hunter et al., 2022). As such, the unequal nature of the vaccine rollout is clear. By December 2021—12 months after the Covid-19 vaccines became available—richer Western nations had reached 90% vaccine coverage while only around 11% of all people in low-income countries had received at least one dose (Hunter et al., 2022).

According to press releases from governments and pharmaceutical companies, the vaccine would reduce the chance of hospitalisation and death and thereby keep people away from overburdened healthcare systems. Hailed by many commentators and researchers as the historical scientific feat of our time, it was found in numerous studies that the vaccine did precisely this (for example, see: Rahmani et al.'s 2022 systematic review of 54 different trials). Using a mathematical model, Watson et al. (2022: 1299) asserted that in the first year of the Covid-19 vaccination campaign vaccination "*more than halved the potential global death toll due to COVID-19, with an estimated 19.8 million deaths from COVID-19 averted as a result*". The vaccine, however, did not protect against infection (Moghadas et al., 2022) and initial evidence that vaccines were over 90% effective proved erroneous (Green & Fazi, 2023). However, the rhetoric from the President of the USA, Joe Biden (2021), on the eve of Christmas continued to suggest that vaccination prevented illness:

> If you are not fully vaccinated, you have good reason to be concerned. You're at a high risk of getting sick. And if you get sick, you're likely to spread it to others, including friends and family. And the unvaccinated have a significantly higher risk of ending up in a hospital or even dying. Almost everyone who has died from COVID-19 in the past many months has been unvaccinated.

While the term 'fully vaccinated' became a moving target (see: Chapter 5 and 6), the implication from President Biden was that vaccines made the pandemic an issue for the unvaccinated only. While the vaccine significantly reduced the likelihood of death, it did not prevent death. In

America during Autumn 2021, around 3 in 10 adults dying of Covid-19 were vaccinated or boosted (Cox et al., 2022). By January 2022, 4 in 10 deaths occurred in individuals who were vaccinated or boosted. Three months later, in April 2022, the CDC in the USA released data that estimated around 6 in 10 adults dying of Covid-19 were vaccinated or boosted, and this remained to be the case until August 2022 (Cox et al., 2022). As the pandemic recedes into the near past, more evidence emerges that the pharmaceutical companies have not been quite as accurate or forthright as their original claims suggested (see: Green & Fazi, 2023).

Numerous commentators gloss over the significant issues discussed so far, instead dedicating attention to how the rapid rollout was 'unprecedented' in historical terms and that boosters were a welcome addition to stem future virus outbreaks and variant surges (see, for example: Glassman et al., 2022; Prakash, 2022). It is undoubtedly the case that the vaccine rollout in countries such as the UK and USA was a remarkable logistical and operational success in the given timeframe, but it is similarly important to look at the political economic underpinnings of its development and rollout. For many of our participants, however, the quick availability of 'boosters' merely confirmed their initial doubts about the vaccine. For example, this female researcher from the UK in her early 30s said: *"it has been the most eye-opening show of hubristic magical thinking that an airborne virus causing an influenza-like illness can be 'controlled' by manipulating the population and through a vaccine which requires 'numerous boosters'. This, for me, raises so many questions"*.

While we rightly praise the logistical and operational rollout undertaken in some countries, in others they lacked the infrastructure for national distribution which had implications for millions of people. India, a country characterised pre-Covid-19 by a substandard health system and where millions of people live on the poverty line, faced numerous challenges with the organisation and distribution of the vaccine (Pandey et al., 2021). With such delays in accessing the vaccine and without the resources to buy from private hospitals, many Indians could not afford to wait around and carried on with their daily lives trying to earn money to eat and feed their families. In other countries, power abuses were observed when politicians and celebrity elites queued up first to get their vaccine in the wake of slow supply. In Peru, there were governmental resignations after it emerged that many politicians and their families had jumped the queue for the vaccine, depriving the vulnerable and elderly (Taylor, 2021). As the vaccine was distributed across Europe, reports of 'vaccine queue jumping' emerged in other countries including among several Mayors in Austria and politicians in Poland (Harris & Moss, 2021).

New variants also evolved. Alpha and Delta were followed by Omicron, less deadly but more infectious, and which according to some diminished the effectiveness of previous immunity and vaccination (Huang et al., 2022; Mohamed et al., 2022). Having provided the initial solution, pharmaceutical companies were ready to provide boosters to cope with new strains of Covid-19 (Barouch, 2022). This was despite no clinical trials to test whether existing vaccines were even effective against Omicron (Green & Fazi, 2023); they were approved by Western governments for booster jabs without any testing whatsoever. Research in Israel confirms that while the fourth vaccination may have continued to provide some protection to the elderly and vulnerable, its effectiveness dropped from 65.1% at week three to 22% by the end of week ten (Gazit et al., 2022).

In the face of waning immunity, research found that providing boosters would be cost effective, reduce future demand for health services (Li et al., 2022), and further defend against hospitalisation (Link-Gelles et al., 2022). Yet, it was hard to ignore how additional boosters generated further profit for the world's biggest pharmaceutical companies. As countries continued to offer 'boosters', particularly to the most vulnerable groups, shares in Moderna increased by nearly 700% in 2021 (Pilkington et al., 2022). In the first quarter of 2021, three months after the vaccine became available, Pfizer reported profits of $3.5 billion (Robbins & Goodman, 2021). By the end of the year, profitability had grown even further. A report by Oxfam (2021) indicated that within 12 months of developing the vaccine, companies such as Pfizer and Moderna were making around $93.5 million a day which equates to around $65,000 a minute or just over $1000 a second. Indeed, both companies were expected to earn around $60 billion in revenues across 2021–2022 (Altindis, 2022).

Despite this, the evolution of a 'successful vaccine' has generated doubts about vaccine safety, questions about pharmaceutical competence, and product honesty. Heyerdahl et al. (2022: 1196) found in their survey involving 7000 participants across Ukraine, Sweden, Spain, Italy, Germany, France, and Belgium that Covid-19 vaccine rejection was *"upon evidence of vaccine safety"* which *"reflected citizens' misgivings about their governments and pharmaceutical companies"* (also see: Schwarzinger et al., 2021). These findings are also consistent with the history of vaccine hesitancy (see: Leach & Fairhead, 2008). In the words of one of our participants, a female teacher in her mid-50s from the USA: *"I feel misled and biased by pharmaceutical and health authorities who are trying to mandate something they have no liability for"*. In fact, it is not clear who or what is liable for damages post vaccination if a serious AE occurs (Emanuel et al., 2021) given that the 'Emergency Use Authorized status' indemnifies pharmaceutical companies of direct liability (Halabi, 2021). Relatedly, for the global rollout of the Covid-19 vaccines, some of the key phases that were established to ensure a safe and reliable vaccine development and testing were merged to improve the speed of distribution (Mohamed et al., 2022).

Tanveer et al. (2022) suggest that the lack of transparency surrounding the Covid-19 vaccine trial documents and data transparency raised concerns over the use of the inoculations. This was found to be the case with Pfizer. Investigative work by the American journalist Paul Thacker at the end of 2021 found that during the company's pivotal phase III trials in Texas, USA, patients were unblinded, data was falsified, employees were not trained sufficiently to deal/handle vaccines, and there was a tendency for staff to be slow to follow up on AEs reported during the final phase of clinical research, potentially compromising data integrity and regulatory scrutiny (Thacker, 2021). More widely, Rhodes et al. (2021: 5) found that:

> 30 per cent of the Covid-19 vaccines being developed at the time of our research were made by developers based in countries that do not require the reporting of clinical trial summary results within 12 months.

They also claimed:

> Without legally mandated, harmonised, transparent processes and timelines for sharing clinical trial results, pharmaceutical developers can present their data in the most flattering and beneficial light or choose to withhold the data altogether. The immense pressure to rapidly produce treatments and vaccines, combined with the huge amounts of money on offer for effective products, only heightens these risks.

As Green and Fazi (2023) note, the pharmaceutical companies are among the most distrusted companies in the world and the Covid-19 vaccine process did nothing to allay those fears. We are certainly not suggesting that there was a global conspiracy to vaccinate everyone (see Chapter 5 on conspiracy). However, while no single explanation accounts for any phenomenon, a range of motivations and pressures converge. If, instead of 'following the science', we 'follow the money', it is clear that Big Pharma gained considerably. However, their history of corruption and reckless profiteering, along with the rapid development of Covid-19 vaccines, left many of our respondents with unanswered questions hinging upon mistrust and scepticism.

Harmalogical Pharmacology

Given the rapid nature of the Covid-19 vaccine development, no studies exist on the potential medium- to long-term side effects or health consequences of its administration. The swift uptake of the vaccine, much like the ideological nudging into social compliance (Chapter 2), occurred at a time when people were frightened or craving the return of their old lives and routines. For many of us, vaccinations are not uncommon. We are vaccinated as children, for travel purposes, and many have winter flu jabs. For most people, the idea of vaccination is unproblematic. In the context of severe and prolonged Covid-19 restrictions, the vaccine promised protection and the means to return to pre-pandemic life (Telford et al., 2022). As we will see, others required vaccination to retain their employment and risked dismissal if they refused (Chapters 5 and 6).

Nevertheless, an important minority continued to be vaccine hesitant and anti-vaccine mandate while a smaller group, who had been compliant and received the vaccine until then, also started to express doubts. From the 5–11 age group through to the elderly, many governments' recommendations for vaccination continued regardless of both the differentiated risks that Covid-19 clearly presented and if one had previously been infected (Bardosh et al., 2022). Meanwhile, global pharmaceutical companies gained unprecedented profit margins without any risk or downside. However, vaccine take-up rates were slow across parts of the world for both young people and children. For example, Williams (2022) outlines how in the UK in January 2022 only one in eight Black Caribbean and Gypsy/Roma 12–15-year-olds had received the inoculation and schools that contained more than half of pupils receiving free school meals possessed a median vaccination rate of 29%. At the same time, studies continued to emerge confirming that natural immunity was at least equivalent or more effective than the protection afforded by the vaccine (for instance: Kojima & Klausner, 2022; Shenai, et al., 2021).

With questions arising over the vaccine's efficacy and the requirement of boosters other issues started to surface, which cast doubt about the balance of risk between the virus and the vaccine (Briggs et al., 2021a). Numerous issues, significantly downplayed by the pharmaceutical companies, became evident. As of January 2022, the VAERS had documented various side effects from the vaccine (Table 3.1).

Initially, the VAERS was created by the CDC and FDA, and it is designed to monitor AEs after vaccination. The system is open to receive reports from vaccine manufacturers, health care providers, and the public. Other countries such as the UK have an equivalent system called the Medicines and Healthcare products Regulatory Agency (MHRA). Yet, Shimabukuro et al. (2015) describe how the VAERS system has major discrepancies for each entry and does not signify a direct (or even indirect) causal relationship between vaccination and the cases. Moreover, the VAERS database is based on passive surveillance

Table 3.1 Constitutional symptoms reported to the VAERS (see Mushtaq et al., 2022: 5)

Symptoms	Vaccine manufacturer		
	Pfizer-BioNTech	Moderna	Janssen
Chills	52,401	51,189	12,590
Dizziness	57,390	32,472	9186
Dyspnea	40,930	20,218	4887
Fatigue	82,486	57,543	12,248
Headache	97,265	67,239	17,831
Injection site pain	13,090	25,668	4029
Nausea	55,440	38,089	9082
Pain in extremity	46,927	38,874	6753
Pyrexia	73,542	63,024	15,097
Total	519,471	394,316	91,703

and could contain errors resulting from reporting bias, while underreporting is also a problem (Shimabukuro et al., 2015). Because of the large number of vaccines administered and the prevalence of serious AEs in the population, it is claimed some cases may occur by chance during the post-vaccination period and are unrelated to the vaccines themselves (Mushtaq et al., 2022). Reporting to these systems, suggests Provost (2023), could be flawed because of numerous clinical, systemic, political, and media influences. This potentially helps to understand the testimonies from a male Filmmaker and a female Lettings Manager who outline how their initial doubts about taking the vaccine because of AEs were confirmed:

> I see them as victims *[people who are vaccinated]*, in more ways than one. Psychologically and physiologically. Anecdotal evidence, but having not known a single person in my extended circles that had more than a bad cold from COVID-19 (my elderly and vulnerable relatives included), I now know of several, if not dozens of people that have had varying degrees of adverse reactions to the 'cure'. Everything from strange rashes, nerve damage and eyesight loss, to heart attacks, strokes, blood clots and Bell's Palsy. One of my friends had thrombotic events in his arms and legs, with clots travelling to the lungs, thankfully caught just in time. Another friend has a leg that turned black, and has developed severe palpitations. My friend's dad had a heart attack two days after receiving his second

dose. Many people I know lost elderly relatives a matter of days after receiving jabs. The list is genuinely endless, and as Orwell put it, I refuse to ignore the evidence of my eyes and ears: the truth is like water. It can be held back for a time, but it always finds a way. Always. (Male, 31, Filmmaker, UK)

I am frightened by the pressure to have the vaccine. I know many people that have had side effects some serious. This is not been spoken about and being denied in some cases. MPs who speak in parliament have been deleted from YouTube. I'm worried about the coercion of my children (who have had Covid anyway). The whole thing feels weird and creepy. There is no honesty so you cannot trust. (Female, 53, Lettings Manager, UK)

Critical questioning based on real experiences and/or real concern became radical dissent, warranting censorship and blanket labelling as 'conspiracy theories' (Briggs et al., 2021b). Nevertheless, the data highlights concerns related to the Covid-19 vaccine. As the rollout was encouraged with younger age groups, even children who are not at serious risk from the disease felt obliged to take it to 'protect their families and loved ones'. Reports of myocarditis (inflammation of the heart muscle) and pericarditis (swelling and irritation of the tissue surrounding the heart), though, started to be associated with the Covid-19 vaccines throughout 2021. Occurring particularly among young men after the second dose of the mRNA vaccines such as Pfizer and Moderna (Knudsen & Prasad, 2023; Pillay et al., 2022), viral vector vaccines were instead recommended as an alternative for patients with a history of either known or unknown cardiac issues. A systematic review by Knudsen and Prasad (2023) that covered studies in Europe, North America, and Asia ascertained that incidences of myocarditis post Covid-19 vaccination vary profoundly. While by June 2022 VAERS reported 4.64 cases per 100,000 doses for those aged 12–15, Knudsen and Prasad (2023: 8) assert *"the incidence of myocarditis after dose 2 of the Moderna vaccine in men under age 40 ranged from 2.4 to 30 cases per 100,000 persons"*.

Thrombosis, or what is more commonly known as blood clotting, and cerebral venous thrombosis (CVT)[4] was reported in 2021 as a rare AE after viral vector vaccination. This was primarily from the AstraZeneca inoculation, which is a viral vector vaccine. Andrews et al. (2022: 10) discerned an increased risk of a thrombotic event after a first dose of the AstraZeneca vaccine for those aged 15–39, claiming the risk is "*highest in under 40-year-olds, at 16.1 and 36.3 per million doses respectively for a CVT or other thrombosis event*". By March 2021, many European countries paused the rollout of this vaccine including Norway, Denmark, Italy, Latvia, and Luxembourg (Wise, 2021). The early prospect of one of the main pharmaceutical manufacturers having their product removed from distribution was found to have led to increased vaccine hesitancy (Houghton et al., 2022). However, nobody in our sample reported such an AE to a formalised reporting system like MHRA or VAERS or the like. In fact, most participants had never heard of these processes. Despite concerns about AE, a recent analysis of randomised control trials found that viral vector vaccines such as AstraZeneca were associated with lower risk of overall mortality compared to mRNA vaccines such as Pfizer or Moderna (Benn et al., 2023). Clearly, this is a complex and evolving picture.

Considering the evidence presented in this chapter, it is evident that pharmaceutical corporations often work in collaboration with government agencies to minimise negative outcomes and ensure necessary approvals to further bolster their market share and profitability. In this chapter, we have briefly considered some of the historical violations of such companies, occasionally drawing attention to the broader context of neoliberal capitalism. It should have been no surprise that when a new contagious virus was transmitted around the world, these same companies championed profit-enabling strategies. Of course, it is undeniable that the Covid-19 vaccines have saved millions of lives by shoring up immunity levels, though they have also had negative consequences for some people that need to be documented. As we will encounter in the

---

[4] This refers to a blood clot in the brain.

next chapter, the rollout of the Covid-19 vaccines also provided the opportunity for increased levels of social control and digital surveillance.

References

Altindis, E. (2022). Inequitable COVID-19 vaccine distribution and the intellectual property rights prolong the pandemic. *Expert Review of Vaccines, 21*(4), 427–430.

Amgen. (n.d.). About Amgen. *Amgen*. Accessed on 25/04/2023. https://www.amgen.com/about

Andrews, N., Stowe, J., Ramsay, M., & Miller, E. (2022). Risk of venous thrombotic events and thrombocytopenia in sequential time periods after ChAdOx1 and BNT162b2 COVID-19 vaccines: A national cohort study in England. *The Lancet Regional Health, 13*, 1–10.

Arguedas-Ramírez, G. (2022). A call to action against persistent lack of transparency in vaccine pricing practices during the COVID-19 pandemic. *Annals of Global Health, 88*(1), 1–6.

Attaran, A., & Gillespie-White, L. (2001). Do patents for antiretroviral drugs constrain access to AIDS treatment in Africa? *JAMA Network, 286*(15), 1886–1892.

Baker, J. (2003). The pertussis vaccine controversy in Great Britain, 1974–1986. *Vaccine, 21*, 4003–4010.

Bardosh, K., Figueiredo, A., Gur-Arie, R., Jamrozik, E., Doidge, J., Lemmens, T., Keshavjee, S., Graham, J., & Baral, S. (2022). The unintended consequences of COVID-19 vaccine policy: Why mandates, passports and restrictions may cause more harm than good. *British Medical Journal Global Health, 7*, 1–14.

Barouch, D. (2022). Covid-19 Vaccines—Immunity, variants, boosters. *New England Journal of Medicine, 387*, 1011–1020.

Benn, C. S., Schaltz-Buchholzer, F., Nielsen, S., Netea, M. G., & Aaby, P. (2023). Randomised clinical trials of COVID-19 vaccines: Do adenovirus-vector vaccines have beneficial non-specific effects? *iScience, 26*, 106733.

Bhattacharya, J., Bienen, L., Duriseti, R., Hoeg, T., Kulldorff, M., Makary, M., Smelkinson, M., & Templeton, S. (2023). *Questions for COVID-19 commission*. The Norfolk Group.

Biddle, J. (2007). Lessons from the Vioxx debacle: What the privatization of science can teach us about social epistemology. *Social Epistemology, 21*(1), 21–39.

Biden, J. (2021). Remarks by President Biden on the fight against COVID-19. *The White House*. Accessed on 25/04/2023. https://www.whitehouse.gov/briefing-room/speeches-remarks/2021/12/21/remarks-by-president-biden-on-the-fight-against-covid-19/

Black, S. (1997). Epidemiology of pertussis. *The Paediatric Infectious Disease Journal, 16*(4), 85–89.

Briggs, D., Telford, L., Lloyd, A., Ellis, A., & Kotzé, J. (2021a). *Lockdown: social harm in the Covid-19 era*. Palgrave Macmillan.

Briggs, D., Ellis, A., Lloyd, A., & Telford, L. (2021b). *Researching the Covid-19 pandemic: A critical blueprint for the social sciences*. Policy Press Rapid Response Series.

Brower, V. (2010). FDA finalizes REMS program for ESAs; Amgen continues to study risks. *Journal of the National Cancer Institute, 102*(9), 592–593.

Brown, K., Long, S., Ramsey, M., Hudson, M., Green, J., Vincent, C., Kroll, J., Fraser, G., & Sevdalis, N. (2012). UK parents' decision-making about measles-mumps-rubella (MMR) vaccine 10 years after the MMR-autism controversy: A qualitative analysis. *Vaccine, 30*(10), 1855–1864.

Burd, E. (2003). Human papillomavirus and cervical cancer. *Clinical Microbiology Reviews, 16*(1), 1–17.

Butler, T. (2014). Plague history: Yersin's discovery of the causative bacterium in 1894 enabled, in the subsequent century, scientific progress in understanding the disease and the development of treatments and vaccines. *Clinical Microbiology and Infection, 20*(3), 202–209.

Chan, K., Chen, Z., Wen, Y., & Tong, X. (2022). COVID-19 vaccines and global stock markets. *Financial Research Letters, 47*, 1–9.

Chen, M., Mott, N., Clark, S., Harper, D., Shuman, A., Prince, M., & Dossett, L. (2021). HPV vaccination among young adults in the US. *JAMA Network, 325*(16), 1673–1674.

Clem, A. (2011). Fundamentals of vaccine immunology. *Journal of Global Infectious Diseases, 3*(1), 73–78.

Cohen, J. (2021). The dream vaccine. *Science, 372*(6539), 227–231.

Corbie-Smith, G. (1999). The continuing legacy of the Tuskegee Syphilis study: Considerations for clinical investigation. *The American Journal of the Medical Sciences, 317*(1), 5–8.

Cox, C., Amin, K., Kates, J., & Michaud, J. (2022). *Why do vaccinated people represent most COVID-19 deaths right now?* Kaiser Family Foundation.

Accessed on 10/04/2023. https://www.kff.org/policy-watch/why-do-vaccinated-people-represent-most-covid-19-deaths-right-now/

Cyranoski, D. (2018). Chinese maker of faulty rabies vaccines fined billions of yuan. *Nature News*. Accessed on 03/05/2023. https://www.nature.com/articles/d41586-018-07136-z#:~:text=China's%20national%20drug%20regulator%20announced,licence%20to%20make%20rabies%20vaccines

Decker, M., & Edwards, K. (2021). Pertussis (whooping cough). *The Journal of Infectious Diseases, 224*, 310–320.

Dyer, O. (2018). Chinese government fines vaccine company £1bn for string of violations. *British Medical Journal 363*.

Dyer, O. (2019a). Bayer and Janssen pay $775m to settle Xarelto misinformation claims. *British Medical Journal 364*.

Dyer, O. (2019b). Philippines measles outbreak is deadliest yet as vaccine scepticism spurs disease comeback. *British Medical Journal, 364*, 1–2.

Editorial. (2018). Vaccine scandal and confidence crisis in China. *The Lancet, 392*(10145), 360.

Editorial. (2021). COVID-19 vaccine equity and booster doses. *The Lancet Infectious Diseases, 21*(9), 1193.

Emanuel, E., Buchanan, A., Chan, S., Fabre, C., Halliday, D., Heath, J., Herzog, L., Leland, R., McCoy, M., Norheim, O., Saenz, C., Schaefer, G., Tan, K., Wellman, C., Wolff, J., & Persad, G. (2021). What are the obligations of pharmaceutical companies in a global health emergency? *The Lancet, 398*(10304), 1015–1020.

European Commission. (2020). *EU support for vaccines*. European Commission. Accessed on 04/05/2023. https://research-and-innovation.ec.europa.eu/research-area/health/coronavirus/vaccines_en

Fenner, F., Henderson, D., Arita, I., Jezek, Z., & Ladnyi, I. (1988). The development of the global smallpox eradication programme, 1958–1966. IN *Smallpox and its eradication* (pp. 365–420). World Health Organization.

Flaherty, D. (2011). The vaccine-autism connection: A public health crisis caused by unethical medical practices and fraudulent science. *The Annals of Pharmacotherapy, 45*(10), 1302–1304.

Ford, N., Calmy, A., & Mills, E. (2011). The first decade of antiretroviral therapy in Africa. *Globalization and Health, 7*(33), 1–6.

Gaynes, R. (2017). The discovery of penicillin—New insights after more than 75 years of clinical use. *Emerging Infectious Diseases, 23*(5), 849–853.

Gazit, S., Saciuk, Y., Perez, G., Peretz, A., Pitzer, E., & Patalon, T. (2022). Short term, relative effectiveness of four doses versus three doses of

BNT162b2 vaccine in people aged 60 years and older in Israel: Retrospective, test negative, case-control study. *British Medical Journal, 377*, 1–9.

Ghose, R., Forati, A., & Mantsch, J. (2022). Impact of the Covid-19 pandemic on opioid overdose deaths: A spatiotemporal analysis. *Journal of Urban Health, 99*, 316–327.

Glassman, A., Charles, K., & Yang, G. (2022). *COVID-19 vaccine development and rollout in historical perspective* (Working Paper 607). Washington: Centre for Global Development.

Graham, R., Donaldson, E., & Baric, R. (2013). A decade after SARS: Strategies for controlling emerging coronaviruses. *Nature Reviews Microbiology, 11*, 836–848.

Green, T., & Fazi, T. (2023). *The Covid consensus: The global assault on democracy and the poor—A critique from the left*. Hurst Publishers.

Grimes, D. (2016). We know it's effective: So why is there opposition to the HPV vaccine? *The Guardian*. Accessed on 03/05/2023. https://www.theguardian.com/science/blog/2016/jan/11/why-is-there-opposition-hpv-vaccine-cervical-cancer

Guiso, N., Meade, B., & Konig, C. (2020). Pertussis vaccines: The first hundred years. *Vaccine, 38*, 1271–1276.

Halabi, S. (2021). Solving the pandemic vaccine product liability problem. *UC Irvine Law Review, 12*(1), 111–160.

Harris, G. (2009). Pfizer pays 2.9 billion to settle marketing case. *New York Times*. Accessed on 25/04/2023. https://www.nytimes.com/2009/09/03/business/03health.html

Harris, P., & Moss, D. (2021). Managing through the Covid second wave: Public affairs and the challenge of Covid vaccination. *Journal of Public Affairs, 21*(1), 1–2.

Harvey, D. (2010). *The enigma of capital*. Profile.

Hawksbee, L., McKee, M., & King, L. (2022). Don't worry about the drug industry's profits when considering a waiver on covid-19 intellectual property rights. *British Medical Journal, 376*, 1–5.

Heyerdahl, L., Vray, M., Lana, B., Tvardik, N., Gobat, N., Wanat, M., Tonkin-Crine, S., Anthierens, S., Goossens, H., & Giles-Vernick, T. (2022). Conditionality of COVID-19 vaccine acceptance in European countries. *Vaccine, 40*(9), 1191–1197.

Hobsbawm, E. (1987). *The age of empire: 1875–1914*. Weidenfeld & Nicolson.

Houghton, D., Wysokinski, W., Casanegra, A., Padrnos, L., Shah, S., Wysokinska, E., Pruthi, R., Ashrani, A., Sridharan, M., Baumann-Kreuziger,

L., McBane, R., & Padmanabhan, A. (2022). Risk of venous thromboembolism after COVID-19 vaccination. *Journal of Thrombosis and Haemostasis, 20*, 1638–1644.

Hutchings, M., Truman, A., & Wilkinson, B. (2019). Antibiotics: Past, present and future. *Current Opinion in Microbiology, 51*, 72–80.

Hoyt, K. (2006). Vaccine innovation: Lessons from World War II. *Journal of Public Health Policy, 27*, 38–57.

Huang, Z., Su, Y., Zhang, T., & Xia, N. (2022). A review of the safety and efficacy of current COVID-19 vaccines. *Frontiers of Medicine, 16*, 39–55.

Hunter, D., Abdool Karim, S., Baden, L., Farrar, J., Hamel, M., Longo, D., Morrissey, S., & Rubin, E. (2022). Addressing vaccine inequity—Covid-19 vaccines as a global public good. *The New England Journal of Medicine, 386*, 1176–179.

Jegede, A. (2007). What led to the Nigerian boycott of the polio vaccination campaign? *PLoS Medicine, 4*(3), 417–422.

Jones, L., & Hameiri, S. (2022). COVID-19 and the failure of the neoliberal regulatory state. *Review of International Political Economy, 29*(4), 1027–1052.

Kanai, K. (1980). Japan's experience in pertussis epidemiology and vaccination in the past thirty years. *Japanese Journal of Medical Science and Biology, 33*, 107–143.

Kaufmann, S. (2017). Remembering Emil von Behring: From tetanus treatment to antibody cooperation with phagocytes. *mBio, 8*(1), 1–7.

Keefe, P. R. (2021). *Empire of pain: The secret history of the Sackler Dynasty*. Picador.

Khan, M., Adil, S., Alkhathlan, H., Tahir, M. N., Saif, S., Khan, M., & Khan, S. T. (2021). COVID-19: A global challenge with old history, epidemiology and progress so far. *Molecules, 26*(39), 1–25.

Kmietowicz, Z. (2013). Johnson & Johnson to pay $2.2bn to settle charges of false marketing on three drugs. *British Medical Journal, 347*, 1–2.

Knudsen, B., & Prasad, V. (2023). COVID-19 vaccine induced myocarditis in young males: A systematic review. *European Journal of Clinical Investigation, 53*(4), 1–14.

Kojima, N., & Klausner, J. (2022). Protective immunity after recovery from SARS-CoV-2 infection. *The Lancet Infectious Diseases, 22*, 12–13.

Krumholz, H., Ross, J., Presler, A., & Egilman, D. (2007). What have we learnt from Vioxx? *British Medical Journal, 334*, 120–123.

Lalani, H., Avorn, J., & Kesselheim, A. (2022). US taxpayers heavily funded the discovery of COVID-19 vaccines. *Clinical Pharmacology & Therapeutics, 111*(3), 542–544.

Lasco, G., & Yu, V. (2021). Communicating COVID-19 vaccines: Lessons from the dengue vaccine controversy in the Philippines. *British Medical Journal Global Health, 6*, 1–3.

Leach, M., & Fairhead, J. (2008). *Vaccine anxieties: Global science, child health and society*. Routledge.

Lenzer, J. (2006). Secret report surfaces showing that Pfizer was at fault in Nigerian drug tests. *British Medical Journal, 332*(7552), 1233.

Li, J. (2014). *Blockbuster drugs: The rise and fall of the pharmaceutical industry*. Oxford University Press.

Li, R., Liu, H., Fairley, C., Zou, Z., Xie, L., Li, X., Shen, M., Li, Y., & Zhang, L. (2022). Cost-effectiveness analysis of BNT162b2 COVID-19 booster vaccination in the United States. *International Journal of Infectious Diseases, 119*, 87–94.

Liebenau, J. (1990). The rise of the British pharmaceutical industry. *British Medical Journal, 301*, 724–728.

Lind, P. (2014). U.S. court pays $6 million to Gardasil victims. *The Washington Times*. Accessed on 02/05/2025. https://www.washingtontimes.com/news/2014/dec/31/us-court-pays-6-million-gardasil-victims/

Link-Gelles, R., Ciesla, A., Fleming-Dutra, K., Smith, Z., Britton, A., Wiegand, R., Miller, J., Accorsi, E., Schrag, S., Verani, J., Shang, N., Derado, G., & Pilishvili, T. (2022). Effectiveness of bivalent mRNA vaccines in preventing symptomatic SARS-CoV-2 infection—Increasing community access to testing program, United States, September–November 2022. *Morbidity and Mortality Weekly Report, 71*(48), 1526–1540.

Lloyd, A. (2018). *The harms of work: An ultra-realist account of the service economy*. Policy Press.

Malakoff, D. (2001). Nigerian families Sue Pfizer, testing the reach of U.S. law. *Science, 293*(5536), 1742.

Malerba, F. and Orsenigo, L. (2015). The evolution of the pharmaceutical industry. *Business History, 57*(5), 664–687

McLean, B. (2016). The Valeant meltdown and Wall Street's major drug problem. *Vanity Fair*. Accessed on 23/04/2023. https://www.vanityfair.com/news/2016/06/the-valeant-meltdown-and-wall-streets-major-drug-problem

Meier, B. (2020). *Pain killer: An empire of deceit and the origins of America's opioid epidemic*. Sceptre.

Mendoza, R., Dayrit, M., Alfonso, C., & Ong, M. (2021). Public trust and the COVID-19 vaccination campaign: Lessons from the Philippines as it emerges from the Dengvaxia controversy. *International Journal of Health Planning and Management, 36*(6), 2048–2055.

Miller, D., Ross, M., Alderslade, R., Bellman, M., & Rawson, N. S. (1981). Pertussis immunisation and serious acute neurological illness in children. *British Medical Journal, 282*, 1595–1599.

Millward, G. (2017). A disability Act? The Vaccine Damage Payments Act 1979 and the British government's response to the pertussis vaccine scare. *Social History of Medicine, 30*(2), 429–447.

Millward, G. (2019). *Vaccinating Britain: Mass vaccination and the public since the Second World War*. Manchester University Press.

Mitchell, W., & Fazi, T. (2017). *Reclaiming the state: A progressive vision of sovereignty for a post-neoliberal world*. Pluto Press.

Moghadas, S., Vilches, T., Zhang, K., Wells, C., Shoukat, A., Singer, B., Meyers, L., Neuzil, K., Langley, J., Fitzpatrick, M., & Galvani, A. (2022). The impact of vaccination on coronavirus disease 2019 (COVID-19) outbreaks in the United States. *Clinical Infectious Diseases, 73*(12), 2257–2264.

Mohamed, K., Rzymski, P., Islam, M. S., Makuku, R., Mushtaq, A., Khan, A., Ivanovska, M., Makka, S. A., Hashem, F., Marquez, L., Cseprekal, O., Filgueiras, I. S., Fonseca, D. L. M., Mickael, E., Ling, I., Arero, A. G., Cuschieri, S., Minakova, K., Rodríguez-Román, E., ..., Rezaei, N. (2022). COVID-19 vaccinations: The unknowns, challenges, and hopes. *Journal of Medical Virology, 94*, 1336–1349.

Mohammed, I., Nasidi, A., Alkali, A., Garbati, M., Ajayi-Obe, E., Audu, K., Usman, A., & Abdullahi, S. (2000). A severe epidemic of meningococcal meningitis in Nigeria, 1996. *Transactions of the Royal Society of Tropical Medicine and Hygiene, 94*(3), 265–270.

Mushtaq, H., Khedr, A., Koritala, T., Bartlett, B., Jain, N., & Khan, S. (2022). A review of adverse effects of COVID-19 vaccines. *Infez Med, 30*(1), 1–10.

Oltermann, P. (2022). Germany hits record Covid infection rate since start of pandemic. *The Guardian*. Accessed on 23/03/2023. https://www.theguardian.com/world/2022/mar/16/germany-hits-record-covid-infection-rate-since-start-of-pandemic

Oxfam. (2021). *Pfizer, BioNTech and Moderna making $1,000 profit every second while world's poorest countries remain largely unvaccinated*. Oxfam.

Accessed on 20/04/2023. https://www.oxfam.org/fr/node/18366#:~:text=New%20figures%20from%20the%20Peoples,profits%20of%20%2465%2C000%20every%20minute

Pandey, A., Sah, P., Moghadas, S., Mandal, S., Banerjee, S., Hotez, P., & Galvani, A. (2021). Challenges facing COVID-19 vaccination in India: Lessons from the initial vaccine rollout. *Journal of Global Health, 11*, 1–5.

Payette, P., & Davis, H. (2001). History of vaccines and positioning of current trends. *Infectious Disorders, 1*, 241–247.

Philips, N. (2018). Chinese vaccine scandal unlikely to dent childhood immunization rates. *Nature Communication News*. Accessed on 18/04/2023. https://www.nature.com/articles/d41586-018-05835-1

Pilkington, V., Keestra, S., & Hill, A. (2022). Global COVID-19 vaccine inequity: Failures in the first year of distribution and potential solutions for the future. *Frontiers in Public Health, 10*, 1–8.

Pillay, J., Gaudet, L., Wingert, A., Bialy, L., Mackie, A., Paterson, I., & Hartling, L. (2022). Incidence, risk factors, natural history, and hypothesised mechanisms of myocarditis and pericarditis following Covid-19 vaccination: Living evidence syntheses and review. *The British Medical Journal, 378*, 1–17.

Plotkin, S., & Plotkin, S. (2011). The development of vaccines: How the past led to the future. *Nature Reviews: Microbiology, 9*, 889–893.

Plotkin, S. (2014). History of vaccination. *Proceedings of the National Academy of Sciences of the United States of America, 111*(34), 12283–12287.

Pollack, E. (2012). Agmen agrees to pay 762 million in drug case. *New York Times*. Accessed on 15/04/2023. https://www.nytimes.com/2012/12/19/business/amgen-agrees-to-pay-762-million-in-drug-case.html

Prakash, S. (2022). Development of COVID 19 vaccine: A summarized review on global trials, efficacy, and effectiveness on variants. *Diabetes & Metabolic Syndrome: Clinical Research & Reviews, 16*, 1–9.

Provost, P. (2023). The blind spot in COVID-19 vaccination policies: Underreported adverse events. *International Journal of Vaccine Theory, Practice and Research, 3*(1), 707–726.

Rahmani, K., Shavaleh, R., Forouhi, M., Disfani, H. F., Kamandi, M., Oskooi, R. K., Foogerdi, M., Soltani, M., Rahchamani, M., Mohaddespour, M., & Dianatinasab, M. (2022). The effectiveness of COVID-19 vaccines in reducing the incidence, hospitalization, and mortality from COVID-19: A systematic review and meta-analysis. *Frontiers in Public Health, 10*, 1–25.

Rappuoli, R. (2007). Bridging the knowledge gaps in vaccine design. *Nature Biotechnology, 25*(12), 1361–1366.

Ratner, M. (2009). Pfizer settles largest ever fraud suit for off-label promotion. *Nature Biotechnology, 27*, 961–962.

Raymen, T. (2022). *The enigma of social harm: The problem of liberalism.* Routledge.

Rhodes, N., Wright, T., Rusu, V., Bakharti, H., Cushing, J., & Kohler, J. (2021). *For whose benefit? Transparency in the development of the Covid-19 vaccines.* University of Toronto Press.

Riedel, S. (2005). Edward Jenner and the history of smallpox and vaccination. *Baylor University Medical Center Proceedings, 18*(1), 21–25.

Robbins, R., & Goodman, S. (2021). Pfizer Reaps hundreds of millions in profits from Covid vaccine. *New York Times.* Accessed on 18/04/2023. https://www.nytimes.com/2021/05/04/business/pfizer-covid-vaccine-profits.html

Roberts, H., Clark, D., Kalina, C., Sherman, C., Brislin, S., Heitzeg, M., & Hicks, B. (2022). To vax or not to vax? Predictors of anti-vax attitudes and COVID-19 vaccine hesitancy prior to widespread vaccine availability. *PLoS ONE, 17*(2), 1–19.

Roscoe, M. (2022). BREAKING: European Parliament MEP calls EU Covid vaccine purchases "biggest CORRUPTION SCANDAL in history". *EuroWeekly News.* Accessed on 25/04/2023. https://euroweeklynews.com/2022/10/12/breaking-european-parliaments-mislav-kolakusic-calls-eus-covid-vaccine-purchases-biggest-corruption-scandal-in-history/

Saleh, A., Qama, S., Tekin, A., Singh, R., & Kashyap, R. (2021). Vaccine development throughout history. *Cureus, 13*(7), 1–7.

Shimabukuro, T., Nguyen, M., Martin, D., & DeStefano, F. (2015). Safety monitoring in the Vaccine Adverse Event Reporting System (VAERS). *Vaccine, 33*, 4398–4405.

Schultz, J., & Soreide, T. (2008). Corruption in emergency procurement. *Disasters, 32*(4), 516–536.

Schwarzinger, M., Watson, V., Arwidson, F., Alla, F., & Luchini, S. (2021). COVID-19 vaccine hesitancy in a representative working-age population in France: A survey experiment based on vaccine characteristics. *Lancet Public Health, 6*(4), 210–221.

Senior, M. (2013). Amgen find $762 million. *Nature Biotechnology, 31*(3), 182.

Shenai, M. B., Rahme, R., & Noorchashm, H. (2021). Equivalency of protection from natural immunity in COVID-19 recovered versus fully vaccinated persons: A systematic review and pooled analysis. *Cureus, 13*(10), 1–15.

Stern, A., & Markel, H. (2005). The history of vaccines and immunization: Familiar patterns, new challenges. *Health Affairs, 24*(3), 611–621.

Stevens, D., Debackere, K., Goldman, M., Mahony, R., Stevens, P., & Huys, I. (2017). *Vaccines: Accelerating innovation and access, global challenges report*. World Intellectual Property Organisation.

Tahamtan, A., Charostad, J., Hoseini Shokouh, S. J., & Barati, M. (2017). An overview of history, evolution, and manufacturing of various generations of vaccines. *Journal of Archives in Military Medicine, 5*(3), 1–7.

Tanveer, S., Rowhani-Farid, A., Hong, K., Jeferson, T., & Doshi, P. (2022). Transparency of COVID-19 vaccine trials: decisions without data. *British Medical Journal Evidence-Based Medicine, 27*, 199–205.

Taylor, L. (2021). Scandal over COVID vaccine trial at Peruvian universities prompts outrage. *Nature News, 592*, 174–175.

Telford, L., Bushell, M., & Hodgkinson, O. (2022). Passport to neoliberal normality? A critical exploration of COVID-19 vaccine passports. *Journal of Contemporary Crime, Harm, Ethics, 2*(1), 42–61.

Thacker, P. (2021). Covid-19: Researcher blows the whistle on data integrity issues in Pfizer's vaccine trial. *British Medical Journal, 375*, 1–3.

Thanh Le, T., Andreadakis, A., Kumar, A., Gómez-Román, R., Tollefsen, S., Saville, M., & Mayhew, S. (2020). The COVID-19 vaccine development landscape. *Nature Reviews, 19*, 305–306.

Tully, D., & Griffiths, C. (2021). Dengvaxia: The world's first vaccine for prevention of secondary dengue. *Therapeutic Advances in Vaccines and Immunotherapy, 9*, 1–8.

Vichnin, M., Bonanni, P., Klein, N., Garland, S., Block, S., Kjaer, S., Sings, H., Perez, G., Haupt, R., Saah, A., Lievano, F., Velicer, C., Drury, R., & Kuter, B. (2015). An overview of quadrivalent human papillomavirus vaccine safety 2006 to 2015. *The Pediatric Infectious Disease Journal, 34*(9), 983–991.

Wadman, M. (2007). Merck settles Vioxx lawsuits for $4.85 billion. *Nature*.

Wakefield, A., Murch, S., Anthony, A., Linnell, J., Casson, D., Malik, M., Berelowitz, M., Dhillon, A., Thomson, M., Harvey, P., Valentine, A., Davies, S., & Walker-Smith, J. (1998). RETRACTED: Illeal-lymphoid-nodular hyperplasia, non-specific colitis, and pervasive developmental disorder in children. *The Lancet, 351*(9103), 637–641.

Watson, O., Barnsley, G., Toor, J., Hogan, A., Winskill, P., & Ghani, A. (2022). Global impact of the first year of COVID-19 vaccination: a mathematical modelling study. *The Lancet Infectious Diseases, 22*(9), 1293–1302.

Williams, S. (2022). COVID vaccines for children: Uptake in the UK is slow—Here's why parents might be hesitant. *The Conversation*. Accessed on 04/05/2023. https://theconversation.com/covid-vaccines-for-children-uptake-in-the-uk-is-slow-heres-why-parents-might-be-hesitant-183881

Wise, J. (2021). Covid-19: European countries suspend use of Oxford-AstraZeneca vaccine after reports of blood clots. *British Medical Journal, 372*, 1.

Yahya, M. (2007). Polio vaccines—"No thank you!" barriers to polio eradication in Northern Nigeria. *African Affairs, 106*(423), 185–204.

4

Technocratic Feudalism, Digital Apartheids, and the New Surveillance Governance

> Lockdown measures considerably curtail people's freedom. Immunity passports would potentially allow some proportion of the population to access more freedoms during lockdown periods. It is unethical to restrict freedom unless there is a real risk to other people. If we have the technology to decide who is not at risk, we should use it. (Brown et al., 2021: e61)

This statement made by healthcare professionals and academics in the UK and Australia positions 'immunity passports' within the context of severe restrictions on movement and the opportunities presented by technology. Vaccination and immunity status for overseas travel is not new (Brown et al., 2021). For example, immunisation for yellow fever is required for many countries, along with recommendations for vaccination against diseases such as Polio. However, "*population-wide adult mandates, passports, and segregated restrictions are unprecedented and have never been implemented*" on the scale witnessed during the pandemic (Bardosh et al., 2022: 2). Meanwhile, contact tracing has been a proven public health containment measure for over a century (Brandt, 2022).

It is, therefore, hardly surprising to see public health officials advocating their implementation and usage during the Covid-19 pandemic (also see: Woolhouse, 2022). However, as digital technologies develop and advance, public health officials, along with technology companies, national governments, pharmaceutical companies, and other actors have increasingly called for 'digital solutions' to public health crises (Lewis, 2021).

The value of technology in predicting, tracking, and tracing infectious diseases became a key discussion point early into the Covid-19 pandemic as countries floundered in their official responses (Green & Fazi, 2023). However, the use of technology to manage public health emergencies opens a wide range of topics that require further investigation, including the impact of digital technology in terms of regimes of surveillance and governance, the creation and exacerbation of digital divisions and social inequalities, the ethical considerations around freedom and autonomy, and the perceived motivations of corporate actors and national governments. Mobilising digital tools to manage a public health emergency tap into various social, cultural, and political issues that inform the context of vaccine hesitancy. Indeed, many of our participants raised concerns about various forms of pandemic management that called upon these wider debates around surveillance and control. It also raised the spectre of conspiracy theory, which we address shortly. The previous chapters connected the power of pharmaceutical companies with their influence over national government as well as the role of the media in shaping a consistent narrative around 'The Science'. In this chapter, we connect a final limb—the technology sector—to complete what Green and Fazi (2023: 442) refer to as the 'techno-media-pharma (TMP) complex'. In that sense, this chapter hears from those individuals who are less 'anti-vaxxers' and more 'anti-vaccine mandate'.

Surveillance Technologies and Regimes of Control

> The pandemic is being opportunistically employed by governments for increase in surveillance (including self-surveillance via our digital devices) and to use 'shock doctrine' tactics to gain more controls for suppression of their dissenters. (Male, 46, Marketing Researcher, Australia)

> No, the whole thing has been about control, mass surveillance, everything that is outlined in the Great Reset. (Female, 50, Former NHS nurse, Wales)

> It's the beginning of tighter digital surveillance, there will never be an end if we don't say no. (Female, 50, Area manager, Scotland)

What makes the participants quoted here think this is where we are heading? Why do some people believe that pandemic management tools are a backdoor to tyranny, suppression, and a dystopian future of mass surveillance? As with all aspects of the pandemic, Covid-19 overlays already existing trends and developments within society and in some cases accelerates if not turbo-charges movement in particular directions (see: Raymen & Smith, 2022; Winlow & Winlow, 2022). This is certainly the case with the role of digital and surveillance technologies. The quotations above show the concerns that many people had about growing trends in digital surveillance, government overreach and plans to reshape the world in favour of political and economic elites. Importantly, these concerns did not emerge irrationally or without some basis in reality. Equally so, some hesitancy around vaccination programmes and the explicit linkage between vaccination status and personal freedoms was attendant to wider debates about surveillance technologies.

It is probably an understatement to suggest that digital technologies have transformed the social world on an individual and collective level in the last three decades (Flyverbom, 2019; Schildt, 2020). There are very few aspects of our lives not impacted by the development of the internet (see: Bridle, 2018; Carr, 2011), and the nanotechnology that enhanced processing power in smaller devices such as the Smartphone. The way we live, work, play, interact, travel, find, and process information have, to some degree or another, become integrated with systems of digital and information technology to the point where Flyverbom (2019) argues that the online world is no longer separate from the offline. The birth of the internet was initially heralded as a utopian space of freedom and discovery (Jeffries, 2021). However, despite the beliefs of early online advocates such as John Perry Barlow (1996), the internet was from the outset a military experiment (Naughton, 2016). Although it did, for a brief period in the 1990s, become tied up with tech-utopianism and the belief in a truly free online community, from the turn of the twenty-first century two competing imperatives have shaped the online world in which we live today: commercialism and security.

On the one hand, advocates of information sharing and networking including the founders of Google, Apple, Microsoft, and more found that an ostensible 'free' online experience limited the ability to profit from users' engagement with search engines and proto-social media sites. Rather than selling advertising space, technology companies realised that selling users' metadata to other companies represented an unparalleled commercial opportunity (Mau, 2019; Pasquale, 2015). In the capitalist societies of the West, digital metadata has been the preserve of the technology companies and the last two decades has seen a 'data gold rush' as companies seek to acquire as much knowledge about our lives, our searches, our likes, and our desires to generate vast revenue streams. To do so effectively requires the development of algorithms capable of processing vast amounts of data (Kalpokas, 2019). As technology has advanced further, algorithms have become much more central to the normal functioning of our lives. From the recommendations on Netflix or Amazon to screening job applications (Schildt, 2020). From efficient management of workplace processes (Pasquale, 2015) to predictive forms of policing (Brayne, 2021; Van Brakel, 2021). From fitness trackers to smart kitchen appliances (Beer, 2016). Digital platforms require masses of data from users for algorithms to become more accurate and efficient.

This is not new information. But it is essential for understanding technology and surveillance during the Covid-19 pandemic because it creates what David Lyon (2018) calls a 'culture of surveillance'. As consumers we often agree to terms and conditions without reading the fine print. We willingly give away our data, often without a second thought. Lyon (2018: 2) effectively captures this process by observing how:

> Today's surveillance is made possible by our own clicks on websites, our texting messages and exchanging photos. Ordinary people contribute to surveillance as never before. User-generated content engenders the data by which daily doings are monitored. This is how surveillance culture takes place.

We often comply with this culture of surveillance not necessarily out of fear or being compelled to do so but out of ease and a sense of fun. Convenience often dictates our choices around digital surveillance and our willingness to hand over data without any real knowledge of its future uses. Pasquale (2015) terms this a 'black-box society' whereby our data is handed to corporations whose proprietary algorithmic technology turns it into value for the company without our knowledge of how that data is used or how it may affect us in the future. That may be an algorithm mistakenly flagging our credit rating or targeting us with exclusive content of a particular political position (Gusterson, 2019).

The second imperative underpinning digital technology is security. The Snowden leaks demonstrated how US security services responded to the intelligence failures of 9/11 by growing the surveillance state to unprecedented levels (Snowden, 2020). State surveillance has always utilised the available technologies of the time and in response to 9/11, digital technology was used to collect vast troves of data on everyone from persons of interest to US citizens without any legal foundation and in contravention of privacy laws (Zuboff, 2019). Those technology companies seeking to monetise metadata entered symbiotic relationships with government security services in the name of 'homeland security' and the prevention of terrorism, often engaging in racial profiling and monitoring 'suspect populations' (Nagra & Maurutto, 2020). Indeed, laws may prevent government from collecting certain forms of data but once data brokers such as Facebook have harvested vast amounts of personal information, nothing prevents the state from buying, demanding, or hacking that data (Pasquale, 2015).

Mau (2019) accurately notes that the ability to record, track, and evidence many if not most of our everyday actions is within the power of the technologies around us. Which roads we cross, where we stopped, how long we walked for, which shops we enter, which websites we visit. Our Smartphones, tablets, Fitbits, televisions, cars, and household appliances track our activity thanks to a vague sense of compliance from us as users (Beer, 2016). As more activity such as banking moves online (Ford, 2016), most of our purchases are now tracked (Scott, 2022). Meanwhile, CCTV tracks our movement through public and private space. A security-conscious society can track and monitor individuals and groups with much greater efficacy, assuming that data is shared and that systems are compatible (Lyon, 2018). As the Snowden leaks showed, respect for the rule of law is subservient to national security concerns and surveillance in the name of security grew exponentially (Snowden, 2020). Critically, for our discussion of the Covid-19 pandemic, infrastructure created in the name of security following 9/11 has a long legacy and significant concern about 'mission creep' (Kuldova, 2022; Snowden, 2020). What was created to tackle an imminent emergency has become an established fact of life.

Surveillance Capitalism in the Covid-19 Era

In the years prior to the Covid-19 pandemic, questions about digital security, big data, and 'surveillance capitalism' (Zuboff, 2019) remained unanswered. The response to the pandemic, as outlined in Chapter 2, not only deviated from established protocols for pandemic management but also represented unprecedented reach into the lives of people across the world (Briggs et al., 2021a, 2021b; Foster et al., 2021). It is through these lenses that some people from our sample viewed the implementation of digital track and trace systems like this female patient transport driver from the UK who said: "*vaccinations and track and trace are a tool of compliance being used to implement digital surveillance*".

Of course, track and trace systems for pandemic management are about population surveillance. It is, as noted above, an established measure for understanding and containing viral spread. However, the concern voiced by our participants about the implementation of surveillance regimes must be understood in the context of wider debates and concerns about digital surveillance. Conspiracy theories are an attempt to bring into the light something hidden or secret. The scale and nature of digital surveillance has been an established part of the public record for years prior to the pandemic, so to raise concerns about digital surveillance in the context of pandemic management is far from the reproduction of conspiracy theory. However, as Green and Fazi (2023) note at length, the story of the pandemic is one of repeated examples whereby alternative points that clash with an official narrative are dismissed as conspiracy. In the UK, the implementation of a digital track and trace system was almost immediately followed by revelations of data breaches in the handling of personal information (Marsh & Hern, 2020), while the NHS was criticised for plans to store personal information for up to 20 years which was in direct breach of GDPR rules (Field, 2020). Essentially, concerns about 'data grabbing' and long-term surveillance reflect poor trust in government to manage our data appropriately and in the ways they promised.

When states and companies have histories of hidden surveillance or using our data without our knowledge, this erodes public trust and undermines the stated intention of a track and trace system. Public trust in government is alarmingly low (Goodwin, 2023; Hochuli et al., 2021; Winlow et al., 2017) and this was reflected in our data. This retired woman from Scotland provided a good example of this when she suggested that the future would be: "*one of universal surveillance and total control of the individual with no freedom of movement, speech or any opinion which is in opposition to those of authority. The future looks bleak in every respect unless one enjoys technology and virtual reality*". Indeed, OECD data (2023) on trust in government shows that less than 40% of UK respondents had confidence or trust in the government. For the USA, it was 31%. These numbers do not tell us the reasons why trust is so low and there is no doubt many contributing factors. However, the statistics illustrate a key point: when the public do not trust or have confidence in the government, it has implications in terms of a willingness to believe that governments are both effective and acting in our interests.

In particular, the upswell in populism in the post 2008 financial crisis era has been seen, by some, to reflect a failure of mainstream politics to represent and speak for those who are increasingly disadvantaged, desperate and desire social change (Babones, 2018; Telford, 2022; Winlow & Hall, 2022). Repeated revelations about apparent corruption, cronyism, or the symbiotic relationship between the state and financial, technology, media, and other sectors damages trust and has resulted in an increasingly cynical public who have lost faith in what our leaders say (Fisher, 2009). As mentioned in Chapter 1, the epoch of capitalist realism has brought about a culture of atomised individualism, cynicism, and scepticism. People are very quick to assume an ulterior motive. Politics is also incredibly divided, with the electorates of the UK, USA, and Europe often on opposite sides of the key issues of our time: Brexit, immigration, the economy, crime, and cultural values (Goodwin, 2023). Pandemic management was overlaid on existing political fault lines: those who supported Donald Trump were likely to agree with his strategy for managing the pandemic while those who thought Boris Johnson was a preening buffoon almost instinctively advocated for the opposite approach (Green & Fazi, 2023). For some, digital surveillance in the hands of untrusted leaders results in a cynical and mistrustful response.

Never Let a Serious Crisis Go to Waste

Naomi Klein (2007) argues that capitalists take advantage of a crisis to implement reforms that would have been politically unacceptable even months before. The reconstruction of New Orleans following Hurricane Katrina in 2005, or the market opportunities presented by the USA-led invasion of Iraq in 2003, are two examples set out in Klein's work. In the context of the pandemic, some of our respondents mirrored analysis from commentators and academics (ourselves included—see Briggs et al., 2021a) to argue that powerful elites with their hands on the political and economic levers of global capitalism would use the pandemic as an opportunity to consolidate wealth and power and to shape the world in ways that best suit their agenda. In some respects, this corresponds with Mirowski's (2013) belief that neoliberalism never lets a serious crisis go to waste. Similarly, Dardot and Laval (2019) argue that the logic of neoliberalism is one that self-aggravates crisis, that is, neoliberalism constructs situations or intensifies dynamics that create crisis conditions that indirectly compel the implementation of neoliberal solutions. Much like the opportunities around conceiving a vaccine for Covid-19 (Chapter 3), whether 'disaster capitalism' or 'crisis capitalism', there is prevailing wisdom that crisis creates opportunities for those that seek to use the situation to their advantage (Harvey, 2023). This female Doctor in her mid-50s suggested:

> This has not been about a virus, this is about implementing changes to society under the guise of a "global epidemic". I fear for the generations that come after me, our world is a sick place under a constant battle by Governments to instigate totalitarian control! I am just happy that millions of people are prepared to stand up to tyranny - say NO and bite back!

This relates to other comments from our participants about the pandemic as a pretext for the implementation of 'The Great Reset'. Discussion of 'The Great Reset' is shaded by a wider dismissal of conspiracy theory but as noted above, conspiracy exists in the shadows whereas the primary supporter for the Great Reset, World Economic Forum (WEF) head Klaus Schwab, has openly advocated for this on numerous platforms including the book-length treatise referred to in Chapter 1 (Schwab & Malleret, 2020). Rather than dismiss it as *conspiracy* and those who fear its implementation as 'gullible' or 'crackpots', it is worth considering what it is and how it relates to the current discussion of digital technology, control and surveillance. Many people, like this male gas engineer from Ireland whose experience of working on the frontline of the Covid-19 pandemic didn't correlate with the same panic presented in the media, see this as transparent:

> What else is there to say except please people cotton on soon or you may have to get used to the idea of global governance, centralised digital citizen passports and a new restrictive way of life. Just look at the World Economic Forum's website for a preview.

When people see gaps between their own experience and the accepted narrative and begin to question the suppression of public debate, their search for answers leads them to any available explanations, some of which are not entirely baseless and some of which are more outlandish. found answers in explanations that have some basis in reality yet are also categorised as conspiracy. Based in Davos, Switzerland, the WEF is an independent international organisation that brings together the powerful and elite from the worlds of politics, economics, and business. Headed by Klaus Schwab since its founding in 1971, the WEF aims to shape global agendas and future directions of markets, politics, and economies. It also lobbies for greater public–private co-operation and identifies 'future leaders' who will be at the forefront of driving the global economy. In the years prior to the pandemic, Schwab (2017) argued that global economies must move towards a 'fourth industrial revolution' predicated on the significant leaps forward offered by interconnectivity, advanced robots, artificial intelligence, and smart automation. The integration of these technologies represents a new phase of human development and maximising the benefits of these advancements was a challenge to be embraced. With the onset of the pandemic, Schwab, along with co-writer Thierry Malleret, published a new treatise titled *The Great Reset* (2020). In this short book, Schwab and Malleret argue that global capitalism has created more losers than winners and that the political turmoil characterised by the return of populism indicates that the global order is on the wrong track. The pandemic will accelerate changes that were already on their way, such as the integration of big data and artificial intelligence. However, the economic and social upheaval wrought by Covid-19 will have destructive and harmful consequences for many in the form of unemployment, growing mental ill health, and other inequalities and it will be incumbent upon nations to provide the support mechanisms previously unseen during neoliberal governance. They effectively suggest that neoliberalism is dead, social safety nets will be required, alongside processes of deglobalisation, shorter supply chains and massive labour market upheaval (also see: Gerbaudo, 2021).

Schwab argues that there is no going back to 'normal' as we knew it before the pandemic. In this sense, the pandemic acts as a catalyst for change and those changes will be largely to the advantage of the elite networks of corporations and politicians that the WEF entertains. While their treatise makes positive noises about reducing inequality, ultimately the 'Great Reset' is a call for capitalism to reinvigorate itself through the opportunities presented by technology, artificial intelligence, and automation. Advocacy for greater integration of smart technology into our lives is, by its supporters, believed to be key in ensuring optimisation and efficiency. Technology allows us to be the best version of ourselves, with the data and metrics to support us to make changes necessary to improve and thrive (Beer, 2016). For those sceptical of the greater integration of algorithmic governance and digital technology in all aspects of our lives, these plans sound like creeping surveillance and measures to further control populations and curtail freedoms.

The shift from shareholder to stakeholder capitalism is one prediction of the future. The economic upheaval wrought by Covid-19 and the range of interventions made by governments around the world seemingly indicate that we are on the verge of the next political economic shift (Raymen & Smith, 2022; Winlow & Hall, 2022). For some, this will be characterised by neo-feudalism: a more stratified society with wealth concentrated at the top, primarily by tech oligarchs, who also control information pipelines and tools of surveillance (Kotkin, 2020). Rather than outlandish 'conspiracy', these forms of political and economic analysis are carefully considered and nuanced. The Great Reset has become a lightning rod for concern that a new social order is being formed and one that will create winners and losers. Enough evidence existed before and during the pandemic that tech oligarchs mine our data for profit (Srnicek, 2017) while working in close proximity with governments who track and survey their citizens with impunity (Snowden, 2020; Zuboff, 2019). For many of our respondents, the pandemic response raised concerns about forms of digital feudalism best represented by phrases such as 'The Great Reset' and spoke to concerns about the loss of control in an increasingly uncertain, fractured, and changing world:

> Probably not but more importantly it will probably facilitate the various agendas that those who've propagated this whole episode have planned. Surveillance, control to name but a few. To venture down the murky river of eugenics is probably a step too far but one might suggest that

the restrictions that the west has become acclimatised to fit in nicely with what comes next. Western governments know that their mission creep allows them to lock down as and when they wish as the subservient masses are mentally prepared for it. (Male, 47, Financial Services, UK)

The restrictions have taken on a life of their own. No State can back down anymore, as this would involve acknowledging they were wrong from the very beginning. There are too many (financial!) interests vested in aspects of the management and continuation. The apps, the PPE, the surveillance and policing, the vaccination subscriptions, the media, the platforms, the online sales, and so forth… Every single job that has been created to sustain the restrictions in one way or another, everyone involved who benefits will fight tooth and nail to prevent this gravy train from coming off the rails. (Female, 55, Housewife, UK)

To these people, the pandemic comes across as 'planned' because dissenting voices were hushed and alternative debates were silenced. They invest in WEF literature by means of looking for a logic to explain the situation and its direction. Furthermore, these quotations show us that there is a sense of disquiet and a concern about several interconnected issues. Surveillance, restrictions, and mission creep all linked to a subservient public and a government unable to change direction while vaguely connected to 'various agendas' and 'what comes next'. While some respondents might not be able to articulate a clear and coherent argument about the interrelationship between these factors, they are hinting at the symbiotic relationship between government and private business; what Green and Fazi (2023) call the 'techno-media-pharma complex' and its impact upon government decision-making.

The vested interests that benefit from the restrictions, pandemic management, and vaccine programmes put profit before public health and seek to solidify their power and position. They correspond to Green and Fazi's (2023) command for us to 'follow the politics' instead of the science. Our respondents appear to be cognisant of the ways in which governments and corporations seek to maximise opportunities in times of crisis and this fuels their scepticism of official narratives and agendas. They questioned the underlying motives behind pandemic management decisions and asked 'who benefits'? Concerns around digital surveillance reflected hesitation about a perceived relationship between vaccine take-up and personal freedom, rather than traditional 'anti-vax' attitudes that predated that pandemic. Their concerns about freedom were also tied into the absence of debate and the role of media companies in censoring alternative perspectives.

Digital Censorship

Kotkin (2020) describes neo-feudalism as driven by tech oligarchs able to control media platforms and information flows. Our participants identified this control of information by mainstream and social media, which further fuelled scepticism of both official narratives and government policy:

> The combined censorship and manipulation by; MSM, Government, social media, and medical professional, also the long-standing infiltration of Government, royal families and large NGO's by eugenicists for over the past 5 decades. (Male, Retired, UK)

> Constant government and media (both mainstream and social media) bombardment appears to be trying to force the vaccine onto the population. (Male, 53, self-employed, New Zealand)

> It's an experimental drug still in a trial phase and with no proper tracking or monitoring as would usually occur in a Phase 3 trial. So people are basically the guinea pigs for the trial. Who gives such things to their children? People are not being fully informed of all information around these vaccines. There is one global narrative and no opposition to it. Any opposition is de-platformed or censored particularly on social media. That tells me something isn't right. Many aren't aware that in all previous studies of mRNA vaccines involving animals prior to 2018 showed that ALL of those animals died. The vaccines worked initially, then destroyed the immune system, neurological system or circulatory systems. I read this research long before this pandemic, but it's now been wiped from the Internet. They also skipped proper animal trials for these vaccines. Very convenient & ridiculously dangerous IMHO. (Female, 48, self-employed, UK)

The scale and reach of technology platforms such as Google, Facebook, and Twitter are unprecedented. Digital technology and social media have, to a large extent, driven traditional media platforms to the margins and now represent the most popular avenues for news content and information. On one level, this represents the evolution of market forces through technological innovation and the competitive capitalist imperative. Tech platforms innovate through digital technology and surpass traditional news markets in providing consumers with news and information. At this point, digital technology and a monopolistic control on platforms gives these tech giants the power to control flows of information. In the wake of the 2016 Brexit vote and the election of Donald Trump, the power of Facebook to reach swing voters in targeted ways and to be manipulated by foreign interference became a significant talking point (for example: Hall, 2022; Moody-Ramirez & Church, 2019).

Green and Fazi (2023) note the emergence of the Trusted News Initiative (TNI), a collective of mainstream news companies such as the BBC, technology platforms such as Google and social media sites like Facebook, which was created to combat 'fake news' and 'disinformation'. From the beginning of the pandemic, a single narrative around Covid-19 emerged and any dissent from that position was treated as disinformation and removed from social media sites, blocked from publication or discredited. At the time of writing (Spring 2023), evidence now exists in the public domain to support positions which, at the height of the pandemic, were disqualified as disinformation or conspiracy theory (Green & Fazi, 2023; Kheriaty, 2022). For example, consensus opinion on the efficacy of lockdown has shifted but only after public criticism of lockdown was costly for individuals willing to voice those perspectives. As previously mentioned, scientific evidence questions the efficacy of face coverings in public and the vaccines do not prevent infection; but at various points these statements would be shut down as problematic or conspiracy. Facebook and Twitter effectively censored alternative opinions to the mainstream narrative which has been questioned as both unscientific (Kheriaty, 2022) and undemocratic (Green & Fazi, 2023). For example, this participant said:

Because of this many eminent experts were censored and silenced for trying to warn us, and they are still being censored. Censorship is a sure sign that truth is being hidden, for only the truth is censored. 'Misinformation' and lies are easily outed through debate. Asks yourselves why debate was shut down from day one. Conflicts of interest are absolutely everywhere and there is a spider's web of corruption. All of the key influencers on SAGE are paid or funded directly or indirectly by the pharmaceutical industry. Why on Earth would anyone listen to a word they say? They are nothing more than snake oil salesman. (Biochemical engineer, male, 36, UK)

When debate on issues as crucial as the decision to restrict people's freedom of movement, the ability to access education and workplaces, to associate with family and neighbours, is restricted and dissenting voices dismissed (Wagner, 2022), our participants suggested that censorship was taking place and that it was important to resist such pressure. Science is messy and the search for the truth through experiment, randomised control trials, peer-review, and scrutiny is essential to determine the best course of action. However, dissent or deviation from an official narrative has been systematically met with professional sanctions, social media attacks, and censorship (Green & Fazi, 2023). At this point, people who asked questions and refused to accept the official narrative were labelled and dismissed as 'anti-vaxxers' and excluded from public discourse by technology companies and social media sites (Kheriaty, 2022). For many of the people in our study, it was the *outright rejection of alternative positions* as 'fake news' or conspiracy which raised deep questions that were never really adequately addressed. The lack of answers led to some people to grasp on to the very same 'conspiracies' resulting in scepticism and cynicism not only in the overall handling of the pandemic but in the motives for certain measures such as lockdown (see Briggs et al., 2021b) and the vaccine mandate.

Biosecurity and Digital Apartheid

> Delia: I work at the restaurant at the door and as a waitress and I am supposed to check everyone's vaccine status on entry. I am not doing it because I am against it. I had some guests telling me to check it but I said to them sure its fine, I guess you wouldn't try to sit inside unless you had the vaccine. But they got so angry with me because they wanted me to check that they had that privilege. I wasn't bothered about seeing it. Like is this what it has come down to, you have got the vaccine and want everyone to know you did it, how righteous you are?" (Switzerland)

Meanwhile on the other side of the world:

> Reporter: "So you've basically said, you probably don't see it like this, but two different classes of people. If you're vaccinated or unvaccinated. You have all these rights if you are vaccinated…"
> Jacinda Ardern (former Prime Minister of New Zealand): "That is what it is, so…yep."

Equally, when restaurant customers are obliging a waitress to confirm their moral superiority through vaccination and a national leader admits that they have created a two-tier society divided according to vaccination status, it is self-evident that new regimes of exclusion have emerged in response to the pandemic. It may well be the case that those regimes of exclusion are necessary to fight the virus; but the consequences are the same as some people are afforded privileges based on vaccination status and others, regardless of reason or circumstance, are excluded. Biosecurity has been a feature of modern life since 9/11 and the emergence of the modern security state (Kheriaty, 2022). Biometric technology such as facial recognition uses algorithms to match faces to images in a database and has been regularly used by police and security services in anti-terror programmes (Lyon, 2018).

However, we have seen the more widespread deployment of biometric technologies within our daily lives, normalising its use and instrumentalising the body as a tool of transaction (Kheriaty, 2022). We use biometrics to unlock Smartphones, for children to pay for lunch at school, for tracking our fitness and exercise regimes, and monitoring our sleep patterns (Crary, 2014). We have, over the last decade, become used to both giving up data related to our bodily functions and using the body to facilitate transactions. Returning to Lyon (2018), the ease of use is a significant draw for subjects looking for a frictionless consumer experience or the pursuit of optimised performance (Kalpokas, 2019). However, the 'black box' phenomenon persists whereby we give up data and biometric information to apps and systems that are opaque, have the potential to reinforce existing inequalities, or create what Pasquale (2015) terms 'cascading disadvantages' (see also: Eubanks, 2018; O'Neil, 2016).

Laura Dodsworth (2021) outlines the use of behavioural economics or 'nudge' theory throughout the UK Government's pandemic management. In relation to vaccine passports this approach is clear. The suggestion was floated on several occasions to test public attitudes and to embed the idea. As Bardosh et al. (2022: 4) note, "*Citing the potential for backlash and resistance, in December 2020, the director of the WHO's immunisation department stated: "I don't think we envision any countries creating a mandate for* [COVID-19] *vaccinations". Many governments originally followed with similar public statements, only to shift positions, often suddenly*".

Despite numerous retractions, eventually the government announced its intention to develop both digital and paper forms of vaccine certification. In fact, digital identification has been a feature of security discussions for two decades, but it is also a key feature of debate surrounding identity in general and health in particular. For example, the European Union's suggested 'Green Pass' for vaccination status was first mooted in 2018 (Kheriaty, 2022). Leading political figures such as Tony Blair have long called for identity cards and more recently claimed that technology facilitates the creation of digital identity cards that hold all of our critical information. Some countries, such as Estonia, have introduced digital identification. Technology certainly provides the means to do so but debate regarding privacy and security have been significant both before and after the pandemic. The concern about biosecurity was aptly summarised by this retired Canadian woman:

> The risks outweigh benefits [of the vaccine vs getting the virus]. There are no long-term safety studies, there is a danger of digital surveillance and a biosecurity state; no informed consent possible, ergo, a violation of the Nuremberg Code.

The relationship between digital surveillance and biosecurity is resoundingly clear in concerns from our participants. As Green and Fazi (2023: 174–175) point out, scepticism and a lack of trust in government are often based on real factors and evidence and leave people suspicious of motives. This quotation above makes connections between the speed of vaccine development and the absence of long-term safety studies with the 'dangers' of digital surveillance and biosecurity. Vaccine hesitancy is situated within this wider context. The long-term discussion of digital identification and biosecurity measures coalesced during the pandemic in a coordinated call for the implementation of vaccine passports or health status certificates (Beduschi, 2022; Hall & Studdert, 2021).

As mentioned, with the emergence of a virus without any known treatments and vaccines governments implemented lockdown policies and other non-pharmaceutical interventions as containment measures seemingly to be kept in place until vaccines arrived. From the outset, discussion of vaccines was accompanied by renewed calls for health status certificates or vaccine passports (Telford et al., 2022). As noted at the start of this chapter, health certificates and vaccination status were already in limited use, but this proposal was much broader. Indeed, Hall and Studdert (2021), while acknowledging the divisive nature of immunity passports, called for a clear distinction between vaccine passports and vaccine mandates. Brown et al. (2021) suggested that the ethical argument for vaccine passports was that it removed the need for lockdown measures. But in their discussion on the scientific and ethical feasibility of immunity passports, the authors noted the suspicion that surveillance and monitoring of activity would be within the proposed scope. Digital privacy and the protection of data has been a feature of critical commentary on technology for some time (see: Pasquale, 2015); but in terms of vaccine certification it was an immediate concern. Beducschi (2022) notes that although the right to privacy may be curtailed in certain circumstances, a number of incidents whereby data on contact tracing was disclosed or leaked raises significant questions about data access, storage, and purpose limitation.

While vaccine passports were initially mooted as necessary for facilitating foreign travel, they were soon repurposed to limit and regulate access to social and recreational activity such as entry to restaurants (Hall & Studdert, 2021; Telford et al., 2022). For example, New York's 'Excelsior Pass' permitted attendance at theatres, arenas, event venues, and large weddings (Hall & Studdert, 2021). Israel trialled a 'green pass' digital certification following its rapid mass vaccination programme, while the EU launched its Digital Covid Certificate in July 2021 (Green & Fazi, 2023). As noted by a high proportion of our participants, the curtailment of rights according to one's vaccination status was unprecedented and raised significant concerns about freedom and privacy. Cristina, a Spanish photographer we interviewed, said at the height of the implementation of the digital vaccine pass that:

> There are places around here in Valencia which require the vaccine to dine in or drink in. Outside they have these notices which intimidate you 'STOP COVID', prepare your Covid passport. Lately there have been loads of raids where the police stop the parties and have checked all the covid passports. This weekend just gone, there was a few young women who were dragged by force out of the disco because of this as if they had committed a serious crime.

Indeed, vaccine passports for international travel had mutated into vaccine mandates for significant parts of daily life. In several countries, including the UK and USA, certain workplaces demanded proof of vaccination to retain employment (Kheriaty, 2022; Poyiadji et al., 2022; Chapters 5 and 6). In the UK, health care and social care workers were mandated to be double vaccinated by April 2022 otherwise they would be forced to leave the profession. What counted as 'fully vaccinated' for the purposes of vaccine certification was also temporary and subject to change: once booster jabs were approved, three and then four vaccinations were required to be fully vaccinated and for vaccine certification to be valid (Green & Fazi, 2023). Kheriaty (2022) noted that social exclusion was baked into the system in a way that meant the unvaccinated would be pressured into compliance through the withdrawal of freedoms or the penalisation of non-vaccination. As people began to lose their jobs in late 2021 and early 2022, the link between biosecurity and vaccination status further fuelled anxiety and mistrust in some sections of the population.

One of the central pillars of vaccine passports and mandates was the initial claim from the pharmaceutical companies responsible for the vaccines that protection was significant, and that viral escape was not possible. Being vaccinated meant you could no longer catch Covid-19 and that your immunity justified the use of a vaccine passport as you were no longer a risk to others (Telford et al., 2022). However, evidence continued to emerge that this was grossly inaccurate and viral escape was not only significant but, in fact, vaccination in some cases increased the likelihood of infection (Israel et al., 2021; Vivaldi et al., 2022). The justification for a system of digital apartheid collapsed. In response, governments eventually began removing the requirement for digital certification or vaccine mandates.

Bill Gates is as much seen as a rich humanitarian trying to do good in the best way he knows how as he is seen as an evil figure seeking to implement systems of control that will further his own agendas. Nevertheless, there is enough of a breadcrumb trail to connect his funding of and influence upon organisations like the WHO, his support for vaccination programmes and development, and his advocacy of digital identification, to create scepticism about official narratives. One of the themes running through our data is a clear absence of trust in terms of such leaders and influential global figures. For many of our participants, that lack of trust manifested in significant concern about the rationale for vaccine passports. Indeed, some even made connections between digital identification, vaccine mandates, and the Chinese social credit system:

> I don't know whether Covid-19 actually exists. If it does, then I believe it was created. I believe that global powers are using it as a way to bring about a bio-techno surveillance state, with a Chinese style social credit system. I believe that the vaccine is a vehicle to instigate vaccine passports, and vaccine passports are a vehicle to bring in digital ID/ surveillance. (Female, 36, Psychotherapist, England)

We can't comply our way out of tyranny. The plan has always been to use this public health crisis to roll out long-desired social credit scoring systems, the printing of trillions of dollars by central banks & increased global surveillance/censorship. (Male, 46, IT worker, USA)

The suggestion that Western democracies were seeking to implement Chinese-style restrictions using digital technologies and forms of surveillance governance, has been dismissed as 'conspiracy theory' and wild speculation. Yet there may be some truth to it. First, it is important to understand what the Chinese social credit system is and then consider its potential influence or application in the West. According to Chin and Lin (2022), the Chinese model of state surveillance utilises cutting edge technologies including facial recognition and biometric technology, as well as digital tracking systems, to monitor its citizens' behaviour and activity. At its most authoritarian and problematic, this technology is used to track and persecute the Uighur tribes in the Northwest of the country. In its most widespread application, it regulates behaviour of individuals and companies by incentivising 'good' behaviours and practices and punishing 'bad' behaviour through blocking access to certain services. For example, the untrustworthy are unable to purchase high-speed rail or plane tickets. The pressure of being blacklisted compels individuals and companies to fulfil their legal obligations. However, while the popular discourse in the West has focused on this system as a 'big brother' or all-encompassing form of totalitarian control, research has shown that while this might be the aim, in practice it is less than totalising (Chin & Lin, 2022; Liang et al., 2018). It is a complicated system that has prioritised financial and commercial activities (Liang et al., 2018), with more success in terms of business rather than individual compliance (Chin & Lin, 2022).

The Chinese model has been interpreted by some, including many of our participants, as a system destined for rollout in the West. The reliance on the Chinese as the world's factory has seen Western companies outsource production to China (Streeck, 2016; Varoufakis, 2015). While Silicon Valley technology companies invented many of the surveillance tools utilised in China's authoritarian surveillance state (Chin &

Lin, 2022), China has subsequently exported the tools of state surveillance—digital tracking systems—to countries around the world, both in developing regions and in the West. China's influence on the West, particularly its corporations and governments, has been more significant than is perhaps often understood despite the Chinese approach being incompatible with the West's deeply held belief in freedom (Žižek, 2020). Indeed, China's willingness to impose lockdown restrictions on Wuhan at the start of the pandemic created a precedent that Western nations almost immediately followed (Žižek, 2020, 2021).

China also put digital surveillance technologies at the forefront of its pandemic response. In its general use of digital technologies as tools of tracking and surveillance, it leads the world. In showing technology companies, security services, and national governments what is possible, the Chinese perhaps create a blueprint or template for those with vested interests in the proliferation of digital surveillance to follow. While it remains to be seen whether a Chinese social credit system is the end point of the West's embrace of digital identification, biometric security, and health certification, it has been possible for many people to connect the dots and raise concerns. As Kuldova (2022) notes, the implementation of digital technology and algorithmic governance has often resulted in a form of 'mission creep' where the original purpose and intention makes way for greater use of the technology once it is established. For some of our participants, the creeping intrusion of digital surveillance and biometric security will result in a totalitarian nightmare of unfreedom. Rather than 'anti-vax' per se, this is a core concern that underpins their hesitancy to Covid-19 vaccination and digital forms of certification.

References

Babones, S. (2018). *The new authoritarianism*. Polity.
Bardosh, K., Figueiredo, A., Gur-Arie, R., Jamrozik, E., Doidge, J., Lemmens, T., Keshavjee, S., Graham, J., & Baral, S. (2022). The unintended consequences of COVID-19 vaccine policy: Why mandates, passports and

restrictions may cause more harm than good. *British Medical Journal Global Health, 7*, 1–14.

Barlow, J. P. (1996). *A declaration of the independence of cyberspace*. Electronic Frontier Foundation. Accessed on 5 March 2023. https://www.eff.org/cyberspace-independence

Beduschi, A. (2022). Taking stock of COVID-19 health status certificates: Legal implications for data privacy and human rights. *Big Data & Society, 9*(1), 1–5.

Beer, D. (2016). *Metric society*. Palgrave.

Brandt, A. M. (2022). The history of contact tracing and the future of public health. *American Journal of Public Health, 112*(8), 1097–1099.

Brayne, S. (2021). *Predict and surveil: Data, discretion, and the future of policing*. Oxford University Press.

Bridle, J. (2018). *The new dark age: Technology and the end of the future*. Verso.

Briggs, D., Ellis, A., Lloyd, A., & Telford, L. (2021a). *Researching the COVID-19 pandemic: A critical blueprint for the social sciences*. Policy Press Rapid Response Series.

Briggs, D., Telford, L., Lloyd, A., Ellis, A., & Kotzé, J. (2021b). *Lockdown: Social harm in the Covid-19 era*. Palgrave.

Brown, R. C. H., Kelly, D., Wilkinson, D., & Savulescu, K. (2021). The scientific and ethical feasibility of immunity passports. *The Lancet Infectious Diseases, 21*(3), E58–63.

Carr, N. (2011). *The shallows: How the internet is changing the way we think, read, and remember*. Atlantic Books.

Crary, J. (2014). *Late Capitalism and the Ends of Sleep*. Verso.

Chin, J., & Lin, L. (2022). *Surveillance state: Inside China's quest to launch a new era of social control*. St Martin's Press.

Dardot, P. Laval, C. (2019). *Never-Ending Nightmare: The Neoliberal Assault on Democracy*. Verso.

Dodsworth, L. (2021). *A state of fear: How the UK government weaponised fear during the Covid-19 pandemic*. Pinter & Martin Ltd.

Eubanks, V. (2018). *Automating inequality: How high-tech tools profile, police and punish the poor*. Picador.

Field, M. (2020). NHS under fire for plans to store track and trace data for 20 years. *The Telegraph*. Accessed 15 March 2023. https://www.telegraph.co.uk/technology/2020/05/28/nhs-fire-plans-store-track-trace-data-20-years/

Fisher, M. (2009). *Capitalist realism: Is there no alternative?* Zero.

Flyverbom, M. (2019). *The digital prism: Transparency and managed visibilities in a datafied world*. Cambridge University Press.

Ford, M. (2016). *The rise of the robots: Technology and the threat of mass unemployment.* Oneworld Publications.

Foster, G., Frijters, P., & Baker, M. (2021). *The great Covid panic: What happened, why, and what to do next.* Brownstone Institute.

Gerbaudo, P. (2021). *The great recoil: Politics after populism and pandemic.* Verso.

Goodwin, M. (2023). *Values, voice and virtue: The new British politics.* Penguin.

Green, T., & Fazi, T. (2023). *The Covid consensus: The global assault on democracy and the poor—A critique from the left.* Hurst & Company.

Gusterson, H. (2019) 'Introduction: Robohumans'. In C. Besteman & H. Gusterson (Eds.), *Life by algorithms: How roboprocesses are remaking our world.* University of Chicago Press.

Hall, M. A., & Studdert, D. M. (2021). 'Vaccine passport' Certification—Policy and ethical considerations. *The New England Journal of Medicine, 385*(11), e32(1–3).

Hall, N. A. (2022). Understanding brexit on Facebook: Developing close-up, qualitative methodologies for social media research. *Sociological Research Online, 27*(3), 707–723.

Harvey, D. (2023). *A companion to Marx's Grundrisse.* Verso.

Hochuli, A., Hoare, G., & Cunliffe, P. (2021). *The end of the end of history: Politics in the twenty-first century.* Zero Books.

Israel, A., Merzon, E., Schaffer, A., Shenhar, Y., Green, I., Goldan-Cohen, A., Ruppin, E., Magen, E., & Vinker, S. (2021). Elapsed time since BNT162b2 vaccine and risk of SARS-CoV-2 infection: Test negative design study. *British Medical Journal, 375,* 1–7.

Jeffries, S (2021). *Everything, all the time, everywhere: How we became postmodern.* Verso.

Kalpokas, I. (2019). *Algorithmic governance: Politics and law in the post-human era.* Palgrave Pivot.

Kheriaty, A. (2022). *The new abnormal: The rise of the biomedical security state.* Regnery Publishing.

Klein, N. (2007). *The Shock Doctrine: The Rise of Disaster Capitalism.* Penguin.

Kotkin, J. (2020). *The coming neo-feudalism.* Encounter Books.

Kuldova, T. (2022). *The compliance-industrial complex: The operating system of a pre-crime society.* Palgrave Pivot.

Lewis, M. (2021). *The premonition: A pandemic story.* Allen Lane.

Liang, F., Das, V., Kostyuk, N., & Hussain, M. M. (2018). Constructing a data-driven society: China's social credit system as a state surveillance infrastructure. *Policy & Internet, 10*(4), 415–453.

Lyon, D. (2018). *The culture of surveillance*. Polity.
Marsh, S., & Hern, A. (2020). Government admits breaking privacy law with NHS test and trace. *The Guardian*. Accessed on 10 March 2023. https://www.theguardian.com/technology/2020/jul/20/uk-government-admits-breaking-privacy-law-with-test-and-trace-contact-tracing-data-breaches-coronavirus#:~:text=Government%20admits%20breaking%20privacy%20law%20with%20NHS%20test%20and%20trace,-This%20article%20is&text=The%20UK%20government%20broke%20the,admitted%20after%20a%20legal%20challenge
Mau, S (2019). *The metric society: On the quantification of the social*. Polity.
Mirowski, P. (2013). *Never Let a Good Crisis go to Waste: How Neoliberalism Survived the Financial Meltdown*. Verso.
Moody-Ramirez, M., & Church, A. (2019). Analysis of Facebook meme groups used during the 2016 US presidential election. *Social Media + Society, 5*, 1–11.
Nagra, B., & Maurutto, P. (2020). No-Fly lists, national security and race: The experiences of Canadian Muslims. *The British Journal of Criminology, 60*(3), 600–619.
Naughton, J. (2016). The evolution of the internet: From military experiment to general purpose technology. *Journal of Cyber Policy, 1*(1), 5–28.
OECD. (2023). *Trust in government (indicator)*. Accessed 8 March 2023. https://data.oecd.org/gga/trust-in-government.htm
O'Neil, C. (2016). *Weapons of math destruction: How big data increases inequality and threatens democracy*. Penguin.
Pasquale, F. (2015). *The black box society: The secret algorithms that control money and information*. Harvard University Press.
Poyiadji, N., Tassopoulos, A., Myers, D. T., Wolf, L., & Griffith, B. (2022). Covid-19 vaccine mandates: Impact on radiology department operations and mitigation strategies. *Journal of the American College of Radiology, 19*(3), 437–445.
Raymen, T., & Smith, O. (2022). The post-Covid future of the environmental crisis industry and its implications for green criminology and Zemiology. *Journal of Contemporary Crime, Harm, Ethics, 1*(1), 63–87.
Schildt, H. (2020). *The data imperative: How digitalization is reshaping management, organizing, and work*. Oxford University Press.
Schwab, K. (2017). *The fourth industrial revolution*. Penguin.
Schwab, K., & Malleret, T. (2020). *Covid-19: The great reset*. Forum Publishing.
Scott, B. (2022). *Cloudmoney: Cash, cards, crypto and the war for our wallets*. The Bodley Head.

Snowden, E. (2020). *Permanent record.* Pan Books.
Srnicek, N. (2017). *Platform capitalism.* Polity.
Streeck, W. G. (2016). *When will capitalism end?* Verso.
Telford, L. (2022). *English nationalism and its ghost towns.* Routledge.
Telford, L., Bushell, M., & Hodgkinson, O. (2022). Passport to neoliberal normality? A critical exploration of COVID-19 vaccine passports. *Journal of Contemporary Crime, Harm and Ethics, 2*(1), 42–61.
Van Brakel, R. (2021). Rethinking predictive policing: Towards a holistic framework of democratic algorithmic governance. In M. Schuilenberg & R. Peeters (Eds.), *The algorithmic society: Technology, power, and knowledge.* Routledge.
Varoufakis, Y. (2015). *The global minotaur: America, Europe and the future of the global economy.* Zed Books.
Vivaldi, G., Jolliffe, D., Holt, J., Tydeman, F., Talaei, M., Davies, G., Lyons, R., Griffiths, C., Kee, F., Sheikh, A., Shaheen, S., & Martineau, A. (2022). Risk factors for SARS-CoV-2 infection after primary vaccination with ChAdOx1 nCoV-19 or BNT162b2 and after booster vaccination with BNT162b2 or MRNA-1273: A population-based cohort study (COVIDENCE UK). *The Lancet Regional Health, 22*, 1–18.
Wagner, A. (2022). *Emergency state: How we lost our freedoms in the pandemic and why it matters.* The Bodley Head.
Winlow, S., & Hall, S. (2022). *The death of the left: Why we must begin from the beginning again.* Policy Press.
Winlow, S., Hall, S., & Treadwell, J. (2017). *The rise of the right.* Policy Press.
Winlow, S., & Winlow, E. (2022). Is the neoliberal era coming to an end? Ideology, history and macroeconomic change in the shadow of COVID-19. *Journal of Contemporary Crime, Harm, Ethics, 2*(1), 1–23.
Woolhouse, M. (2022). *The year the world went mad: A scientific memoir.* Sandstone Press.
Žižek, S. (2020). *Pandemic!: COVID-19 shakes the world.* Polity.
Žižek, S. (2021). *Pandemic! 2: Chronicles of a time lost.* Polity.
Zuboff, S. (2019). *The age of surveillance capitalism.* Profile Books.

5

Asymptomatic Freedom, Resistance, and the 'Anti-vaxxers'

Given the wider context outlined in the book so far, 'vaccine hesitancy' has always existed but had grown prior to the pandemic with fewer people around the world getting vaccinated, sometimes even for basic and treatable diseases (DiResta et al., 2021; WHO, 2019). Eisenstein (2022: 44) suggests that although global vaccine coverage generally increased from the 1970s onwards and reached 85% for various vaccine-preventable diseases in 2014, in the subsequent years *"leading up to the pandemic, we really saw a stagnation of coverage for many of these long-established vaccines"*. Much of this was driven by concern over vaccine safety (Chaney & Lee, 2022), with the WHO suggesting in 2019 that vaccine hesitancy was one of the ten greatest threats to global health (Eisenstein, 2022). Accordingly, regarding framing Covid-19 vaccine rejection we must consider such rejection as part of a downward trend in vaccine confidence. As the Covid-19 restrictions set in and a vaccine was developed, increasing governmental persuasion became directed towards taking the inoculation to 'achieve herd immunity' and move out of the pandemic.

This was done with varying levels of success. As of May 2023, 70% of the globe's population had received at least one dose of a Covid-19 vaccine, though this only included 29.8% in low-income countries (Our World in Data, 2023). Quite clearly, a stubborn proportion have significant doubts, which is despite the threat of digital passports and vaccine mandates during the pandemic (Schmelz & Bowles, 2021). In our study, this group traversed a continuum from 'anti-vax' to 'anti-mandate' and often regarded mandatory vaccination as both oppressive and disproportionate to the threat of the virus, particularly once subsequent variants followed the natural evolution of viral reproduction and became much less deadly (Honigsbaum, 2020). Despite this, government ministers and health experts continued to insist on immunisation for everyone, rather than those most at risk (Woolhouse, 2022).

The same behavioural nudging used to instil compliance in lockdown mandates was transferred to vaccine uptake (see Dai et al., 2021). Countries such as Canada, New Zealand, and Australia, where Covid-19 infection, hospitalisation, and death rates had been less severe than places like the UK, USA, and Spain, followed strict lockdown measures with strong demands for vaccination. Some countries, such as the USA, made the vaccine mandatory in certain employment sectors and threatened the unvaccinated with dismissal. In the UK, for example, thousands of health and care home workers left their jobs following efforts to enforce vaccine mandates in the workplace. Across Europe, the President of the European Commission, Ursula von der Leyen, advised the member states of the EU to consider mandatory vaccination against Covid-19 and was quoted as saying: "*How we can encourage and potentially think about mandatory vaccination within the EU, this needs discussion*" (Burki, 2022: 27). Those dismissed as anti-vaxxers were accused of preventing the end of the pandemic but remained cautious and unconvinced by the official narrative. Many of this group—diverse in their beliefs, sentiments, and feelings about the vaccine and not necessarily 'anti-vaccine' per se—had already had doubts about the restrictions and continued their forms of resistance. Some were new additions, having felt that Covid-19 did not warrant so many new rules and restrictions while others had grown tired of them. Yet in political discourse they were often grouped together as 'anti-vaxxers' and portrayed as selfish, morally, and ethically absent, or conspiracy theorists (Bardosh et al., 2022; Telford et al., 2022). As we will see in this chapter, however, their wide-ranging doubts and complex views warranted analytical attention regardless of one's opinion on their resistance to Covid-19 vaccination.

Fear, 'Nudging', and the Vaccine Campaigns

In our previous work (Briggs et al., 2021a), we demonstrated how Covid-19 was depicted and presented without the factual nuance around differentiated risk based on age, co-morbidities, and other relevant factors (also see: Chapter 2). In this sense, the risk of illness, hospitalisation, and death was misrepresented. Most information presented to the public particularly during lockdown, came from government briefings, mainstream media, and social media sites which sought to curtail 'misinformation'. This created a single narrative, often underpinned by emotive calls for solidarity and sacrifice, while simultaneously tapping into deep-rooted fears and anxieties. Our data reflects this point:

> I think it is their choice [to vaccinate], but I also think most people have taken the vaccine through fear due to mainstream media constantly posting death and infection rates and making people feel it is the bubonic plague and if they go outside their house they are going to die. I also think that a lot of people have been forced in to having it because of their jobs, or because they are desperate to travel or see family etc. I am concerned for vaccinated people because the long-term impact of the jabs is not yet known. (Female, 49, Wholesaler, Wales)

Fear causes division. A 'responsible citizen' adopted the messaging and reproduced it as compliant behaviour, while a 'negligent citizen' ignored restrictive measures and refused the vaccine. From the outset, future vaccines were presented as the way out of the pandemic and so it became one's social responsibility to be vaccinated; greater levels of immunisation would result in an end to lockdown restrictions and a return to normality. The United Nations Secretary-General Antonio Guterres, for instance, said in 2021 that the only way out of a global pandemic "*is through a global vaccination plan*" (United Nations, 2021). This positioned vaccine uptake as the responsible choice. Consequently, vaccine refusal was cast as damaging to the greater good. In one of many Facebook posts, taken at the time of the vaccine rollouts in December 2020, ideological hope was pinned on such an outcome. Crystal, a young American waitress, wrote in one Facebook forum:

> "With a thankful heart I want to say thank you [name of hospital] for this privilege you have given me and my co-workers to receive our immunizations. Thank you to all those that were behind the scenes whom I may never meet but yet they made these vaccines possible for us 🙏
> I feel blessed and grateful knowing the vaccine I received today is to protect my family, friends and myself. I truly feel this vaccine represents a sign of hope and faith for us all to close this chapter and go back to the days where we were able to hug, visit extended family, travel and create happy memories. This 2020 pandemic has affected everyone worldwide, people have lost businesses, jobs, and financial stability. But the most painful effect of this virus has cause to our human race was losing almost two million loved ones. I can personally testify because I lost my sweet, beloved grandmother. 🥺
> As 2020 comes to a close, I chose to be vaccinated for better tomorrows and new pleasant memories to come!"

Many of our interviewees recognised this in hindsight such as these two friends from Switzerland:

> Delia: I think they [government] don't really know what to do so they go by the 'easy' way into letting people believe that the only way out of this pandemic is the vaccine. (Female, 22, Office administrator)

> Maya: Yes, I slightly disagree but Delia is right in a way. I am a very social person and I was glad to be able to do something for the society. Also, it was like a sunny moment when it felt like the world would soon be 'normal' again. I personally don't completely understand why there are people that don't want the vaccine but at the same time, I don't think that they should have to get it if they don't want to. (Female, 23, Student)

Switzerland saw strong compliance during the first lockdown (Franzen & Wöhner, 2021) and by December 2020 had *"recorded three million downloads, representing an adoption rate of 43%"* (Geber & Ho, 2022: 2) for their contract-tracing app. Like other countries, compliance eventually waned including for vaccine uptake which was markedly troublesome even among Swiss healthcare professionals (Asri et al., 2022). Despite this, Delia and Maya were able to politely disagree on the vaccine and successfully negotiate the increasingly hardened and socially damaging divisions that emerged around pandemic management. Though they differed in opinion, they respected each other's position. However, for most of our participants such common ground was absent. Both sides found fault with the other's position, with the vaccine hesitant as critical of those choosing to vaccinate as the vaccinated were towards the 'anti-vaxxers'. This self-employed psychiatrist was extremely critical of her peers and wider society in general:

> The pressure is everywhere you look. The weaponisation of social conformity was probably their cleverest move *[government, mass media]*. Just go and read the SAGE meeting minutes - it's all there, for all to see, in black and white. The manipulation of social pressure has done a number on many. Except those of us that retain the grey matter to think critically, analyse data, spot propaganda, and see straight through applied behavioural science. (Female, 30, UK)

Alongside this criticism of others, many participants reflected upon their own choices, and some came to regret their decision to be vaccinated or had post-hoc revelations of manipulation and social pressure. Perhaps emblematic of a sense of collective anxiety, this business owner from India reflected how he:

> …was in that deluded state where people thronged the Vax centres for their jabs. I wish we hadn't *[got the vaccine]*. Without realising what we were doing me and my wife queued up and took the first jab in 2021. We had no idea we would suffer such side effects. (Male, 50, Business owner, India)

This business owner was not alone. According to longitudinal surveys undertaken in India, compliance with restrictions, digital forms of track and trace, positive reflections on the government and health system, as well as vaccine uptake, were divided by wealth with greater compliance among high-income groups while hesitation was found more among the rural or urban poor (Umakanthan et al., 2021: 1063). In neighbouring Bangladesh, a cross-sectional survey of 1,377 people found that "*fifty percent of respondents were concerned about the side effects of vaccines, where a considerable number of participants believed the vaccine would not be safe and effective*" and that the increasing prevalence of information was a factor in these attitudes (Hossain et al., 2021: 4028). In hindsight, many of our participants suggested the general populace had been 'manipulated' into believing in the vaccine as the only avenue for exiting the pandemic. They cited the lack of debate on alternative policies and described how a 'one-sided science' had prevailed as this female Communications worker from France indicated:

> Completely mismanaged and over blown *[Covid-19 in general]*. There has never been any focus on early treatment or any public health initiatives to boost general health. There is a lot of fear mongering and a lack of debate.

This corresponds with the absence of trust discussed in Chapter 4. In a lengthy reflection, Nicola, a self-employed female entrepreneur from the USA, articulated a feeling present within our sample. She connects lockdown restrictions with the increase in multiple social problems and recalls how she was considered a 'domestic terrorist' for not aligning herself with the vaccine narrative. She also suggests that alternative treatment methods or solutions were quelled by mainstream media and political discourse:

> Everything was overkill. At the beginning, nobody knew anything so it seemed legit to shut down and ride this thing out. It's been two years so enough already with the restrictions. We have a mental health crisis amongst kids who haven't gotten to live like kids for two years. I'm flabbergasted about how masks and vaccines are promoted so much by the

government while natural immunity isn't recognized and proper nutrition, healthy lifestyle, exercise, vitamin/supplement protocols and early treatment is either completely ignored or totally censored and marked as dangerous misinformation or domestic terrorism. Seriously? I'm a domestic terrorist because I don't agree with or follow the government's 'guidelines'?!? Wear your mask and get your vaccine—are you fucking kidding me?!? That's it? It's completely asinine, it won't work, people who wear masks and get vaccines still get and spread Covid. It's here to stay and its mind boggling how many people go along with it. If the government cared so much about health as they claim to, they would pay fitness instructors and yoga teachers to teach free classes in parks all over the country every single day and promote them like they do masks and vaccines. If they cared about people's health, they would gather all info from doctors who came up with their own Covid protocols to treat their patients successfully and promote the use of these effective treatments as much as they do vaccines and masks. They would mail an effective Covid protocol to every citizen with instructions on how to use it at the first sign of illness. Early intervention treatment would be available at free clinics like vaccines are and promoted like vaccines are. But no, this isn't happening so we're fucked.

Nicola raises some important points about the wider context of public health and healthy lifestyles. However, wavering commitment or doubts about the vaccine were addressed via financial incentives as a means of improving take-up. After saying how the restrictions were *"overbearing"*, this self-employed handyman from Scotland claimed it was *"criminal"* that people were *"vaccinated by the offer of donuts, food vouchers, etc. all in the name of looking after your health"* (Male, 57). Some academic research provided valuable support for the use of incentives (Savulescu et al., 2021). For example, Acharya and Dhakal (2021) reported on the successful use of lotteries to boost vaccine uptake, despite questionable evidence on its efficacy (Thirumurthy et al., 2022). Oxford University experts in the UK such as Professor Julian Savulescu (2021: 84) stated that in the context of the Covid-19 pandemic *"mandatory vaccination can be ethically justified but when risks are more uncertain, payment for vaccination (whether in cash or kind) may be an ethically superior option"* and that:

One attractive benefit would be the freedom to not wear a mask in public places if you carried a vaccination certificate, and not to socially distance. Currently, everyone has to wear a mask and practise social distancing. Relaxing this requirement for those who have been vaccinated (or otherwise have immunity) would be an attractive benefit. Moreover, it would help ameliorate the risks the unvaccinated would pose to others.

There is a clear relationship here between vaccination status and the end of invasive restrictions. There may be epidemiological fact behind these suggestions, but this is communicated in a neoliberalised culture of mistrust and fears about manipulation. In Europe incentives were less prevalent, but differences began to emerge in the treatment of the vaccinated and unvaccinated. Specialised Covid-19 healthcare staff confirmed to us in Spain that the restrictions had been utilised as a means of coercion into vaccination. This exchange took place at one of the many empty vaccination centres dotted around the country in the spring of 2022:

> I am due a Covid-19 booster I'm told. I have already had three calls reminding me/offering me the opportunity. My doubts are mainly related to the fact that I don't think I need it and related to mixing the vaccines (in Spain Johnson & Johnson is no longer available so Pfizer and Moderna are on offer). I approach the walk-in vaccination centre which, having driven past it most days, is as empty as it has been for the last six months. For some reason though, it has expanded somewhat and more white tents and clinical staff sit around on their mobiles. I approach the nurse who comes over and I say how I am surprised it is both empty and the compound is bigger. *"Well we made it bigger at the end of last year thinking that there would be a flood of people to get the vaccination but many people, including loads of kids, got Covid so they didn't come, they got their immunity through the virus"* she tells me. *"Maybe the campaign was to get the kids but they got the virus first"* I say, and she nods understandingly.
> She asks: *"are you here for a vaccination?"* I reluctantly admit I am considering it but really don't want it and explain how the restrictions are loosening in many countries before expressing some objection about how I felt coerced into having it in the first place. *"Yes, that was the idea...to make it difficult for people, so they almost had no choice but to get it, it was the only way to get people vaccinated"* she says as she sidesteps to keep

herself warm in the wind. "*Really? I think they could have given people a choice*" I say. "*Yes but this is a business now, look at all this infrastructure, they won't dismantle this quickly, there is lots of money at stake*" she concedes. "*Yes I can see that and that is why I am dubious*" I confess.

Five minutes into our discussion she says "*oh yeah, you need a mask to talk to me*" even though no one has said anything yet. She reaches for a box, pulls one out and obliges me to put it on in the open air to continue the conversation. As we continue to carry on talking she offers me half a Moderna booster, which she thinks would be enough for the winter though she then says "*if I were you, I would wait because things may be changing*". Mask restrictions have just been loosened for indoor contexts and in Denmark the vaccination programme has thus been suspended. [Field notes 'Covid concessions' by Daniel Briggs]

Eventually, restrictions were eased just in time for the busy and financially lucrative 2022 summer tourist season. Spain also dropped restrictions which had, for nearly a year, previously deterred unvaccinated people from entering the country. By summer 2022, it was clear that vaccination did not prevent infection or transmission and it had become harder to sustain restrictive measures on the public's lives. However, social divisions had already been caused by around a year of oppressive measures through the hostile vaccine campaign, passports, and mandates.

Expanding Powers on Vaccine Mandates

In comparison to many countries, Spanish citizens queued up for the vaccine. By the summer of 2021, 70% of the population had been double vaccinated. At the end of 2021, this had risen to 80% and reached 86% over the summer of 2022. A study undertaken by Imperial College London in (2021) found that 79% of people in Spain trusted Covid-19 vaccines, compared to 62% in the USA, 56% in France, and 47% in Japan. This was because there was deep trust in the public health system and close-knit family ties, which encouraged people to get the vaccine to protect relatives (Imperial College London, 2021). There were no mandates passed per se which obligated people to get vaccinated. However, forms of division and exclusion did exist, which both made life harder for the unvaccinated and identified them publicly as different or opposed to the majority. The introduction of the vaccine passport to enter bars, restaurants, and entertainment venues such as cinemas and theatres was generally accepted by people yet complimented with subtle reminders of where unvaccinated people belong as these field notes indicate (Fig. 5.1).

> It is approaching the winter of 2021 and I am returning to regular transit between Madrid and Majorca. There is talk of increased Covid cases, but no such variant has yet to present itself. Perhaps as a measure of caution the local government has eased the bureaucratic procedures associated with travelling between the airports for vaccinated travellers. They can pass freely at will down the blue aisle. For those without the vaccine, though, there are a series of white-suited professionals armed with temperature checks and iPads to check the Covid tests are authentic. I'm just off the plane and when I see 99% of the flight follow the blue arrows, and I subsequently follow the red I can feel the looks from my protected contemporaries who breeze into the luggage collection area as I confront a barrage of white coats. Because I don't have the vaccine, I must have a PCR test, wait for the results and should it be positive I will have to self-isolate at home for two weeks. After the test, I am led down to

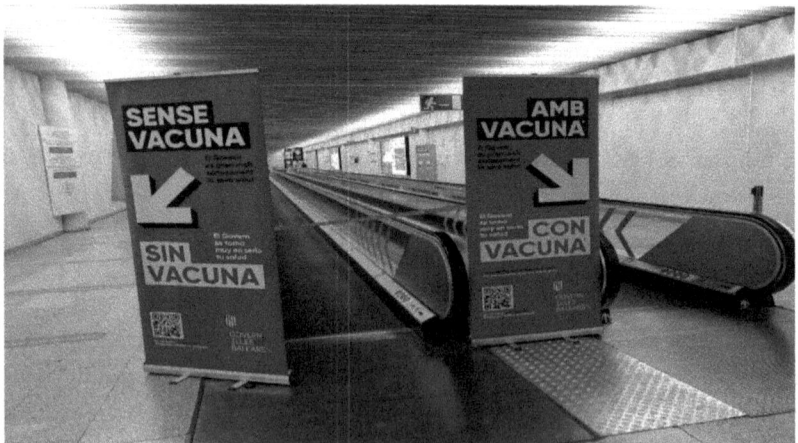

Fig. 5.1 Red without vaccination, blue with vaccination

the quarantine area of the airport which is guarded by more white coats and wait 30 minutes for my notification that I am negative. [Field notes 'Walk of shame' by Daniel Briggs]

By this point, viral escape had been reported meaning that the vaccine did not provide protection from infection or transmission (Green & Fazi, 2023). Meanwhile, much of the discussion of immunity continued to ignore natural immunity associated with previous infection; immunity was provided by the vaccines and nothing else. However, social divisions were amplified based upon one's vaccination status (Bardosh et al., 2022). While our survey was active during the latter stage of 2021 and early part of 2022, US President Joe Biden tried to mandate vaccination for large companies to "*protect their workers, customers, and communities*". The mandate was allowed to stand for health workers and federal employees which elicited disagreement among our respondents. "*Mandatory vaccination is contrary to the principles of the USA*" said one American nurse from Kentucky in her early 40s, while 58-year-old Deena from Texas felt a degree of relief to leave the profession and reject the vaccine in the process:

> I was fired for not getting it. Yes 👎 from a healthcare facility where I worked at 21 years. I was lucky that the timing worked out perfectly so I could retire with full social security and my pension. I feel so sorry for young people these days. No wonder the suicide rate is up 😥

There was equal frustration in Canada. For some months, the Canadian authorities impeded international and domestic travel for unvaccinated people, imposing mandates in workplaces which caused immense stress for people who had doubts about the vaccine. This 32-year-old prison worker said how he "*didn't want it*" and that "*if I have to take one or lose my job, I will try to find another job, if that becomes impossible I will be forced to take a non mRNA vaccine in bad conscience and I will be sick and depressed about what's been done to my bodily autonomy for the rest of my life*". Such pressure was also evident in responses from healthcare staff in the UK, where numerous NHS workers expressed their concern. This former education-based nurse from Wales said:

> None of the policies used were to control transmission, none of them were scientifically sound. It has all been about control of the people, not the pathogen. I left my job in the NHS before the jabs came along, I cannot be part of this mass manipulation.

Another respondent, in her early 30s and now unemployed, conveyed similar views:

> I left my job in the NHS as I knew vaccines would be pushed. I could also see first-hand how ridiculous the pandemic response was. I couldn't work there any longer.

On 9 November 2021, the UK Health Secretary mandated that all NHS staff must be vaccinated against Covid-19 by 1 April 2022, enacting the necessary legislation in a statutory instrument laid before parliament in January 2022 (see: UK Parliament, 2022). Although they present various ethical conundrums (Giubilini et al., 2022; Pugh et al., 2022), the use of mandates has been found to increase vaccine uptake (for instance: Karaivanov et al., 2022; Mills & Rüttenauer, 2022). NHS staff had until 3 February 2022, to receive a first vaccine dose or risk losing their job. The mandate saw almost 130,000 staff come forward to be vaccinated (McKee & Schalkwyk, 2022). Even though the mandate was overturned on 31 January 2022, this pressure led some to regret their decision to receive the inoculation. This male nurse, aged 64 and close to retirement, reflected on how:

> I work in the NHS and one day turned up to work to be told that I was to go first thing and get the vaccine. I wasn't keen but felt I had no option at the time. I have declined the subsequent vaccine boosters as I had adverse reactions to the first and disagree strongly with how they are being strong-armed onto the population.

Research suggests such pressure prompted changes in perceptions of pandemic governance. In New Zealand, surveys by Thaker (2021) taken in the summer of 2020 on the prospect of a Covid-19 vaccine found as many as 26% of people would not want it, largely because of public concerns about how the new type of vaccines are riskier (as is the case with the COVID-19 vaccines), rushed vaccine development, and a perceived corporate agenda behind vaccine development. After a series of strict lockdowns, which tried to control the outbreak of a handful of infections, the government kept the country in isolation until October 2021. Subsequent surveys by Prickett and Chapple (2021) found that low trust in government was correlated with 'vaccine hesitancy'. This hospitality worker in her late 30s concluded that:

> The New Zealand government's initial response seemed reasonable and appeared to be effective. Now our leadership has taken a turn towards control, compliance and obedience, and it no longer feels as though citizen health is the most important thing. Our rights and freedoms are being removed daily and our leadership is now a dictatorship.

Aside from constant pressure from politicians and the mainstream media, vaccine mandates were adopted for people working across Education, Fire and Emergency, Police and Defence Force, as well for all Health and Residential Care workers in October 2021. It is only relatively recently—April 2022—that the mandate was scrapped for some workers in the list above. It was said that such decisions by the New Zealand government were *"strongly and explicitly informed by public health expertise and advice"* even if they did generate some resistance among its electorate (Gauld, 2022: 42).

By December 2021, 70.9% of the German population was fully vaccinated (Fieselmann et al., 2022). However, this was not without criticism about the reduction of various freedoms—*"My country has done nothing in the way of protecting people from any illness or making sure those having it are treated appropriately. They have mainly been busy with restricting the freedom of those citizens who are healthy, and the effectiveness of these measures with respect to the transmission of any disease has never been evaluated by the government"* said one 40-year-old female accountant. *"The problem is that it* [unvaccinated] *is seen as socially wrong"* she added. In agreement, another male UK civil servant in his mid-30s said *"there certainly has been pressure as being vaccinated is the only socially acceptable option"*. There was, it seems, no access to 'normal life' without the vaccine as these three UK participants concurred:

I actually want to get my booster soon to hopefully visit some family. Also it makes life easier, especially since my work now have rules that mean you need to be fully vaccinated, recovered or have a PCR test to work. Being vaccinated is the least amount of hassle. (Female, 61, Tutor, UK)

Well I was, as I explained before it is impossible to have a normal life without the vaccine, so that's where the pressure come from *[so had the vaccine]*. I felt that if I did not have the vaccination I would be excluded from doing things I had been denied during lockdown, such as going to gigs, festivals, travelling etc. (Male, 44, Training Manager, UK)

I think many think it [the vaccine] will protect them. If they looked at the stats dispassionately (CFR and age stratification and risks) they would realise they don't need it. I think the millions who have done it to travel and access normal life are making it much harder for everyone to have a normal life in the long run. I think people have been propagandised, however, and are sort of hypnotised. It's hard to explain. I know people who balk at taking aspirin but who have taken this vaccine and are super healthy. (Female, 49, Journalist, UK)

However, the threat of exclusion from social and cultural life and pre-pandemic leisure activities could be resolved with the use of the Covid-19 passport—an electronic QR code which would confirm vaccination status (Chapter 4). Some responses, however, indicated ways around the system to still participate in cultural life. For example, one participant, Yana, a personal trainer from Ukraine, paid for a vaccine certificate to "*avoid taking a substance I didn't want to cure a virus I didn't think was that bad plus to not be compliant to the State and have them follow me around*". Similarly, one female respondent, 33, who was a carer in Greece claimed:

In a way I am, because in my country there is vaccination passport system. I don't have any pressure from my work, which I think it's most important. When I want to go out with friends or colleagues I have been using someone else's Covid passport, because my country (Estonia) doesn't allow to use negative PCR test instead when going to restaurants etc.

This echoes Child's (2022) research into fake Australian Covid-19 passports, which showed how criminal markets emerged to help the vaccine hesitant circumvent new regimes of certification and exclusion. People seek ways to resist. Moreover, this Estonian woman working in the care sector in Greece had seen enough to make her doubt both the vaccine and the passport. As had happened in Italy, France, and Hungary (see Sokol, 2021) she did not like the way the vaccine had been made mandatory for people working with the vulnerable—"*It makes no difference on infection rates, people transmit this virus even if they are vaccinated*" she added. Early surveys undertaken in Greece in 2020 show doubts among a growing number of people who thought the pandemic was part of a 'hidden agenda' (Holeva et al., 2022). Similarly, data gathered in 2021 from 2,029 participants found nearly a third were undecided on the vaccine and 12% did not want to take it (Costarelli & Michou, 2022). From January 2022, Greece made the vaccine mandatory for everyone older than 60 and those who refused were fined €100 every month thereafter (Burki, 2022). Around this time, approximately 520,000 Greek people older than 60 were unvaccinated (Burki, 2022).

As many regimes around the world instigated vaccine campaigns and mandates, participants questioned the ethics of such approaches. Many people who participated in our study questioned how Covid was managed and whether a vaccine was necessary. Here we apply 'asymptomatic'—or the *absence of symptoms*—in the context of freedom. Many of our respondents who criticised the vaccine and approaches to dealing with Covid-19 believed people who conformed were bereft of freedom. As such, freedom is asymptomatic. This raises an important point which underpins much of our discussion; many of the world's liberal democracies are built upon the ideological foundation of freedom in both a general sense and for the individual (Raymen, 2022). In the context of a health crisis, is there a limit to freedom of choice and bodily autonomy or are these absolute, sacred, and unquestionable? If, as Pemberton (2016) suggests, social harm can be seen in the barrier to autonomy then lockdown and vaccine mandates are problematic impositions on our freedoms. However, if my autonomy harms others—by not following lockdown mandates or choosing to avoid vaccination and potentially putting others at risk, is that not also harmful? These are complex ethical questions which were often side-lined and minimised, routinely replaced with argument, division, and transparent attempts to 'nudge' people into certain responses.

Under Pressure: The Cornering of the Unvaccinated

Ben, the German student we met in Chapters 2 and 3, recognised how the social and governmental tone seemed to change as pressure mounted to increase uptake of the Covid-19 vaccine:

> They started policies which withdrew support from people unless they got the vaccine. 'You need to be double vaccinated to get paid if you are of self-isolating' this kind of thing. It started to get tougher and tougher from then on. That was worrying and made me angry. We talked about solidarity in the beginning but all the political discourse was about the people who don't follow the rules being the bad guys then it was the people without the vaccine doing the damage to the society. So it went from one target to another.

There was significant criticism of what participants identified as a collusion between government and media, generating pressure on the public to take the vaccination. This was further bolstered by those who had accepted the need for the vaccine and applied additional pressure. One young male kitchen porter in his early 20s from the UK who had refused the vaccine and did not declare it to his peers said he was *"fearful of being discriminated at work"*. Another experienced UK female care home worker described how the *"entire country was under pressure"* in the face of *"many losing jobs and livelihoods simply from refusing to take the vaccine"*. Some related it to a form of 'bullying' and were made to feel like 'criminals':

> I was under pressure. I feel I was coerced into accepting a vaccine by the British government. I chose not to take the 3rd 'booster' jab this winter

when it became clear that the English 'plan B' vaccine passports would be scrapped. (Female, 34, Scientist, UK)

I have to make anti-gen tests every day when going to work and I am in fear that I may become 'a criminal' because I carry along a flu like (Covid) disease may be one day. All the media makes people like me feel like we do not care about fellow people and are like criminals. (Female, 55, Account Manager, Scotland)

Yes. Pressure from the government – my natural immunity passport only lasts 6 months yet I have plenty of antibodies. Family and friends are scared because they are misinformed. (Female, 31, Housewife, Australia)

The power of emotive ideological messaging is visible in its reproduction by people who applied additional pressure to the unvaccinated. People were told to get the vaccination for the greater good, to save their health systems, to collaborate and unite against the virus. While most people did, there was no space to discuss public concerns or hesitation. This 49-year-old female translator from Ireland explained how she had been "*verbally abused*" and "*pressured by family & work. I have also been locked out of most social activities in Ireland for over a year now*". In Malta, this mature female student was having a similar experience:

I am a student and to get into my school I need a certificate. At the beginning the tests were valid for 48 hours but all of a sudden they changed it to 24. They also changed the sticks with which they go up our noses and made them thicker. They are trying to make it as unpleasant as possible for us, so we get sick of it and just get the vax. My professors also put me under a lot of pressure.

Many of these experiences were particularly common for young people since they were generally the most likely to resist. Germany had particularly stringent vaccine mandates, which particularly affected students and their social lives:

Since I am studying in Germany, I am under a lot of pressure to get vaccinated. I study design and I cannot attend any cultural events or go to museums to educate myself. From today on, I am not allowed to attend classes live, I need to get access to them via Zoom, while everyone else is present. I might not be allowed to work anymore, since the government is thinking of only allowing vaccinated people to go to small shops. My goal in life is to become a designer and to get the best out of my studies which is heavily impacted by the current restrictions. I am in a class of 20 people, being the only one not vaccinated. My classmates tell me sentences like "you are a threat to the class" or "if you would get the vaccine, you would belong to us again". This is putting me under a lot of social pressure as well. (Female, 21, Student, Germany)

In some instances, the consequences of the Covid-19 restrictions (see Briggs et al., 2021a) compounded preferences to avoid the vaccine, making family and social life more complex. This was true for a female company director in her late 40s who we spoke to at the close of 2021 when the Omicron variant was embryonic in the UK. At this time, delay in vaccination and rejection of the vaccine was being met with further potential mandating:

My family is being cut out of society. I had an offer to work on campus which I had to turn down. At first, I was going to be out of work, but I was subsequently offered online. My daughter is in the middle of a professional degree, which she won't be able to complete due to mandates for campus and she is not vaccinated either. My husband is losing his job of 19 years with the public service next month due to mandates because he is not vaccinated. He works from home, and did so before Covid-19. All of this is coercion and medical tyranny from our Prime Minister's decree/mandates.

Participants reported receiving calls from health services to either get vaccinated or to remind them to get a booster. In a few cases, the regularity of the contact to convince these people to vaccinate seemed excessive. One UK female farmer in her 60s received "*15 text messages, five letters and five phone calls*". In her words, this amounted to "*harassment*". Another woman in her late 40s, a cleaner for McDonalds in the UK, received "*26 messages*". One male American restaurant manager received 30 phone calls and had this to say:

Everyone thought it was some form of cure but myself, my fiancé and many vaccinated co-workers still got Covid. Currently we feel under pressure. The unvaccinated are being bullied, manipulated into getting it for fear of losing their jobs, kids not being able to attend school, no travel, no festivals, locked out of 'inessential' shops.

On the other side of the world a similar pursuit of the unvaccinated via vaccine mandates was underway:

> Yes, I'm under constant pressure as I lost all my income caused by mandating vaccine in my state, restricted movement, separation from my family and friends and no access to non-essential services. (Female, 42, Swimming pool supervisor, Australia)

> I am currently under pressure because I may lose my job. I also live in a different part of the country to my family and it is required to be fully vaccinated to travel. (Female, 38, take away shop worker, Australia)

In Australia, Smith et al. (2022) compared survey findings about vaccinations pre-pandemic in 2017 and during the Covid-19 pandemic in 2021. The 2017 survey found 88% of the participants' agreed vaccines were safe, effective, and necessary. This confidence was dented, though, for only 66% of respondents indicated they would take a coronavirus vaccine in 2021. In addition, 70% of the respondents who indicated hesitancy were concerned about the safety of the vaccine, believing it was developed too quickly. Meanwhile, nearly three quarters of participants (73%) agreed that the government should require a Covid-19 vaccine for work, travel, and study (Smith et al., 2022). This elucidates the forms of division and exclusion we have discussed throughout our book. Faced with these circumstances, some submitted to pressure and received the vaccine while others resisted and navigated new forms of social and cultural exclusion. Katie, a customer services worker in Spain and one of our interviewees, was vocal against the restrictions and the vaccine citing 'bigger plans' under way. Having fallen out with family and friends, and received criticism in an online Facebook forum, she said:

I used to be social before the pandemic but now I am like 'fuck them all'. I used to love people, really. But because all the dopes have fallen for the Covid propaganda and I can't do certain things because of the vaccine, I simply am not interested. I give up on humanity, fuck them all!

People in other countries also reported feeling pressurised:

> I'm under pressure to vaccinate myself and my children. Currently we are avoiding all places that require us to show vaccine passes. We're hoping the government will come back to its senses soon. (Female, 44, Housewife, Pakistan)

The 'Anti-vaxxers'

The term 'anti-vaxxer' became common in political and media discourse as an undifferentiated phrase to label the unvaccinated (for instance: Miyazaki et al., 2022). Although it conflated anti-vaccination with anti-mandate, it came with moral and ethical undertones to suggest they were selfish individuals unconcerned with other peoples' health and wellbeing. The 'anti-vaxxer' was unable to think logically and was also 'anti-science', although as we have discussed there are various problems with this single scientific explanation (also see: Green & Fazi, 2023). Anyone who disagreed with the vaccine narrative was apparently jeopardising the future and people from around the world were critical of this:

> I've been called an 'anti-vaxxer' by work colleagues. Told I was selfish. I made my case for my choice (not that I should have to) and gave data and facts that surprised colleagues and friends. They even double-checked them, they were confused when the examples and data I gave was deemed correct. That silenced their questioning. (Male, 39, Construction worker, Ireland)

> The only pressure that I feel, which I ignore, is through the media and the fact that I am in the minority and they are trying to make us feel that we are in the wrong, we are 'anti-vaxxers' and crazy for not getting it. There

is also a pressure due to the vaccine passports, the mandatory vaccines in the social care settings in the UK, which doesn't impact me directly but I am aware of it. The pressure being put on people is immense and I can see how people would feel forced to have it so they can travel, or not have to isolate if they come in to contact with someone who has Covid, or go to a nightclub or big events. I had numerous text messages and letters from the NHS telling me to book my vaccine but I ignored them. (Female, 43, Self-employed and Student, UK)

I feel under massive pressure as the government has set impossible vaccination targets and pitted the vaccinated to form an angry moral mob to make us 'anti-vaxxers' comply in order to reach their absurd target. I will also not be able to do 'normal' things and my partner may lose his job. We may lose our farm and home. (Male, 62, Disabled with chronic health conditions, New Zealand)

Interestingly, this final respondent ticks several high-risk boxes for Covid-19 including his age and medical condition. Yet, he remains sceptical of the vaccine and governmental pressure to comply. Questions arose within our sample about the demand to comply with the vaccine, its contravention of basic civil liberties, and one's independent bodily autonomy:

I feel immense pressure from family and friends. I also used to travel a lot and haven't travelled for two years now. The more they push the more I know this isn't about my health or even public health. The more stories emerge of serious side effects the more I know I have done the right thing. I will never take the mRNA or adenoviral vector versions. I would consider a more traditional one. But I deeply object to taking it in return for access to my basic civil liberties. I think that's abhorrent. (Female, 49, Journalist, UK)

I felt my life would not be worth living if I took the injection due to my fears around its effects. I have a chronic illness with frequent systems which fluctuate. I would be always worried about how the injection had affected me. Also out of principle, I would not comply with an immoral system which violates the principle of medical choice and bodily autonomy. (Female, 33, unemployed, UK)

Respondents weighed up scientific evidence alongside their scepticism or distrust of media narratives and government agendas. As Woolhouse (2022) notes in his account of his advisory role to the UK and Scottish Governments during the pandemic, it was established early in 2020 that Covid-19 posed a greater risk to the elderly and those with underlying health conditions (Chapter 2). Children were largely unaffected or asymptomatic and the survival rate for most people was generally high. Much of this information was in the public sphere but was often lost in the authoritarian noise or dismissed as 'misinformation'. Many of our respondents were willing to trust these figures and saw no need for vaccination. Many with health conditions also worried about an experimental vaccine and its impact upon underlying health problems. In the context of various pharmaceutical scandals (Chapter 3) trust was low, and cynicism was high. Although reasons varied, they focused on why it was not necessary to get vaccinated:

> I'm not vaccinated and if someone wants the vaccine that's their choice I haven't a problem with that what I have a problem with is people saying you need to get vaccinated to protect others. That's not how a vaccine works it works to protect the individual from getting it but this vaccine doesn't even do that as them who are vaccinated are still getting it and passing it on making the vaccine pointless. (Male, 48, Plant operator, UK)

> I have a genetic mutation that effects how I metabolize drugs. I have significantly higher risk of several complications, listed as side effects. Life threatening ones. I have a medical education, halfway through a graduate program with a 4.0gpa. For me, genetically, the risk is not worth it. I am also sole provider to an adult disabled child so if anything happens to me, their life is then affected. (Non-binary, 47, Caregiver, USA)

> Everyone is feeling pressure from all around them. Media, news, etc. I decided that I won't be pressured into getting the vaccine even if people called me a stupid, ignorant anti-vaxxer. One such person said: what do you know you're just a fucking language teacher. Besides I had COVID twice and don't need the vaccine. I now have natural antibodies. Also I'm allergic to a lot of medicine and I rather stay away from a vaccine that I

don't know what's in it. They are also not forthcoming with all the side effects. If I take any medication I read the pamphlet carefully because I have level 3 kidney failure. I don't just take any medication that can further cause kidney problems. (Female, 60, Lecturer, South Africa)

I am surrounded by friends and family saying 'get the bloody jab' loads of them are now sick through it and saying they are lethargic. But my health is more important. There is no research showing how the vaccine impacts Covid over the long term but enough to show natural immunity is stronger than vaccinated. (Female, 72, Retired, UK)

Those sceptical or mistrustful of government and media narratives found further proof in their concern when countries such as the UK moved the vaccine goalposts. Much like the lockdown 'nudging' (Dodsworth, 2021), initially the UK announced that vaccinating the 15 million most vulnerable citizens would signal the end of lockdown. This mutated into vaccinating as many as possible, then two doses, then children, then boosters, and so on. While this makes good business sense for the vaccine companies (Chapter 3), it further erodes trust and raises questions about motives. What was promised had changed without good reasons or explanation. Perhaps controversially, there were also efforts to vaccinate children—the least affected group from the virus. This lowering and blanket endorsement among all age groups including children made the 'anti-vaxxers' more resolute; many claimed that these attempts to vaccinate were unrelated to health:

I have not, and never will capitulate to this. For me, it no longer has anything to do with health, but a point of principal. But there's no doubt the pressure is intense, and constant. The intentional use of fear, and the weaponisation of social pressure is quite frankly criminal. The way families, friends and social circles have been intentionally turned against each other, is unforgivable. There is now no doubt in my mind that what we are going through right now, supposedly in the name of a virus within the same envelope as seasonal flu, has ANYTHING to do with health and wellbeing. What other conclusion can be drawn now, as we head into a third year of a clearly manufactured 'emergency'? The agendas are clear to anyone with eyes, ears, and a functioning brain. (Male, 71, Retired, UK)

> I have chosen my hill and this is it. I will never, ever take these injections. Not only are they killing and maiming millions of people around the world (VAERS, Yellow Card, EMA), but this is no longer about health, if it ever was. The second they tried to tie my compliance with government medical instructions to my freedom, liberty and very way of life, they made it about far more than health. THEY did that. Not us. (Male, 35, Biotech engineer, UK)

> I think many are deluding themselves they are better off *[those vaccinated]*. Some experts say the vaccine actually diminishes the efficacy of the immune system. It can also cause other issues. In the worst case scenario, the rumours that the vaccines are deliberately causing cancer and other side-effects is true. Also I find it stifling and creepy to be excluded from the participation in public life, by those vaccinated people who happily continue to enjoy theirs. I feel they are hypocritical in their moralising that everyone should get vaccinated and vaccinate their children (!) to protect the risk groups. (Female, 41, Saleswoman, Netherlands)

A Science for Everyone Is a Truth for Nobody

Balanced views on those who were vaccinated and unvaccinated were hard to come by in this study. As the previous section highlights, unvaccinated people generally felt concerned about how the powerful use of ideology based upon one scientific truth through governments and media had eroded logic and common sense in examining issues surrounding the Covid-19 vaccination and mandates. *"They have lost the ability to research or use their intuition and they believe politicians who are professional liars and financially corrupted scientists"* said one man in his mid-50s who was a Physiotherapist in the UK. However, in a world devoid of meaning and belief and 'one's truth' dominates, there is a different version of science to believe in:

> It is their free choice *[to get vaccinated]* but it concerns me that many are not truly informed and are taking the vaccines under coercion to keep their jobs and to be able to travel overseas, not for medical reasons. This is unethical from a medical perspective. Many were also under the

impression that it would only be two jabs but now they realise that they will need multiple boosters to keep their freedoms. In other words, the government owns their bodies. (Male, 56, Biostatistician working in clinical trials, UK)

Falling in line with government and media messaging leaves doubts and suspicion in these peoples' minds. This is particularly because the coalescing of the political, media, and scientific establishment under one science produces a truth for no one. It sends people resistant to the vaccine to the infinite corners of the internet to undertake their own research to try to understand what is happening. This then becomes another source of division and conflict:

They *[the vaccinated]* are doing what they think is best, based on the propaganda they have swallowed. I find some of them quite dispassionate and uncaring about the naughty unvaccinated and their unproven vaccine injuries or ignoring the 'science.' They make huge sweeping assumptions about our views, usually focusing on the absurd end of it. The media are the worst. I worked as a story producer in mainstream media only a few months ago, and cannot believe the lies being spewed out about the vaccine and it's efficacy. Reporters are not asking hard or obvious questions. It has been very eye opening, to such a degree that I'm having sympathy for MAGA[1] supporters now! And only contempt now for the 'Fake News.' How could that happen?" (Female, 50, Self-employed columnist/researcher, New Zealand)

Accordingly, people who don't get the Covid-19 vaccines are "*uneducated*" (Female, 19, Student, Switzerland), are "*selfish wankers who are prolonging the pandemic*" (Gender fluid, 46, Professor, 'European') and "*lack of care for society*" (Female, 41, Teacher, Germany). The pursuit of an alternative science—much of which was relegated to the dark cupboards of history during the Covid-19 pandemic (Briggs et al., 2021a)—is therefore viewed as wrong because these people "*believe that they are more intelligent than all the health officials and institutions in the*

---

[1] MAGA refers to the 'make America great again' movement that supported Donald Trump in the 2016 USA Presidency.

world" (Male, 20, Student, Germany). As such, the 'antivaxx science' is conceived as disinformation:

> I find it very frustrating. There is a lot of disinformation out there, and it annoys me that people are spreading and believing it. I think it's very dangerous. I also find that those who won't take the vaccine more likely to be unwilling to take any precautions with regards to Covid. They tend to moan about Covid the most, but are unwilling to do anything to help the situation. (Female, 39, Radiographer, UK)

According to the vaccinated, the unvaccinated are seen to not take the virus or its medium- to long-term impact seriously. However, the vaccinated are viewed in a similar light since they have received an inoculation which has not been tested over time. As such, they have been "*conned into it*" (Male, 54, Architect, India), "*duped*" (Female, 51, Consultant, Scotland), and "*hoodwinked*" (Female, 42, Self-employed, Wales). This unemployed Canadian woman in her 40s, who lost her job in her local store during the lockdowns, was concerned "*for their welfare given side effects and lack of knowledge on medium-to-long-term impact as well sympathy for either their stupidity or lack of ability to recognise the propaganda*". Some respondents labelled them as 'lab rats' and 'misguided fools' on which unknown experiments were being performed, suggesting they "*didn't have long to live*" (Male, 37, Personal trainer/Nutritionist, Canada) like "*in previous animal-testing of mRNA-platforms*" (Male, 37, High-level software engineer, Sweden). The vaccinated were also described as "*crazy, not using common sense and not thinking of their future, only thinking short-term gains*" (Female, 48, Registered Nurse, Australia). A New Zealand potato farmer in his late 20s reflected:

> I can understand many don't pay attention to what is going on and just want to get on with their lives, they still believe everything will go back to normal if they comply. I feel pity for those who have been pressured into it with their jobs on the line. I hope they haven't all been given a death sentence, been irreversibly turned into mutants, become permanently dependent on immune boosters, or some other weird shit. At the end of the day some of them are morons and sheep but the vast majority are just good normal people.

Similarly, this male HGV driver in his 40s from the UK reasoned:

> For the vulnerable groups the benefits outweigh the risks, but healthy adults queuing up for it have been brainwashed by the media. I think, about half of them had the vaccine, because they fully believe in what the mainstream media say about it. The other half do not believe this, but had the vaccine in order to get some of their freedom back or to keep their jobs. To my mind, everyone should be able to decide this for themselves, based on correct information, as long as the decision is truly free and not taken under pressure.

The divisions and arguments on social media, among families and friends and in public spaces, were felt by one respondent, a Social Policy Assistant in Belgium, to detract attention from more pressing issues:

> It depends on their reasons for not being vaccinated. If they are afraid or are being sceptical in general, I can understand. The mass media has not done much to make people trust the vaccines. However, if they tell me, they prefer to wait until enough of other people get vaccinated, so that the "herd immunity is reached, then I have no understanding at all. To me, this mentality is a symptom of the neoliberal world, in which everyone just thinks of themselves. Another opinion in this matter: for the ruling class, it is very convenient to have such a schism in society (vaccinated vs. non-vaccinated) to keep the sight off of real problems (economic inequality, ecologic disaster threatening future generations because nobody wants to give up bits of the comfort of the crazy consumerism, wealth of one part of the world at the costs of the other, inhuman treatment of some people - refugees etc. etc.). So, it's easier to make people believe their problem are the non-vaccinated (or the other way around) and direct the anger towards them.

This chapter empirically explored various forms of division and exclusion generated by policies surrounding the Covid-19 vaccines, ideological nudging by the media and governments, and vaccine mandates. It detailed how many respondents were highly cynical, mistrustful, and sceptical of the media and governments, occasionally suggesting vaccine mandates were not about the public's health and wellbeing but social manipulation and control. Some of the unvaccinated respondents had lost their jobs during the pandemic due to refusing to get the vaccine, while many of their relations with friends and family subsequently diminished. The transient imposition of vaccine passports to access large parts of civic life in countries around the world created further division and exclusion, cast by some of our respondents as a bio-medical two-tiered society. Although some of the 'anti-vaxxers' offered what could reasonably be cast as conspiratorial views, others weighed up the scientific evidence and believed the potential risk of harm outweighed the benefits. Many others were unsure about the Covid-19 vaccines' mid-long-term safety and were deeply cynical towards the mainstream media, governments, and Big Pharma.

Yet for us it is clear that the political elites and authorities provided substandard leadership and no debate on fundamental issues such as the restrictions and vaccines which abandoned these people to indulge in alternative perspectives often cast as 'conspiracy'. In the next chapter, we further address some of the forms of division and exclusion that were created by many states' authoritarian responses to the unvaccinated. This includes China's and New Zealand's 'Zero-Covid' approach, the curtailing of public protests, and the Canadian Government's response to the 'truckers' in Canada.

References

Acharya, B., & Dhakal, C. (2021). Implementation of state vaccine incentive lottery programs and uptake of COVID-19 vaccinations in the United States. *JAMA Network Open, 4*(12), 1–12.

Asri, A., Asri, V., Renerte, B., Follmi-Heusi, F., Leuppi, J. D., Muser, J., Nuesch, R., Schulder, D., & Fischbacher, U. (2022). Which hospital workers do (not) want the jab? Behavioral correlates of COVID-19 vaccine willingness among employees of Swiss hospitals. *PLOS One, 17*(5), 1–20.

Bardosh, K., Figueiredo, A., Gur-Arie, R., Jamrozik, E., Doidge, J., Lemmens, T., Keshavjee, S., Graham, J., & Baral, S. (2022). The unintended consequences of COVID-19 vaccine policy: Why mandates, passports and restrictions may cause more harm than good. *British Medical Journal Global Health, 7*, 1–14.

Burki, T. (2022). COVID-19 vaccine mandates in Europe. *The Lancet, 22,* 27–28.

Briggs, D., Telford, L., Lloyd, A., Ellis, A., & Kotzé, J. (2021a). *Lockdown: Social harm in the Covid-19 era.* Palgrave Macmillan.

Chaney, D., & Lee, M. S. (2022). COVID-19 vaccines and anti-consumption: Understanding anti-vaxxers hesitancy. *Psychology & Marketing, 39*(4), 741–754.

Childs, A. (2022). *The distribution of fake Australian vaccine digital certificates on an alt-tech platform.* Trends in Organised Crime. Online First: https://doi.org/10.1007/s12117-022-09466-x

Costarelli, V., & Michou, M. (2022). Predictors of COVID-19 vaccine hesitancy and prevention practice in Greece. *International Journal of Health Promotion and Education,* 1–16.

Dai, H., Saccardo, S., Han, M., Roh, L., Raja, N., Vangala, S., Modi, H., Pandya, S., Sloyan, M., & Croymans, D. (2021). Behavioural nudges increase COVID-19 vaccinations. *Nature, 597,* 404–424.

DiResta, R., Cryst, E., & Meyersohn, L. (2021). *Memes, magnets and microchips: Narrative dynamics around Covid-19.* The Virality Project.

Dodsworth, L. (2021). *A state of fear: How the UK government weaponised fear during the Covid-19 pandemic.* Pinter & Martin Ltd.

Eisenstein, M. (2022). A shock to the system: How the COVID-19 pandemic damaged waning childhood vaccination rates around the world. *Nature, 612*(22/29), 44–46.

Fieselmann, J., Annac, K., Erdsiek, F., Yilmaz-Aslan, Y., & Brzoska, P. (2022). What are the reasons for refusing a COVID-19 vaccine? A qualitative analysis of social media in Germany. *BMC Public Health, 22*(846), 1–8.

Franzen, A., & Wöhner, F. (2021). Coronavirus risk perception and compliance with social distancing measures in a sample of young adults: Evidence from Switzerland. *PLOS One, 16*1(2), 1–13.

Gauld, R. (2022). A review of public policies on Covid-19: The New Zealand experience. *Public Administration and Policy: An Asia-Pacific Journal, 26*(1), 10–20. https://doi.org/10.1108/PAP-04-2022-0028

Geber, S., & Ho, S. (2022). Examining the cultural dimension of contact-tracing app adoption during the COVID-19 pandemic: A cross-country study in Singapore and Switzerland. *Information, Communication & Society.* Online First: https://doi.org/10.1080/1369118X.2022.2082880

Giubilini, A., Savulescu, J., Pugh, J., & Wilkinson, D. (2022). Vaccine mandates for healthcare workers beyond COVID-19. *Journal of Medical Ethics, 49*(3), 211–220.

Green, T., & Fazi, T. (2023). *The Covid consensus: The global assault on democracy and the poor—A critique from the Left*. Hurst Publishers.

Holeva, E., Parlapani, V. A., Nikopoulou, I., Nouskas, I., & Diakogiannis, I. (2022). COVID-19 vaccine hesitancy in a sample of Greek adults. *Psychology, Health & Medicine, 27*(1), 113–119.

Honigsbaum, M. (2020). *The pandemic century—A history of global contagion from the spanish flu to COVID-19*. Random House.

Hossain, E., Rana, R., Islam, S., Khan, A., Chakrobortty, S., Ema, N., & Bekun, F. (2021). COVID-19 vaccine-taking hesitancy among Bangladeshi people: Knowledge, perceptions and attitude perspective. *Human Vaccines & Immunotherapeutics, 17*(11), 4028–4037.

Imperial College London. (2021). *Global attitudes towards a COVID-19 vaccine*. Imperial College London.

Karaivanov, A., Kim, D., Lu, S., & Shigeoka, H. (2022). COVID-19 vaccination mandates and vaccine uptake. *Nature Human Behaviour, 6*, 1615–1624.

McKee, M., & Schalkwyk, M. (2022). England's U turn on covid-19 vaccine mandate for NHS staff. *British Medical Journal, 376*, 1–2.

Mills, M., & Rüttenauer, T. (2022). The effect of mandatory COVID-19 certificates on vaccine uptake: Synthetic-control modelling of six countries. *Lancet Public Health, 7*, 15–22.

Miyazaki, K., Uchiba, T., Tanaka, K., & Sasahara, K. (2022). Aggressive behaviour of anti-vaxxers and their toxic replies in English and Japanese. *Humanities and Social Sciences Communications, 9*(229), 1–8.

Our World in Data. (2023). *Coronavirus (COVID-19) vaccinations: Our world in data*. Accessed on 5 May 2023. https://ourworldindata.org/covid-vaccinations

Pemberton, S. (2016). *Harmful societies: Understanding social harm*. Policy Press.

Prickett, K., & Chapple, S. (2021). Trust in government and Covid-19 vaccine hesitancy. *Policy Quarterly, 17*(3), 69–71.

Pugh, J., Savulescu, J., Brown, R., & Wilkinson, D. (2022). The unnaturalistic fallacy: COVID-19 vaccine mandates should not discriminate against natural immunity. *Journal of Medical Ethics, 48*, 371–377.

Raymen, T (2022). *The enigma of social harm: The problem of liberalism*. Routledge.

Savulescu, J. (2021). Good reasons to vaccinate: Mandatory or payment for risk? *Journal of Medical Ethics, 47*, 78–85.

Savulescu, J., Pugh, J., & Wilkinson, J. (2021). Balancing incentives and disincentives for vaccination in a pandemic. *Nature Medicine, 27*, 1500–1509.

Schmelz, K., & Bowles, S. (2021). Overcoming COVID-19 vaccination resistance when alternative policies affect the dynamics of conformism, social norms, and crowding out. *Proceedings of the National Academy of Sciences of the United States of America, 118*(25), 1–7.

Smith, D., Attwell, K., & Evers, U. (2022). Support for a COVID-19 vaccine mandate in the face of safety concerns and political affiliations: An Australian study. *Politics, 42*(4), 480–491.

Sokol, D. (2021). Covid-19 vaccination should be mandatory for healthcare workers. *British Medical Journal, 375*, 1–2.

Telford, L., Bushell, M., & Hodgkinson, O. (2022). Passport to neoliberal normality? A critical exploration of Covid-19 vaccine passports. *Journal of Contemporary Crime, Harm, Ethics, 2*(1), 42–61.

Thaker, J. (2021). The persistence of vaccine hesitancy: COVID-19 vaccination intention in New Zealand. *Journal of Health Communication, 26*(2), 104–111.

Thirumurthy, H., Milkman, K. L., Volpp, K. G., Buttenheim, A., & Pope, D. (2022). Association between statewide financial incentive programs and COVID-19 vaccination rates. *PLOS One, 17*(3), 1–7.

UK Parliament. (2022). *Covid-19: Requirements for employees to be vaccinated* (Vol. 707). House of Commons.

Umakanthan, S., Patil, S., Subramaniam, N., & Sharma, R. (2021). COVID-19 vaccine hesitancy and resistance in India explored through a population-based longitudinal survey. *Vaccines, 9*(10), 1–11.

United Nations. (2021). *UN chief: Global vaccination plan is 'only way out' of pandemic*. United Nations. Accessed on 1 May 2023. https://news.un.org/en/story/2021/11/1106792

Woolhouse, M. (2022). *The year the world went mad: A scientific memoir.* Sandstone Press.

World Health Organisation [WHO]. (2019). *Ten threats to global health in 2019*. Geneva: World Health Organisation. Accessed on 20 April 2023. https://www.who.int/news-room/spotlight/ten-threats-to-global-health-in-2019

6

Heavy Hands and Iron Fists Against High Social Fevers

The continual presence of 'anti-vaxxer' opposition was met with *heavy-handed* governmental responses which became *iron fisted*. Numerous governments including Western liberal democracies refused to listen to dissenting voices; instead, they intensified the legal exclusion of significant numbers of people who for various reasons were frustrated and angry about Covid-19 vaccine mandates. While this occurred in many nations including Austria, Netherlands, Italy, Germany, France, New Zealand, and Australia, perhaps the clearest example was in Canada where tens of thousands of truckers and protestors blocked highways, bridges, border crossings and occupied the space outside parliament in protest at the persistence of Covid-19 restrictions during early 2022.

By virtue of their occupations those engaged in protests had previously been lauded by the Canadian Government as 'heroes' of the pandemic. However, members of the government, including Prime Minister Justin Trudeau, branded them as 'racists' and 'abusers' (Naughtie, 2022) before utilising emergency powers to disperse the truckers. What happened in Canada was an extreme example of the dramatic expansion of the surveillance state (Chapter 4) and the democratic limitations of a state of emergency (Wagner, 2022). This included more powers to seize protest funds, criminalise peaceful protest activity, and track down and prosecute donors to the movement (Saria & Satyogi, 2022). Although some governments began to relax Covid-19 restrictions, this came with the warning that future variants or other states of emergency may require renewed restrictive measures upon the citizenry's civil liberties. This chapter addresses these social divisions and exclusions, particularly the 'Zero-Covid' approach deployed in Australia, New Zealand, and China and the Canadian Government's responses to the truckers.

Upping The 'Ante' on the Anti-vaxxers

> Hans: "It's their personal choice and I'm generally indifferent, people have their own medical histories and fears that they have to deal with and battle. I only have negative feelings towards the unvaccinated who believe the vaccine is about 'control' from the government and continue to complain that everything isn't back to normal. Everyone is already controlled by money and the need to go to work eight hours every day just to survive. The reason things aren't back to normal is because the virus still fills the hospitals. The sad thing about giving people free choice is that statistically, half of the population have less than average intelligence."

It is probably unsurprising that Hans, an actor in his late 40s from Austria, is entirely supportive of the vaccine mandates in his country. Espoused at the height of tensions in Austria related to the vaccination campaign, his comments echo many political remarks and widely read medical 'experts'. Dr Edzard Ernst, for example, a now retired but well-respected British-German physician, was famously quoted as saying how *"anti-vaxxers tend to be uneducated and ignorant"* (Ernst, 2021). Austria had already experienced a harsh first lockdown and kept stringent restrictions in place throughout 2020, which didn't seem to reduce the social devastation caused by the first and most severe wave of Covid-19 infection (Herby et al., 2022; Sonnichsen, 2023). Nonetheless, the government decided to initiate further lockdowns and social distancing at the peak of the second wave in November 2021, which was much less severe.

Vaccination rates in Austria had been among the lowest in Western Europe at this time so government officials, 'guided by the science', passed laws and policies which prohibited unvaccinated Austrians from leaving their homes except to go to work, buy essential supplies, or exercise. In what was arguably the world's first 'lockdown for the unvaccinated', it was hoped that such measures would further encourage people into vaccination. However, survey research in late 2021 indicated unvaccinated people were unlikely to be convinced by public health officials or stringent infringements on their liberty; but they would be more motivated to get the vaccine if there was a financial reward (Stamm et al., 2022). No such scheme was proffered.

Austria was not the only country where political anger and frustration about the anti-vaxxers boiled over. Governments around the world hardened their tone and approach, with particularly political rhetoric and media and social media forums utilised to stigmatise, demonise, and ostracise the unvaccinated (Antonini et al., 2022; Ellis et al., 2021; Popova & Valkov, 2022). In neighbouring France, which had adopted similar limiting measures for unvaccinated people in public spaces, President Emmanuel Macron said he wanted to *"piss off"* the unvaccinated (Bardosh et al., 2022). Australian Prime Minister, Scott Morrison, issued warnings to Kanye West before his tour of the country by saying *"the rules are you have to be fully vaccinated.... Follow the rules – you can come"* (Kelly, 2022). Such pressure affected many people including this grocer in his early 30s, who lived in a suburban community of Sydney: *"I am only considering getting vaccinated in the future to keep my job because of government mandates"*. Scott Morrison and the former Minister for Immigration, Citizenship, Migrant Services and Multicultural affairs—Alex Hawke—were also pivotal in the deportation of professional tennis player, Novak Djokovic, in 2022. As Bardosh et al., (2022: 6) asserts:

> Perhaps the most high-profile case to date involves the deportation of the top-ranked men's tennis player, Novak Djokovic, at the Australian Open 2022, despite having been granted a medical exemption on the basis of documented prior infection. While media outlets were quick at hinting

about problems in his official submission, the Minister of Immigration accepted that he had a valid test result and that he posed only a 'very low' risk to the health of Australians. Yet, the court ruled that it was reasonable for the Minister to conclude that Mr Djokovic's presence could 'foster anti-vaccination sentiment' and thus have a negative impact on vaccination and boosters. It endorsed Mr Djokovic characterisation as a threat to Australian 'civil order and public health.

In some respects, it became difficult to differentiate Western liberal nations from other regimes renowned for more authoritarian forms of political and social life. In the United Arab Emirates (UAE)—a country with limited freedom of speech, arbitrary arrests, detainee abuse and torture, and unlawful attacks on people—similar restrictions to participate in public life were enacted to bolster vaccination compliance. In 2021, the government in Abu Dhabi enacted strict measures to try control the spread of Covid-19 and encourage vaccination. Accessing indoor facilities was restricted to green pass holders of the 'AL-HOSN' app, which contained individual's vaccination status and health information (Kharaba et al., 2022). Most people complied with these measures including an office administrator in her early 40s who lived in the city:

> I had to sacrifice my values and beliefs to be able to earn a living, despite knowing that the 'vaccines' are ineffective in reducing transmission and me not being in any risk category. There is just no observable logic to 'vaccine' mandates. Months later, I still regret not having stood up for my values and refused to get vaccinated and move countries.

Increased associations were made between 'anti-vaxxers' and 'conspiracy theories' as a means of isolating the group further (Nasralah et al., 2022), with direct references to mis- and disinformation becoming the dominant explanations for their doubts about the vaccine across the globe (Lazarus et al., 2022). As we have shown, however, 'anti-vaxxers' constitute a group of people with diverse motivations for rejecting the Covid-19 vaccine. People rejected the vaccine on political, religious, aesthetic, and medical grounds even if, according to Cowden and Yuval-Davis (2022), what appeared to unite them was a strong insistence that the authorities imposing the restrictions were doing so based upon hidden and ulterior motives (Chapter 4). Instead, societies became even more divided and negative perceptions—as well as pro-vaccine stances—created significant divisions. Undoubtedly, this was bolstered by the algorithmic workings of social media. For example, in one study examining the content of 450 Facebook users, Gearhart et al., (2023) found that hostile media 'bias' enhanced negative perceptions of 'bias' about the vaccine.

In the USA, some states issued strict vaccine mandates to compel people into compliance, while in other states vaccine hesitancy was amplified by broadcast messages suggesting vaccine efficacy was minimal (Hao & Shao, 2022). This poignantly highlights the politically polarised nature of Covid-19 information but also how partisan health attitudes hinged more upon political ideology than science (Stevens et al., 2022). This was most evidently reflected in speeches by President Biden, where he placed direct blame for high Covid-19 infection rates on the 'unvaccinated'. At the beginning of October 2021, Biden (2021) said:

> The fact is, this has been a pandemic of the unvaccinated. The unvaccinated overcrowd our hospitals, overrunning emergency rooms and intensive care units. The unvaccinated patients are leaving no room for someone with a heart attack or in need of a cancer operation and so much more because they can't get into the ICU. They can't get into the operating rooms. The unvaccinated also put our economy at risk because people are reluctant to go out. And think about this: Even in places where there is no restriction on going to restaurants and gyms and movie theaters, people are not going in anywhere near the numbers because they're worried they're going to get sick.

A month later, the Occupational Safety and Health Administration (OSHA) declared an Emergency Temporary Standard to 'protect workers from Covid-19'. The Standard obliged all employers with 100 or more workers including airlines to adopt 'vaccinate-or-test' rules in the name of employees' safety. In the speech above, Biden also mandated federal workers to be vaccinated and repeated the incorrect assessment that the vaccinated could not spread the disease.

By mid-January 2022, however, the Standard had been annulled by the Supreme Court, which concluded the President did not have the authority to impose such rules. Despite this, numerous large employers chose to comply with Biden's mandate and obligate employee vaccination, with many offering incentive schemes such as some US airlines who offered bonuses to vaccinated workers (Anderson, 2022; Berkman et al., 2022). Our data shows other companies in countries around the world adopted similar tactics to persuade their unvaccinated employees to 'see the light' and 'get the shot':

> Yes I feel pressured to *[get the vaccine]*. Can't go back to my job because I won't take it and can't apply for a job that I want, that I could get with my degree I just received because of it. I will be homeless before I put some ingredients into my body that I don't know what's in it and seeing how many deaths and injuries from the vaccine. [Female, 47, unemployed, Canada]
>
> No, I haven't had the vaccine, but there is a lot of pressure from the government and media. They are repeatedly asking us to get vaccinated via different media and, in some places, they do door to door campaign. [Female, 33, Writer, India]

And closer to home:

> I have not been vaccinated yet as I am young and healthy as far as I am aware. I can feel the net tightening in work though so unfortunately I might have to succumb in order to feed my family, pay my bills etc. This makes me angry and sad for what has become of our society. [Female, 38, Pilot, Ireland]
>
> Yes. And I had it *[the vaccine]* because of work. Not had any since but initially the info was poor. I took a decision based on probability for caring for my family. Now, I find it incredulous that so many people accepted everything without question but even more egregiously, they attack 10% of the population minority that have doubts. They should turn their ire on government and their puppets! [Female, 46, School teacher, UK]
>
> Yes, my boss is pressuring me to have it stating I could lose my job (I don't work with the public), appearing to gloat that I can't easily travel abroad and that I will be blocked out of society with the covid passport requirements in Scotland, and has also suggested that I may eventually be sectioned under the mental health act if I continue to refuse. He is

planning to phone our branch office to discuss the fact that he has a vaccine refuser on his team. He can fuck off, I still won't get it! [Female, 58, Security analyst, Scotland]

One female American nurse, who left her employment in the wake of the pandemic, was convinced there was no reason for vaccine mandates and aggressive Covid-19 policies. She was a medical coder responsible for translating physicians' reports at the height of the lockdowns but began to question things when certain standard practices were aborted, making it difficult to measure Covid-19 case numbers. These inadequacies led to her refusal to get vaccinated:

> It's a regular flu and they lied *[the government]* saying it *[Covid]* was overwhelming the hospitals - yet the hospitals were empty. They used the PCR test fraudulently to provide 'cases' so they could do a lockdown (all the while rolling out the 5G worldwide). EVERYTHING was coded for the Covid-19 if they had a positive test result and if magnified enough times the PCR test will give a positive on anything, then mandating masks, and now pushing an experimental gene therapy vaccine into people. My country did exactly what was planned to push the agenda they want it to go to. And I was a medical coder until the charts stopped coming in *[from which she was able to do her job]*. That's when I knew they were lying about the hospitals 'overflowing' with patients. There weren't any patient charts to code and when the work trickled down to nothing, they started letting us go. Nurses were putting out dance videos world-wide as they were bored. That's when the research started. When you know they are lying, but why? I didn't go back. I felt like it would be fraud coding the charts as Covid but they were in for something else and just happened to have a PCR test that is known for the false positives so they could use the 'cases' to scare people with. These inconsistencies led me to have no faith in any vaccine associated with what was going on.

In an arena of suppressed information channels and lack of alternative debate, the nurse seeks some foothold in what is happening. Witness the real and evidenced concerns she has which derive from her direct experience of watching Covid-19 cases being, in her words, 'fraudulently' documented. This led her to question the whole foundation for the Covid-19 pandemic. Yet with evident restrictions placed on public debate, her avenues for information and explanation are limited. This opens the door to more peculiar theories propagated across social media such as the link between lockdowns and the rollout of 5G.

In Europe, the 'upping the ante' approach maintained a form of 'moral suasion', especially through the introduction of the digital passport (Chapter 4). This was generally only granted to those who were vaccinated, had evidence of having had Covid-19, or tested negative through an anti-gen test in the previous 48 hours (Vergallo et al., 2022). For our unvaccinated participants, in some countries public life became almost impossible:

> The biggest problem was the fact that without the vaccine, especially in Italy is impossible to keep with your normal life. The vaccination policy in Italy requires you to be full vaccinated to do anything. Now even the Covid test is not valid, just the vaccine for many things although to go to work you still can do just the Covid test. But even then if you are positive, you can't work and many companies won't pay you if you are ill with Covid because they say 'it is your fault for not protecting yourself'. [Male, 26, Student, Italy]

In Germany, requirements were passed for unvaccinated people to take a test or be vaccinated to do basic things like travel on public transport:

> Despite of the fact that it is getting more obvious that the virus can also be transmitted by vaccinated people, Germany is really trying to get the economy going, so bars, clubs, cafés and cultural events mostly are for vaccinated and recovered people only. It feels like excluding unvaccinated people step by step is to show that they actually take action and some form of control of the situation. According to many health care workers speaking up, Germany is supposed to have a massive problem concerning the numbers of intensive care beds and available workers for decades now, which only gets highlighted by the pandemic. So I think, that instead of putting so much pressure onto people that personally don't want to take the vaccine, Germany should rather invest into the health care system. Destabilising people by dividing them into polarised groups where one

6 Heavy Hands and Iron Fists Against High Social Fevers

gets blamed by the other brings up a lot of tension, fear, stress and anger all over the country and this is not a good basis for a healthy population. [Male, 21, Student, Germany]

Such public space and life deprivations (see: Devonish & Dulal-Arthur, 2022) were enough for some to succumb to the pressure and get vaccinated:

Actually, I felt kind of bullied into it, so many were so excited and think it's wonderful, I only had it so that I could travel, but yet again the goalposts have been moved and there's more required to enable travel. I'm not inclined to have any 'booster' it's just another shot, if the first two didn't work why do they imagine more will have any effect? Also the lack of any liability by the manufacturers, plus the nonchalance of the people who 'jab' you I find very disturbing. [Male, 59, Delivery driver, UK]

I think people like myself did what they thought was best at the time, they took it *[the vaccine]* because they were frightened. They trusted what they were being told. I come from a research background, and had some previous work in pharma studies. My daughter had a horrific reaction to the h1n1 vaccine, so I knew last February I'd be looking into the injections before we signed up. As the carrots (lotteries) and sticks increased (mandates and punishments), so did my suspicions. I also started seeing dissenting voices be destroyed, and also heard of first-hand injuries. [Female, 50, Professor, Canada]

However, at the height of the vaccine rollout and increasing use of mandates during 2021 and early 2022, few people in authority publicly questioned the mandates. The logic was they were instigated to create safer spaces where the virus could not be transmitted, though in many instances they were more about creating a *feeling of safety* (Attwell et al., 2022). Many of our participants saw the introduction of these mandates as a further example of governmental overreach (Chapters 4 and 5):

Scotland has turned into dictatorship to control people. The SNP government have destroyed small businesses and the compulsory wearing of masks is being used to muzzle the masses. Cop26 was good example of how the elite can meet and greet with no restrictions in enclosed spaces but just be served by muzzled persons! Now they want everyone vaccinated with something which arguably does very little to protect people from Covid-19! All governments are enjoying the power too much and do not want to relinquish it. [Female, 61, self-employed, Scotland]

Bardosh et al. (2022), suggest such approaches were 'scientifically questionable' and argue they caused more harm than good. They cite restrictions on peoples' ability to work, study, use public transport, and engage in social life as a grave infraction on human rights, generating stigma and social polarisation. They intimate that mandates will also damage trust in government, authority, and science in the medium to long term. These findings were reflected in this exchange with a DJ in Spain who developed scepticism of the Covid-19 restrictions and further distanced himself from government and politics:

> *Social visits continue around the Christmas and the New Year [of 2021/2] and this time we are due to see some friends who we haven't seen much during the pandemic. As our children play in the park, one of their friends joins us. Though mask mandates should oblige us to wear them outside at all times, none of us turn up to meet each other like this. Looking around though, we are in a minority since Pedro Sanchez announced just before Christmas that they were to be mandatory once again at all times, both indoor and outdoor. Since then, the compliance seems to have quickly returned, and we feel like the sinners as we converse in a group talking about all this. I get talking to Raul, a local DJ and event entertainer. Much of his work disappeared throughout 2020 and although it partially recovered in 2021, he still made a loss for the year. Now bookings are up, and almost all his availability is booked for 2022 - "Fingers crossed nothing happens this year"* he says as he looks up towards the skies. Feeling aggrieved by this did not affect his perception of the virus or its potential threat. *"It's nothing for people like you and me, just a bad flu, nothing more, we have no serious problems so we should not worry...I get that it is dangerous for the old people, but really to shut everything down? They should have just protected them better"* he laments.
>
> *His criticism continues on the mask mandates which have dominated much of Spanish Covid policy in the last two years. For the first four months of the pandemic, there were none, then in June 2020 they were mandatory in both indoor and outdoor contexts, changing to indoor contexts only from June 26th, 2021. As the weaker Omicron variant spread, the prime minister*

reintroduced them. "I don't wear it outside it is absurd, ridiculous, makes no sense like many of the policies" *says Raul.* "If I have to wear it, I wear it below my nose so I can breathe through the nose otherwise having it on all the time, I get coughs" *he adds. Much of his work, though, has been cancelled when potential clients have found out he is unvaccinated.* "Many people want that security, even if you can still transmit it and get it with the vaccine, they want to know you have the vaccine so it means I cannot do all my gigs" *he bemoans before adding* "I had another event cancelled on New Year's Eve because the hotel wouldn't let me in without it *[the certificate]*." *He then decided to see some of his friends instead:* "I ask some friends if they want to meet and eventually get invited to a party but a few days beforehand my closest friend of many years calls me and says 'I feel bad about this but you can't come to the party because someone is uncomfortable with the fact that you haven't had the vaccine' and I am like 'wow, what the fuck is happening here, I mean I feel like a social leper".

On the vaccine, he says "I don't need it, I am waiting to see what happens, I do events that permit me and maybe I wear my mask but I don't wear it properly". *We get on to the subject of the campaign to vaccinate 5 to 11 year olds, approved early in December 2021.* "No fucking way are they vaccinating my son, no way on this earth…we are going to wait, sit it out as long as we can, I am not convinced by the vaccine safety and it is strange to me it was available so quickly. The government are criminal to put this on people" *he reflects angrily.* [Field notes 'Social leper' by Daniel Briggs]

Evidently, Raul is economically, socially, and culturally excluded by his decision to remain unvaccinated. Despite the social and economic difficulties that come with this decision, Raul remains resolute and resistant. In fact, a cross-country survey by John et al., (2022) of over 23,000 people in the G7 countries during January to February 2022—one year into the global vaccination campaign—found 13% of people remained unvaccinated across the G7. This includes how a majority of the unvaccinated claimed they did not want to take the vaccine (87%) (John et al., 2022). Such findings suggest it seemed to make no difference whether countries like the UK or USA opted for a softer coercive approach to vaccination in comparison to those taking more harder stances like France, Germany, Italy, Greece, and Canada; the latter two famously adopted fines for unvaccinated elderly people (Briggs et al., 2021a) and increased taxes for those without the vaccine (Dyer, 2022).

High Social Fevers and More Social Protest

Efforts to further corner this cohort of 'anti-vaxxers' resulted in increased discontent and unrest. Marches and protests were organised in numerous countries around the world, with Bardosh et al., (2022: 2), asserting that *"mandate and passport policies have provoked community and political resistance including energetic mass street protests"*. The main origins of dissatisfaction initially began in the summer of 2020 particularly in the USA and UK, which seemed to consolidate two groups. The first, according to Martin and Vanderslott (2022), involved pre-existing anti-vaccine groups (perhaps the true 'anti-vaxxers') with a new varied group. Like the American nurse and Spanish DJ, the latter group disagreed about the severity of Covid-19 and questioned the threat it posed. Importantly, they were critical of the measures governments used to limit and manage transmission of the virus. This formed the uniting variable between both groups, who were strongly opposed to vaccine coercion/mandates.

These groups solidified their cause as the pandemic evolved and the perseverance on restrictions took increasingly aggressive forms, leading to various forms of protest and social unrest (Wood et al., 2022). In New York, for example, protests and unrest were reported as the deadline for 'municipal workers'[1] to get vaccinated against Covid-19. Those who had not complied were forced to take unpaid leave or quit their job unless, of course, they got the vaccination (Bellafante, 2021). Across parts of India many people reunited their efforts by protesting against lockdown policies, often resulting in *"episodes of state repression and violent enforcement"* (Campedelli & D'Orsogna, 2021: 5). Protests became more frequent in New Zealand too, where people from varied backgrounds including individuals who were unvaccinated and vaccinated converged to protest against the vaccine mandates (Gauld, 2022).

---

[1] This includes police officers, firefighters, and teachers.

Similarly, one year into the vaccine campaign, increased frustration with the measures and vaccine pressure was felt in Europe. In France, an increase in case infections was met with the increased use of stringent measures to prove people were vaccinated. Therefore, over 100,000 people protested in early January 2022 (Al Jazeera, 2022). This followed up on the previous unrest during the summer of 2021 when around 200,000 people protested France's pass sanitaire (Drew, 2022). In the Netherlands, violent protests erupted in January and November 2021 as the government considered imposing restrictions on the unvaccinated and further lockdowns (Neumayer et al., 2023). Some 40,000 people also protested in Vienna, the capital of Austria, which was only a few weeks away from making the vaccine *compulsory* for all citizens (Al Jazeera, 2022). While protests also occurred in Germany and Italy, media and political institutions were quick to label the dissent as 'a minority'.

Towards the end of January 2022, similar protests evolved in cities across the Netherlands after the country experienced a hard lockdown over the Christmas period (De Wouw, 2022). This was in the wake of previous protests in 2021, where police shot at protestors who had started fires and threw rocks and fireworks at officers (BBC, 2021). The violence that erupted was downplayed by the Prime Minister, Mark Rutte, who called the protestors 'idiots' who 'threatened democracy' (Rankin, 2022). In neighbouring Belgium, there were similar protests against the vaccine pass and making it compulsory for healthcare staff (Rankin, 2022).

In the UK, resurgent variants in the form of Omicron and high infection rates—but not increased hospitalisations or deaths—also produced knee-jerk political responses that seemed to be directed at health and social care staff. During the summer of 2021, political discussion started to circulate about ways to prevent future infection rates. This was in the face of growing evidence that while the vaccine had significant impact on preventing hospitalisation, it did not prevent infection (Stokel-Walker, 2022). Consequently, a petition was circulated which demanded *"health and social care workers are given the right to exercise free will in relation to any medical procedure and so to be able to refuse to take the covid 19 vaccination without fear of facing discrimination at work or in wider society"* (see: UK Government and Parliament Petition, 2021). On learning of the possible mandatory vaccination, one of our participants, Susan, a former care home manager, described it as *"unethical, illegal, discriminatory tyranny"*. Susan then handed her notice in, having worked in the sector for over 30 years. Reflecting on her decision, she said *"I am sad to be losing my job in four weeks, but I won't be threatened to stay in work"*.

The UK Government then targeted NHS staff by announcing new similar requisites for mandatory vaccination towards the end of 2021 as the Delta variant continued to circulate. This was despite evidence that suggested healthcare workers—regardless of their own vaccination status—were opposed to mandatory vaccination. Staff were told to get vaccinated before 1 April 2022, or lose their job (Rimmer, 2021). From a survey of 5,633 NHS workers between 21st April and 26th June 2021, only one in six respondents favoured mandatory vaccination (Woolf et al., 2022: 11), believing that *"building trust, educating, and supporting HCWs who are hesitant about vaccination may be more acceptable, effective, and equitable"*.

The UK Government launched a consultation where 90,000 staff responded, overwhelmingly rejecting the motion with 90% supporting its withdrawal (Unison, 2022). Days before the deadline, the motion was abandoned by the Health Secretary as it was felt the country 'was better prepared' in light of increased vaccination among health care workers. The threat seemed to have worked. From September 2021 to February 2022, 127,000 staff came forward to get the vaccination (Iacobucci, 2022). Nevertheless, this approach harmed the NHS labour force. Iacobucci (2022) outlines how by January 2022, 80,092 staff (5.4% of the total NHS workforce) remained unvaccinated while estimates suggest mandatory vaccination led to the loss of 40,000 staff in care homes. For many NHS staff who opted to stay in the profession, they remain highly stressed, burnt out, and often suffer from mental health problems (Lloyd et al., 2023).

While the political and scientific establishment further used media entities to disseminate their policy messages on vaccines, other institutions also compelled unvaccinated people to 'get protected'. Although we can critically question the degree to which governments pay attention to academic research, many academics reinforced the call for vaccination. The sociologist Liao (2022: 4) analysed protest slogans and public sentiment of those opposed to the vaccine and concluded: *"the only way forward is to correct the misinformation/disinformation about vaccination and to emphasize each citizen's civic responsibilities for the collective good"*. Writing in one of the most prestigious scientific journals, *Nature*, Hotez (2022: 525) placed blame upon the unvaccinated, claiming even though the vaccine had become widely available during the summer of 2021 *"at least 200,000 unvaccinated Americans have lost their lives potentially needlessly because they refused to have a Covid immunization"*. Hotez (2022: 526) concluded how the barrier to complete vaccination was:

> An organized, well-funded and empowered anti-science movement now threatens to spill over and threaten all childhood immunizations in the USA and globally...Anti-vaccine activism now costs human lives on scales that exceed global terrorism or other established threats. We must recognize the depth and breadth of anti-vaccine activism and its detriment to global security.

The new wave of anti-vaxxers were now responsible for jeopardising future immunisation efforts, even if vaccine hesitancy/rejection has always been a feature of the history surrounding vaccines and was increasing pre-Covid-19 (Chapter 3). However, while many frown upon these protests, whether because they pose a risk in terms of viral transmission or in political opposition, it is incumbent upon social scientists to listen and make sense of these concerns. Working on a government funded-research project, German researchers claimed that such protests produced sizable increases in infection rates (of up to 35%) in activists' home regions after they had concluded (Lange & Monscheuer, 2022). However, while infection rates may have inevitably increased among protest attendees as social distancing measures were broken, other more robust evidence generated by the Center for Health Economics & Policy Studies (CHEPS) at San Diego State University suggests that such events did little to a country's overall infection rate. In their study funded by a philanthropic foundation. Dave et al. (2020) used data from 286 US cities where Black Lives Matter protests took place and found:

the protests had little effect on the spread of COVID-19 for the entire population of the counties with protests during the more than five weeks following protest onset. (34)

We feel it is illustrative of the political atmosphere and media pressure about Covid-19 restrictions and the vaccine that a *government-funded study* indicates such protests are a 'public health threat' but causes such as Black Lives Matter seem to, by comparison, raise few alarm bells. This represents what Kampmark (2020) notes as the 'politicisation of public health science'.

From Heavy Hand to Iron Fist: New State Powers

How far would the emergency powers granted to tackle the pandemic actually stretch? The answer was, in Canada's case, as far as it took. By early 2022, the Omicron variant had superseded the earlier Delta variant and was circulating in many countries. Canadian Prime Minister, Justin Trudeau, seemingly unsatisfied with the already high vaccination rate in his country (87% of five and older have one shot and 80% were fully vaccinated, one of the highest in the world), required children under 12 to show proof of vaccination for indoor sports activities and then started to turn further on the 'unvaccinated population'. In a speech which seemed to be a toned-down version of Macron's blast against the unvaccinated, Trudeau declared that it was in fact *"fellow Canadians"* who were *"angry and frustrated"* about *"people who still refuse to get vaccinated"* (Hodder-Williams, 2022; see also Robbins, 2022). One of our Canadian participants, an electrical engineer in her early 40s, recognised this and told us how *"the restrictions suck"*. She then drew a line from *"false positive Covid-19 test systems"*, which facilitated *"interest in contracting corrupt big pharma for vaccines as a solution"*. This in turn led to *"public questions silenced by bent politicians"*, which manifested in protests due to *"extreme vaccine mandates that are based on fear and bias opinion polls"*. A Canadian estate agent in her early 30s was also critical of the handling of Covid-19 and the basis for the restrictions:

> Canada has handled Covid-19 horribly. My country is punishing all to help a select few. We seem to have more stringent control efforts in place than many other countries and it doesn't seem to have a very positive outcome. Studies have shown that masks do not help stop the spread. And yet the government insists on us wearing them. The vaccine has shown little efficacy when it comes to transmission so what is the point in taking a vaccine that will not stop you from getting Covid. The government here has completely gone beyond the scope of its authority by forcing citizens to take the vaccine for a virus that has little more effect than a common flu would have.

Despite the social pressure placed upon these two women, they had managed to navigate their daily lives without taking the vaccine. It was people like them who would be in the Prime Minister's authoritarian line of rhetorical and policy fire as Omicron continued to spread and heightened political attention turned to the unvaccinated. Trudeau (Cited in Zimonjic, 2022) concluded they were *"irresponsible"* and *"remained a problem"*. In an appeal in Parliament, he said:

> It's not just about governments and health workers frustrated that there are Canadians who still continue to choose to not get vaccinated. It's fellow Canadians as well. When people are seeing cancer treatments and elective surgeries put off because beds are filled with people who chose not to get vaccinated, they're frustrated. When people see that we are in lockdowns or serious public health restrictions right now because of the risk posed to all of us by unvaccinated people, people get angry.

Trudeau eventually passed a mandate which would require them to be fully vaccinated. Although the truckers were initially heralded as 'heroes' during the country's first lockdown as they continued to work transporting goods around the country, they were now in the opposing corner as threats to public health. With an election looming in April 2022, this looked to be Trudeau's attempt to shore up his own popularity by singling out the unvaccinated as responsible for increased Covid-19 infections (Briggs et al., 2021a). Canadian media outlets such as CTV reiterated governmental concern in numerous reports, citing 'projected' hospitalisation rates due to the unvaccinated (Zaida, 2022). However, these projections failed to materialise.

The vaccine mandate imposed by Trudeau, though, was met with quick opposition. By the end of January 2022, a convoy of truckers had made its way to Ottawa in protest at the new restrictions. Naming themselves the Freedom Convoy, their motivations did not only derive from the vaccine mandate but also a reflection of the general frustration with the pandemic management and associated interventions. Bubba, one of our participants, a Canadian trucker who regularly crossed the US border, told us *"I sit alone in my truck, I hardly talk to anyone, who am I going to infect? I mean come on, man! We aren't even talking about a deadly disease. Most folks I know, including myself, just got a bad cold for a few days…we are being told to fear everything when there is nothing to fear. We WANT FREEDOM from this tyranny, man"*.

Bubba had left his family at home and set up his truck on the main central area on Parliament Hill in the centre of Ottawa. At the time, this place was becoming the arrival point for hundreds of heavy-duty trucks, pickup trucks, and other vehicles, operated by individuals who said they were fed up with the social restrictions and vaccine mandates. The movement grew and truckers also started to block other roads and even US border crossings, interrupting supply chains between the two countries. Protest banners demanded restoration of rights and freedom to travel, and the abandonment of rules associated with the management of Covid-19, such as requiring vaccination to either work, travel, or eat at a local restaurant.

As the protests continued and gathered some public support, Trudeau labelled the movement *"a threat to national security"* and labelled the protestors a *"fringe minority"* who *"disrespected science"* (Naughtie, 2022). Trudeau alleged that the *"racist"* protestors were causing *"hate and division"* by exercising their right to protest (Al Jazeera, 2022), while other commentators cast them as a right-wing extremist fringe movement engaged in violence (Saria & Satyogi, 2022). This mass gathering provoked Trudeau to engage the National Emergency Act legislation, which is normally initiated in the event of public health, public order, and international threats to sovereignty crises. The Act enabled orders to be issued to ban protests, which were believed to lead to illegal activity, deter gatherings near or around border crossings, and grant licence to tow trucks to assist in the removal of the vehicles. Four days later on February 18, heavily armed police moved into the area to disperse the protestors. It took two days to move the convoy, resulting in 200 arrests, 400 criminal charges predominately related to obstruction, and the removal of 115 vehicles (Canadian Press, 2022). The demonstration had lasted just 23 days.

In keeping with Wagner's (2022) caution about the expansive and concentrated powers provided by a state of emergency, other powers were granted under the Act including the confiscation of funds used to support the protests. The Canadian authorities issued warrants to crowdfunding websites and other payment-processing companies such as PayPal to declare the names of those who donated money in support of the truckers. Overall, $3 million was seized and over 200 bank accounts belonging to a mixture of companies and individuals were frozen. In a subsequent letter written to lawmakers, representatives of the Freedom Convoy claimed police engaged in *"violent tactics"* and warned politicians about the precedent the Trudeau Government was setting (Cited in Vieira, 2022). Although accounts were unfrozen on February 21 and the emergency powers dropped on February 23, it is important to bear in mind the Freedom Convoy's statement (Cited in Vieira, 2022) below:

> This is no longer a partisan subject or a matter of political opinion. We must ask ourselves with the long-term implication in mind: how far can the police be allowed to go against peaceful demonstrations?

While many Western liberal societies chose to undertake an authoritarian set of lockdown policies to manage Covid-19, other countries went a step further and adopted an eradication strategy commonly referred to as 'Zero-Covid'. The containment measures associated with these approaches included lockdowns, quarantine for travellers, contact tracing and isolation, routine testing of key populations, and community-wide screening. Such approaches also generated a mixture of compliance and unrest (Bleakley, 2021) as aggressive government pursuit of viral eradication faltered. Woolhouse (2022) notes that eradication of Covid-19 was always unlikely given the slow responses to its emergence. As such, its persistence was perhaps blamed, unfairly, on compliance levels or not being aggressive enough. In places like Australia and New Zealand, liberal Governments engaged such approaches and closed their borders for lengthy periods in an effort to reach 'Zero Covid', as did more authoritarian countries such as China.

When Covid-19 hit the shores of Australia early in 2020, the government acted quickly. During March 2020, borders were closed, and quarantine hotels were established for those residents wishing to return home. Individual states also closed their borders, opening them periodically between detected local outbreaks. Social distancing was promoted, and non-essential services were closed such as restaurants, bars, and clubs leaving the operation of construction, manufacturing, and many retail organisations. As an outbreak of Covid occurred during the summer of 2020, a strict lockdown was called particularly in the Victoria territory with the army called in along with helicopters to secure high vigilance and compliance (see: Bleakley, 2021). Such an approach set a precedent for later outbreaks in Sydney and Melbourne during the summer of 2021 when the Delta variant started to circulate.

Unsurprisingly, Mitch, a marketing manager from Victoria who had reluctantly taken the vaccine under pressure, said: *"vaccines are wildly popular, generally. I think the negative government narrative on unvaccinated people, the hysteria in the media towards the unvaccinated and the mandating of the vaccine in places like Victoria is actually working towards increasing the number of people who will resist taking this vaccine"*. Maisie, a female student in her late 20s from the same area, said:

> My country has overreacted to the point the harm of their actions is greater to people of all ages than any harm the virus could have done. Health, well-being and life is about more than controlling the transmission of a single virus but this has been forgotten. All this harm for a virus which doesn't pose a significant risk to the majority. My country has turned into a nightmare and I feel as if I've been set on fire for some greater good I'm not a part of, and my mental and physical health has been destroyed. No public health measures should cause such immense harm. (Female, 27, Student, Australia)

Bernadette, an unemployed woman in Sydney, described the above as representing *"the erasing of history"*, intimating that the pressure to vaccinate is something which *"cracks you"*. She added:

> One day with all this shit around you and you are tired and exhausted. I just avoid those people, for my own mental health. These people who put on Facebook how they believe in science and they say 'I am double vaccinated'. I am not vaccinated and at Christmas they invited me to meals. I was told to do a self-test. We all made the test and I couldn't believe I was doing it. It is so funny, it is like a Dali painting, it is so funny.

Understandably, given these words, Bernadette was critical of the *"government overreach"* feeling that *"there is no journalism. There is no politician speaking out. There are just odd groups of people like me scattered around who see what is going on"*. She suggested the most disturbing aspect was— *"I mean, the quarantine camps topped them all, I mean what is going on with society?"* She refers to the policy some Australian states took up to quarantine people who could not safely self-isolate at home. Designed for both vaccinated and unvaccinated people, the camps were constructed to temporarily house people in these situations, the former staying a shorter period of seven days while the latter 14 days until 'covid-free'. Once again, the effectiveness of such an approach was found to be more harmful to people, particularly on their mental health, compared to the initial potential risk of infection (Grout et al., 2021).

Throughout the two-year period in which Australia's borders were closed to international travellers, localised and intense lockdowns were used to facilitate exhaustive contact tracing of new outbreaks. The app that was supposed to facilitate such tracing, much like its UK equivalent (Briggs et al., 2021a), similarly failed and *"was not sufficiently effective to make a meaningful contribution to the Covid-19 response"* (Vogt et al., 2022: e250). Public pressure grew on the government in the form of 'freedom rallies' as it became clear that such stringent measures could not be maintained. By July 2021, the Australian Government's rhetoric started to shift towards 'living with the virus' and a return to zero tolerance of dissent was discarded. Perhaps reluctant to relinquish its accumulated power structures and control mechanisms (see: Wagner, 2022 on states of emergency), the Australian Government wanted to move towards such a scenario on their own terms.

Much of the discontent, though apparent also in the cities of Sydney, Brisbane, Perth, and Adelaide, was concentrated in Melbourne in the territory of Victoria. According to Victoria Premier (political leader) Daniel Andrews, the transition to 'living with Covid', was to make use of the Public Health and Wellbeing (Pandemic Management) Bill 2021. Such a Bill was to permit the *"Premier to make an indefinite declaration of a pandemic and state of emergency, give the health minister power to make broad public health orders, and grant authorised officers the power to detain people under quarantine"* (Convery, 2021). In fact, the Premier had been attempting to speed up the bill before Australia's emergency powers expired on 15 December 2021. Like Trudeau in Canada, the political elite in Australia were attempting to push through stringent policies on social control to endure into the post-Covid period (Chapter 4).

Many of these protestors had been branded as *"white supremacists"* and the *"racist far right"*, and their presence generated a smaller and more insignificant counter demonstration by the Campaign Against Racism and Fascism (CARF). CARF, a coalition of progressive activists and left-wing organisations, declared their gathering was to highlight the *"conspiracy theorists"* and *"far right"* present at the 'freedom rallies' (Convery, 2021). As she took to the stage, one activist said that *"hostility to vaccines and other important health measures has become a gateway to the far-right globally"*, and how the group would *"not allow fascist groups to propagate their bigotry and occupy our streets without resistance"* (Convery, 2021).

New Zealand also seemed to be a breeding ground for similar *"bigots"*, *"racists"* and *"white supremacist"* anti-vaxx opposition (Miller, 2023). Yet New Zealand had followed the similar 'zero tolerance' pathway to Australia. The country quickly closed its borders to non-citizens mid-way through March 2020, and had begun isolating new arrivals in quarantine hotels by 10 April 2020. The country also entered a strict lockdown, whereby people were told that to avoid transmission they should avoid meeting in public or even talking to their neighbours. In a Facebook live broadcast on 20 April 2020, Jacinda Ardern (Cited in McGuire et al., 2020: 372), spoke of how:

> I think the way that I would describe it is that success doesn't mean zero Covid cases, because we still get cases. It means zero tolerance for cases. It means as soon as we know we have a case, we go in straight away, we're testing around that person, we're isolating them ... we contact trace, we find out all the people who may have been in contact with them while they could have passed it on. That's how we keep stamping out Covid cases whenever they come up. That's quite a different strategy from other countries.

This strategy was considered a success by the summer of 2020, with the country lasting 102 days without any community transmission (Cumming, 2022). However, when four people from one family in Auckland tested positive early in August 2020, the whole city was placed into a strict lockdown. Despite the relatively few cases that were detected from this small outbreak, the city remained under tight Covid restrictions for the best part of two months. There seemed to be some opposition to this approach in the form of social protest of a few thousand people. There then followed other small outbreaks and temporary restrictions in February, March, and June of 2021 before a three-day national lockdown and one week lockdown in Auckland were declared in August 2021 on the detection of one Covid case in Auckland (Dyer, 2021). This was the nation's first domestic transmission of the virus in six months (Dyer, 2021). Despite the lockdown, case numbers continued to rise until the government conceded that the Zero-Covid strategy had failed, citing the contagiousness of the new Delta variant.

There was almost no mention or acknowledgement of the protests which took place as the Autumn progressed to Winter in 2021 when the Prime Minister Jacinda Ardern announced that people working in health, disability, corrections, and education sectors as well as in business and hospitality needed to be vaccinated (Kukutai et al., 2021). Simultaneously, Ardern made proof of vaccination necessary to gain access to gyms, hairdressers, events, cafes, and restaurants (Miller, 2023). Trnka (2022) describes how protests ensued late into 2021 and across February–March

2022, whereby around 3,000 protestors marched outside Parliament in the capital, Wellington, for 23 days before police were able to disband them. Ardern refused to speak to representatives of the movement and *"went as far as describing the protestors as under the spell of foreign powers, declaring that their movement 'feels imported to me' as 'it's not the way we protest in New Zealand'"* (Cited in Trnka, 2022: 219).

The answer many Western liberal nations had to potential opposition and unrest has been crushingly aggressive and often followed by increased public threats about the anti-vaxxer group and disproportionate treatment. These nations were not dissimilar, in some ways, to authoritarian dictatorship regimes. In Russia, for example, a long-standing mistrust with the state apparatus significantly affected the motivation for Russians to get the Covid-19 vaccine. King and Mukhina (2021) point out that one of the main reasons why Russia remained one of the lowest vaccinated countries was because of the fraught relations between the government and its citizens; vaccine decision-making became an arena for the enactment of resistance to the state. Indeed, as of April 2023, the rate of fully vaccinated Russian citizens was around 55 per 100 people (Statista, 2023).

Even though hospitalisation and mortality rates have been difficult to ascertain—primarily because the Russian authorities counted only patients who demonstrably died from Covid-19 and used generic and ambiguous diagnoses such as 'atypical pneumonia'—the pandemic context and lack of interest from the government with putting in measures generated significant discontent. Perhaps used to how dissent is dealt with in public spaces, the Russians took to online platforms to flood the internet with critical messages against the government (Bodrunova, 2020). However, these platforms were quickly censored, and the daily business of co-optation and repression resumed.

For nearly three years, parallel suppression of opposition to governmental measures against Covid-19 took place in China. Like Australia and New Zealand, the Chinese governmental apparatus opted to pursue a Zero-Covid policy with any detection of Covid cases resulting in significant and quick lockdowns (Ong, 2023). In some instances, lengthy lockdowns were bolstered by stringent policing and severe consequences for those in breach. Even then, those who tested positive were forced to stay in quarantine camps. Complemented by social distancing, masks, mass testing, and track and trace applications, these measures were reported to be an initial success although there was little faith in the official statistics on 'cases', 'hospitalisations', and 'deaths' (Yerulshalmy, 2022).

However, numerous lockdowns and associated distancing measures meant people had very little exposure to the virus—and the vaccination rate remains lower than in many similar countries. Furthermore, China devised their own vaccine and refused to import other, more effective vaccines developed in the West. But infectious variants and low immunisation of the most vulnerable group resulted in increased infections and deaths (Shridhar, 2022). Much anger and frustration bubbled under the public surface until a series of events intensified it. In September 2022, a 'quarantine bus' crashed killing all the passengers (Ong, 2023) in the province of Guizhou where, over two and a half years, it was reported that only two people had died of Covid-19 (Thomas & Jalil, 2022). A fire also broke out in an apartment block in Urumqi, Xinjiang province, late in October 2022. The residents in the block, fearful of the consequences of leaving their homes because of the repercussions from the state police, remained in their apartments resulting in the loss of ten lives. The next day, collective indignation began to accumulate when angry neighbours spilled out on to the street to protest.

The continual stress and strain on the economy and peoples' everyday lives culminated in widespread social protests across Chinese cities particularly in late 2022, whereby particularly students gathered in opposition against the continual use of Covid restrictions (Ong, 2023). The police were quick to arrest young people who were found with specific apps like Telegram and regarded as possible protest organisers. By December 2022, the protests had resulted in a governmental shift towards the management of Covid-19 and the state quarantine camps were abandoned, allowing people to isolate at home if they had mild or no symptoms. Tests were also discarded, and people were allowed to travel more freely inside the country. Of course, Zero-Covid was always an impossibility and anti-scientific policy; but under *"China's stifling political climate, this notion cannot be uttered, let alone debated"* (Kirby, 2022: 1026).

At the outset of the pandemic, China's swift and decisive approach became the model that most of the world would follow. Almost three years later, ironically, protests at the authoritarian, divisive, and exclusionary policies enacted throughout the pandemic spread from the rest of the world back to China. The potential consequences of this sudden and unanticipated shift towards authoritarianism, particularly in what were purportedly liberal democracies, and the evidence of both submission and resistance to this from sections of their populations, will now be the focus of the next and final chapter of our book.

References

Al Jazeera. (2022). *Anti-vaccine protesters rally in France, Germany, Austria, Italy.* Accessed on 2 April 2023. https://www.aljazeera.com/news/2022/1/9/more-than-100000-rally-in-france-against-covid-vaccine-rules

Anderson, J. (2022). COVID-19 in the Airline Industry: The good, the bad, and the necessary. *Comment and Controversy, 32*(2), 92–99.

Antonini, M., Eid, M. A., Falkenbach, M., Rosenbluth, S. T., Prieto, P. A., Brammli-Greenberg, S., McMeekin, P., & Paolucci, F. (2022). An analysis of the COVID-19 vaccination campaigns in France, Israel, Italy and Spain and their impact on health and economic outcomes. *Health Policy Technology, 11*(2), 1–13.

Attwell, K., Roberts, L., & Ji, J. (2022). COVID-19 Vaccine Mandates: Attitudes and effects on holdouts in a large Australian University population. *International Journal of Environmental Research on Public Health, 19*(6), 1–19.

Bardosh, K., Figueiredo, A., Gur-Arie, R., Jamrozik, E., Doidge, J., Lemmens, T., Keshavjee, S., Graham, J., & Baral, S. (2022). The unintended consequences of COVID-19 vaccine policy: Why mandates, passports and restrictions may cause more harm than good. *British Medical Journal of Global Health, 7*, 1–14.

BBC. (2021). *Covid-19: Dutch police break up anti-lockdown protest. BBC.* Accessed on 30 April 2023. https://www.bbc.co.uk/news/world-europe-56393820

Bellafante, G. (2021). What the antivaxxers actually want. *New York Times*. Accessed on 29 April 2023. https://www.nytimes.com/2021/10/29/nyregion/anti-vaccine-protests.html

Berkman, B., Miner, S., Wendler, D., & Grady, C. (2022). The ethics of encouraging employees to get the COVID-19 vaccination. *Journal of Public Health Policy, 43*(2), 311–319.

Biden, J. (2021). *Remarks by President Biden on the importance of COVID-19 vaccine requirements*. The White House.

Bleakley, P. (2021). The fight to remain compliant: Public sentiment, pandemic and policing the second 2020 Victorian lockdown. *Journal of Contemporary Crime, Harm, Ethics, 1*(1), 23–44.

Briggs, D., Telford, L., Lloyd, A., Ellis, A., & Kotzé, J. (2021a). *Lockdown: social harm in the Covid-19 era*. Palgrave Macmillan.

Bodrrunova, S. (2020). Contributive action: Socially mediated activities of Russians during the COVID-19 lockdown. *Media International Australia, 177*(1), 139–143.

Campedelli, G., & D'Orsogna, M. (2021). Temporal clustering of disorder events during the COVID-19 pandemic. *PLoS ONE, 16*(4), 1–27.

Canadian Press. (2022). Nearly 400 criminal charges laid, 79 vehicles towed. *Ottowa City News*. Accessed on 15 April 2023. https://ottawa.citynews.ca/police-beat/nearly-400-people-facing-criminal-charges-ops-5085098

Convery, S. (2021). Australia Covid protests: Threats against 'traitorous' politicians as thousands rally in capital cities. *The Guardian*. Accessed on 20 April 2023. https://www.theguardian.com/australia-news/2021/nov/20/australia-covid-protests-threats-against-traitorous-politicians-as-thousands-rally-in-capital-cities

Cowden, S., & Yuval-Davis, N. (2022). Contested narratives of the pandemic crisis: The far right, anti-vaxxers and freedom of speech. *Feminist Dissent, 6*, 96–132.

Cumming, J. (2022). Going hard and early: Aotearoa New Zealand's response to Covid-19. *Health, Economics, Policy and Law, 17*, 107–119.

Dave, D., Friedson, A., Matsuzawa, K., Sabia, J., & Safford, S. (2020). Black Lives Matter and risk avoidance: The case for civil unrest during a pandemic. Working Paper 27408. National Bureau of Economic Research.

Devonish, D., & Dulal-Arthur, T. (2022). Perceived COVID-19 vaccine pressure in the Caribbean: Exploring a new stressor-strain phenomenon in the pandemic. *Vaccines, 10*(238), 1–14.

De Wouw, P. (2022). Protest in Netherlands against coronavirus measures. *Reuters*. Accessed on 18 April 2023. https://www.reuters.com/world/europe/protest-netherlands-against-coronavirus-measures-2022-01-16/

Drew, L. (2022). Did COVID vaccine mandates work? What the data say. *Nature News, 607*, 22–25.

Dyer, O. (2021). Covid-19: Australian outbreak surges as New Zealand sees first domestic cases in six months. *British Medical Journal, 374*, 1–2.

Dyer, O. (2022). Covid-19: Quebec to tax the unvaccinated as vaccine mandates spread in Europe. *British Medical Journal, 376*, 1–2.

Ernst, E. (2021). *Anti-vaxers tend to be uneducated and ignorant – THOSE WHO KNOW NOTHING MUST BELIEVE EVERYTHING.* Edzard Ernst. Accessed on 28 April 2023. https://edzardernst.com/2021/12/anti-vaxers-tend-to-be-uneducated-and-ignorant-those-who-know-nothing-must-believe-everything/

Ellis, A., Briggs, D., Lloyd, A., & Telford, L. (2021). A ticking time bomb of future harm: Lockdown, child abuse and future violence. *Abuse: An International Impact Journal, 2*(1), 37–48.

Gauld, R. (2022). A review of public policies on Covid-19: The New Zealand experience. *Public Administration and Policy*. https://doi.org/10.1108/PAP-04-2022-0028

Gearhart, S., Coman, I., Moe, A., & Brammer, S. (2023). Facebook comments influence perceptions of journalistic bias: Testing hostile media bias in the COVID-19 social media environment. *Electronic News, 17*(1), 3–18.

Grout, L., Katar, A., Ouakrim, D., Summers, J., Kvalsvig, A., Baker, M., & Blakely, T. (2021). Estimating the failure risk of quarantine systems for preventing COVID-19 outbreaks in Australia and New Zealand. *The Medical Journal of Australia, 215*(7), 320–324.

Herby, J., Jonung, L., & Hanke, S. (2022). *A literature review and meta-analysis of the effects of lockdowns on COVID-19 mortality. Studies in Applied Economics*. John Hopkins Institute for Applied Economics, Global Health, and the Study of Business Enterprise.

Hao, F., & Shao, W. (2022, March 25). Understanding the influence of political orientation, social network, and economic recovery on COVID-19 vaccine uptake among Americans. *Vaccine, 40*(14), 2191–2201.

Hodder-Williams, P. (2022). *Public opinion polls and British politics*. Routledge.

Hotez, P. J. (2022). Will anti-vaccine activism in the USA reverse global goals? *Nature Reviews: Immunology, 22*, 525–526.

John, P., Loewen, P., Savani, M., Nyha, B., McAndrews, J., Banerjee, S., Koenig, R., & Lee-Whiting, B. (2022). *Overcoming barriers to vaccination by empowering citizens to make deliberate choices.* The British Academy.

Kampmark, B. (2020). Protesting in pandemic times: COVID-19, public health, and black lives matter, contention. *The Multidisciplinary Journal of Social Protest, 8*(2). https://doi.org/10.3167/cont.2020.080202

Kelly, L. (2022). Kanye West must 'be fully vaccinated' before any concert tour in Australia. *The Sunday Times.* Accessed on 15 April 2023. https://www.timeslive.co.za/sunday-times/lifestyle/2022-02-01-kanye-west-must-be-fully-vaccinated-before-any-concert-tour-in-australia/

Kharaba, Z., Ahmed, R., Khalil, A., Al-Ahmed, R., Said, A., Elnour, A., Cherri, S., Jirjees, F., Afifi, H., Ashmawy, N., Mahboub, B., & Alfoteih, Y. (2022). Parents' perception, acceptance, and hesitancy to vaccinate their children against COVID-19: Results from a national study in the UAE. *Vaccines, 10,* 1–16.

King, S., & Mukhina, A. (2021). Making sense of COVID-19 vaccine hesitancy in Russia: Lessons from the past and present. *The Conversation.* Accessed on 16 April 2023. https://theconversation.com/making-sense-of-covid-19-vaccine-hesitancy-in-russia-lessons-from-the-past-and-present-165716

Kirby, W. (2022). Editorial: Zeroing out on zero-COVID. *Science, 367,* 1026.

Kukutai, T., Clark, V., Mika, J., Muru-Lanning, M., Pouwhare, R., Sterling, R., Teague, V., Watts, D., & Cassim, S. (2021). *The COVID-19 domestic vaccine pass: Implications for Maori.* University of Waikato.

Iacobucci, G. (2022). Covid-19: Government abandons mandatory vaccination of NHS staff. *British Medical Journal, 376,* 1.

Lange, M., & Monscheuer, O. (2022). Spreading the disease: Protest in times of pandemics. *Health Economics, 31,* 2664–2679.

Lazarus, J., Wyka, K., White, T., Picchio, C., Gostin, L., Larson, H., Rabin, K., Ratzan, S., Kamarulzaman, A., & El-Mohandes, A. (2022). A survey of COVID-19 vaccine acceptance across 23 countries in 2022. *Nature Medicine, 29,* 366–375.

Liao, T. (2022). Understanding anti-COVID-19 vaccination protest slogans in the US. *Frontiers in Communication, 7,* 1–5.

Lloyd, A., Briggs, D., Ellis, A., & Telford, L. (2023). Critical reflections on the COVID-19 pandemic from the NHS frontline. *Sociological Research Online,* 1–18. https://doi.org/10.1177/13607804231156293

Martin, S., & Vanderslott, S. (2022). "Any idea how fast 'It's just a mask!' can turn into 'It's just a vaccine!'": From mask mandates to vaccine mandates during the COVID-19 pandemic. *Vaccine, 40*, 7488–7499.

McGuire, D., Cunningham, J., Reynolds, K., & Matthews-Smith, G. (2020). Beating the virus: An examination of the crisis communication approach taken by New Zealand Prime Minister Jacinda Ardern during the Covid-19 pandemic. *Human Resource Development International, 23*(4), 361–379.

Miller, M. (2023). Ardern's covid policy was her 'greatest legacy'— but also her undoing. *The Washington Post*. Accessed on 25 April 2023. https://www.washingtonpost.com/world/2023/01/20/jacinda-ardern-new-zealand-covid-resignation/

Nasralah, T., Elnoshokaty, A., El-Gayar, O., Al-Ramahi, M., & Wahbeh, A. (2022). A comparative analysis of anti-vax discourse on twitter before and after COVID-19 onset. *Health Informatics Journal, 28*(4), 1–17.

Naughtie, A. (2022). Trudeau accuses Canada truckers of 'hate, abuse and racism' as he tests positive for Covid after evacuation. *The Independent*. Accessed on 20 April 2023. https://www.independent.co.uk/news/world/americas/justin-trudeau-covid-canada-convoy-b2004245.html

Neumayer, E., Pfaff, K., & Plumper, T. (2023). Protest against Covid-19 containment policies in European Countries. *Journal of Peace Research*. https://doi.org/10.1177/00223433221135335

Ong, L. (2023). The CCP after the zero-covid fail. *Journal of Democracy, 34*(2), 32–46.

Popova, M., & Valkov, I. (2022). Media representations and the politics of the COVID-19 pandemic in Bulgaria. *Journal of Media Ethics*. https://doi.org/10.1080/23736992.2022.2057313

Rankin, J. (2022). *Violent anti-lockdown protesters are idiots, says Dutch PM*. Accessed on 20 April 2023. https://www.theguardian.com/world/2021/nov/22/violent-anti-lockdown-protesters-are-idiots-says-dutch-pm

Rimmer, A. (2021). Covid vaccination to be mandatory for NHS staff in England from spring 2022. *British Medical Journal, 375*, 1.

Robbins, C. (2022). How Trudeau Botched the Trucker Protests Response. *Foreign Policy*. Accessed on 5 April 2023. https://foreignpolicy.com/2022/03/04/trudeau-trucker-vaccine-protests-canada-communications/

Saria, V., & Satyogi, P. (2022). Crowds and COVID-19: An introduction. *Medicine Anthropology Today, 9*(2), 1–9.

Shridhar, D. (2022). China's Covid crisis demands terrible choices. The world will suffer if this goes wrong. *The Guardian*. Accessed on

14 April 2023. https://www.theguardian.com/commentisfree/2022/nov/28/china-abandon-zero-covid-protests-mass-vaccination

Sonnichsen, A. (2023). Collateral effects of lockdown to combat the COVID-19 pandemic in Austria. *Collateral Global*. Accessed on 7 May 2023. https://collateralglobal.org/article/collateral-effects-of-lockdown-to-combat-the-covid-19-pandemic-in-austria/#fnref-14

Stamm, T., Partheymuller, J., Mosor, E., Ritschl, V., Kritzinger, S., & Moritz, E. (2022). Coronavirus vaccine hesitancy among unvaccinated Austrians: Assessing underlying motivations and the effectiveness of interventions based on a cross-sectional survey with two embedded conjoint experiments. *The Lancet Regional Health – Europe, 17*, 1–12.

Statista. (2023). Number of people vaccinated and fully vaccinated against COVID-19 per 100 population in Russia from December 15, 2020 to April 3, 2023. *Statista*. Accessed on 26 April 2023. https://www.statista.com/statistics/1239299/covid-19-vaccination-rate-in-russia/#:~:text=Russia's%20COVID%2D19%20vaccination%20rate,among%20the%20lowest%20in%20Europe

Stevens, H., Rasul, M., & Oh, Y. (2022). Emotions and incivility in vaccine mandate discourse: Natural language processing insights. *Journal of Medical Internet Research, 22*(2), 1–13.

Stokel-Walker, C. (2022). What do we know about covid vaccines and preventing transmission? *British Medical Journal, 376*, 1–2.

Thomas, M., & Jalil, Z. (2022). China Covid: Quarantine bus crash kills 27 and injures 20. *BBC*. Accessed on 21 April 2023. https://www.bbc.co.uk/news/world-asia-62947897

Trnka, S. (2022). States reimagined: COVID-19, the ordinary, and extraordinary in Aotearoa/New Zealand. *Anthropological Forum, 32*(3), 207–233.

UK Government and Parliament Petition. (2021). *Closed Petition: Do not require health and social care workers to take Covid-19 vaccination*. Accessed on 28 April 2023. https://petition.parliament.uk/petitions/577842

Unison. (2022). *Vaccination as a condition of deployment (VCOD) for health and care workers (England) Frequently Asked Questions*. Unison. Accessed on 22 April 2023. https://www.unison.org.uk/health-news/2022/01/mandatory-covid-vaccination-of-health-and-care-workers-england/

Vergallo, G., Del Rio, A., & Zaami, N. (2022). COVID-19 vaccine mandates: What are the current European public perspectives? *European Review for Medical and Pharmacological Sciences, 26*, 643–652.

Vieira, P. (2022). What is the freedom convoy? Trucker protests in Canada explained. *The Wall Street Journal*. Accessed on 12

April 2023. https://www.wsj.com/articles/freedom-convoy-canada-trucker-protest-what-11644441237

Wagner, A. (2022). *Emergency state: How we lost our freedoms in the pandemic and why it matters.* The Bodley Head.

Wood, R., Reinhardt, G., RezaeeDaryakenari, B., & Windsor, L. (2022). Resisting lockdown: The influence of COVID-19 restrictions on social unrest. *International Studies Quarterly, 66*, 1–16.

Woolf, K., Gogoi, M., Martin, C., Papineni, P., Lagrata, S., Nellums, L., McManus, I., Guyatt, A., Melbourne, C., Bryant, L., Gupta, A., John, C., Carr, S., Tobin, M., Simpson, S., Gregary, B., Aujayeb, A., Zingwe, S., Reza, R., Gray, L., Khunti, K., & Pareek, M. (2022). Healthcare workers' views on mandatory SARS-CoV-2 vaccination in the UK: A cross-sectional, mixed-methods analysis from the UK-REACH study. *eClinicalMedicine, 46*, 1–15.

Woolhouse, M. (2022). *The year the world went mad: A scientific memoir.* Sandstone Press.

Vogt, F., Haire, B., Selvey, L., Katelaris, A., & Kaldor, J. (2022). Effectiveness evaluation of digital contract tracing for COVID-19 in New South Wales, Australia. *Lancet Public Health, 7*, 250–258.

Yerulshalmy, J. (2022). Zero-Covid policy: Why is China still having severe lockdowns? *The Guardian.* Accessed on 14 April 2023. https://www.theguardian.com/world/2022/nov/29/china-zero-covid-policy-what-is-it-and-why-lockdowns-quarantine-protests

Zaida, D. (2022). COVID-19 hospitalizations due to Omicron are vastly underreported: Grassroots organization. *CTV News.* Accessed on 7 March 2023. https://www.ctvnews.ca/health/coronavirus/covid-19-hospitalizations-due-to-omicron-are-vastly-underreported-grassroots-organization-1.6030947

Zimonjic, P. (2022). Trudeau says Canadians are 'angry' and 'frustrated' with the unvaccinated. *CBC.* Accessed on 24 April 2023. https://www.cbc.ca/news/politics/trudeau-unvaccinated-canadians-covid-hospitals-1.6305159#:~:text=It's%20fellow%20Canadians%20as%20well,vaccinated%2C%20they're%20frustrated

7

New Futures of Exclusion

We write this just after the 3rd anniversary of the WHO declaration that the global spread of Covid-19 was a pandemic and the subsequent announcement of lockdowns around the world. Yet by May 2023, the very same organisation (WHO) announced that Covid-19 is no longer a public health emergency of international concern. Unsurprisingly, perhaps then that, for many people, Covid-19 has receded into the background of social life. It has all but vanished from public consciousness. As many politicians announced throughout 2022, we have learned to live with the virus. People continue to catch Covid-19. Some people require hospital treatment. Some people die. In the UK in early 2023, JCVI announced booster vaccinations for high-risk groups such as the elderly and those with underlying conditions (Department of Health & Social Care, 2023). Otherwise, life seemingly goes on as normal and our attention is diverted to high levels of inflation, a cost-of-living crisis, war in Ukraine, climate change, and the other issues that led Adam Tooze (2022) to refer to our age as one of 'poly-crisis'.

Given that most countries dropped vaccine passports, digital certificates, and mandatory vaccinations in 2022 (Telford et al., 2022), is it possible to discuss new regimes of exclusion when, for the most part,

Covid-19 has fallen out of our lives? We believe so, yes. By focusing attention upon the vaccine hesitant and those resistant to enforceable mandates, we have pulled together several threads that not only speak to forms of exclusion *during the state of emergency* but exclusions and divisions that will continue to reverberate as the pandemic continues to quickly fade further into the past. In much the same way that we argue the conditions leading up to the pandemic informed the way in which governments, institutions, and people responded during the crisis, the impact of Covid-19 and how it was managed will inform our societies going forward into the future. As we noted, aside from the multidimensional damage we continue to suffer as a consequence of lockdowns and other Covid-19 restrictions (Chapter 2) as well as the vaccine and its mandates (Chapters 5 and 6), there is an ever-present residue of the pandemic all around us (Hadas, 2022), which now lives on in our politics, in our schools and workplaces, in our social relations, in our media and social media activity.

While we have presented a critical account of the Covid-19 vaccine rollout and government mandates, we feel it is important to reiterate that the development of vaccines was an incredible scientific achievement and they have good benefit to the public health and wellbeing of societies around the world. But the evidence we present in this book leads us to conclude that while the vaccine may have 'saved the lives of some vulnerable people' (Watson et al., 2022), it has equally harmed many people who were not at serious risk from the virus. In the current polarised political climate, simplistic frames of *only* good or *only* bad drown out critical analysis and nuance. For this reason, we believed the Covid-19 vaccines, their development and rollout, as well as the public response, required a critical appraisal. Considering this, we conclude that new forms of social exclusion and division emerged in response to the vaccines. Some of which appear to have receded, such as digital vaccine certificates, and others continue to inform our ongoing social relations including the divisive relationship between the vaccinated majority and the 'anti-vax' minority. More concerning, perhaps, is a lasting division over the relationship to authority. The anti-vaxxers have profoundly lost faith in the State, corporate businesses, and medical science. As we noted in Chapter 1, such institutions were weak going into the pandemic but the consequences of the pandemic and its management will further erode both the efficacy and the faith in public institutions. Ineffective and hollowed-out institutions, what Streeck (2016) calls a process of 'under-institutionalisation' creates significant risks in the future where further crises cannot be dealt with effectively and a real and active political temptation to exercise and inflict authoritarian measures emerges instead. We forecast this will fuel further alienation among the public which may prompt further authoritarian responses and thus recalibrate new futures of exclusion.

For Better, For Worse, For Richer, For Poorer, in Sickness and in Health

One of the critical points raised in this book is the political economy of medicine. The importance of understanding neoliberal capitalism and the conditions it created prior to the pandemic has been made clear particularly in relation to health and economic inequalities (Bambra et al., 2023), patterns of work (Lloyd, 2022), and education and living arrangements (Briggs et al., 2021). As the pandemic cleaved to existing forms of social inequality, it was important to assess the neoliberal trajectory leading up to 2020. In the same vein, it is important to situate the pharmaceutical industry in the context of neoliberal capitalism because concerns regarding vaccine development, the motives of companies like Pfizer, individuals such as Bill Gates, and national governments stem from this political economic reality.

As we noted in Chapter 3, vaccines and other drug development have done much good in the world but in an increasingly under-regulated and profit-driven industry, corners have been cut in relation to patient safety and clinical trials. In addition, political lobbying and pressure has worked in favour of giant corporations, and the bottom line of maximising profitability is often the driving factor in drug development. When we look at the rapid and unbridled profit-making success these companies have had, even in the face of scandals and billion-dollar losses, it feels like we are wedded to the security they provide at times of a public health crisis such as what we witnessed between 2020 and 2022. Echoing the renowned wedding vows, we are bound thus for better, for worse, for richer, for poorer, in sickness and in health.

Nevertheless, all this feeds into a wider neoliberal culture of atomised individualism, distrust, cynicism, and suspicion (Winlow & Hall, 2013). Green and Fazi (2023) conceptualise a techno-media-pharma complex which works in a symbiotic relationship whereby Big Pharma lobbies government to implement their agendas. From early into the pandemic, the government and media narrative—policed by technology companies through digital forms of censorship—presented a single argument that there were no effective treatments for Covid-19 and therefore lockdowns were necessary until a vaccine came along. Although driven by numerous, often conflicting interests and motivations, a consensus quickly emerged that put Big Pharma, some of the most problematic and ethically dubious companies in the world, in the driving seat. Despite a legacy of wrongdoing (Meier, 2020), these companies were waved through without oversight or legal challenge. As if this was not enough, the government, media, and public then often *questioned, ostracised, and silenced the people who found this problematic.*

The relationship between Big Pharma and technology companies existed prior to the pandemic and, in the spirit of Naomi Klein's shock doctrine, saw the pandemic as the necessary crisis to make a forward leap in their own evolution. Advocates for digital identity cards, vaccine certification and the wider implementation of biosecurity measures (Kheriaty, 2022), found in a moment of global crisis the conditions to drive forward their own agenda. This does not have to be an underhanded or conspiratorial development; epidemiologists have increasingly argued that technology will improve the efficiency of contact tracing and Covid-19 represented a real-world emergency where those technologies could be implemented (Woolhouse, 2022). In the absence of convincing political leadership and unanswered questions about the lockdowns led some vaccine hesitant respondents to make connections between the implementation of technology to manage the pandemic with wider and long-standing concerns about privacy and surveillance in a digital age (Pasquale, 2015). As with the political economy of medicine, digital technology and concerns about surveillance predate the pandemic and tap into societal concerns about the use of data, or 'digital gold', and the use of proprietary algorithms to process and make decisions that impact upon our lives (Kuldova, 2022). Many of our participants expressed deep concern about handing over data via contact tracing apps and vaccine certificates, and immediate stories about the mishandling of data did not assuage these concerns.

Divide and Conquer, Exclude and Ostracise

In terms of exclusion, the creation of digital identification based on vaccination status raises significant questions about the formation of what New Zealand's Prime Minister during the pandemic, Jacinda Ardern, admitted would be a two-tier society. As we noted in Chapter 4, pandemic management may in fact require the curtailment of some freedoms or some forms of surveillance to protect either the most vulnerable or the population at large. However, the vaccine passports either proposed or implemented during 2021–2022 created a new social reality whereby individuals were excluded from jobs, travel, and various forms of leisure activity based solely upon vaccination status. While this is undoubtedly a legal issue, it is also a significant sociological issue in terms of the implications of dividing a society in this way and excluding a significant minority of the population. We can begin to observe the effects through social division and antagonism between the two groups, as well as the considerable negative consequences for those now excluded. This included job losses, the inability to travel to see family and loved ones, the economic costs associated with barring people from shops, bars, restaurants, and hotels, not to mention the potential conflicts and flashpoints in each of those locations when people are excluded from entry. While governments may use emergency powers to enact exclusionary laws (Wagner, 2022), it becomes the responsibility of individuals in often low-paying and non-unionised jobs including security guards, shop assistants, bar staff, and taxi drivers to implement those restrictions in practice.

Accordingly, it is perhaps not surprising to see those who feel strongly about vaccination or government mandates resist these developments. As we identified early into the pandemic, the initial solidarity galvanised by ideological governmental messaging when a new 'threat' presented itself quickly dissipated. This was particularly when some peoples' doubts and questions were not addressed about the necessity of lockdowns and the perceived severity of Covid-19. As a mono-science became the central narrative from governments and media institutions and alternative voices were silenced, more people started to resist. These unanswered doubts, as we can see from our participants' testimonies, acted as central foundations for reservations about the vaccine. Governments thereafter started to get heavy handed, and iron fisted with this group. Many states blamed them for subsequent infection increases and labelled their cause as worthless and conspiratorial; the preserve of amoral and unethical individuals concerned only for themselves (Telford et al., 2022).

While many countries rolled back emergency powers and vaccine certification, some cracked down harder and utilised repressive measures. In Chapter 6, we focused on the Zero-Covid approach used in Australia, New Zealand, and China, as well as the Canadian Government's handling of the truckers' protest. This demonstrated how times of crisis can result in governments adopting emergency powers, declaring states of emergency, and circumventing democratic checks and balances with alarming ease (Wagner, 2022). The institutions that we thought would prevent overreach stood by and deployed measures without sufficient oversight or critical questioning. This is perhaps the lesson of Covid-19 in terms of social exclusion. The biosecurity infrastructure created to manage this pandemic is unlikely to disappear simply because the crisis has passed (Green & Fazi, 2023). We are already witnessing the faster shift towards digital currency in terms of banking apps and businesses no longer accepting cash (Scott, 2022). We see this in the increasing use of digital tickets without an offline alternative. QR codes and biometric security are now facts of daily life. The security state created after 9/11 did not vanish once the Taliban were defeated in Afghanistan or Osama Bin Laden was assassinated in 2011. The technological and pharmacological tools that underpin vaccine passports, as well as the technological and media platforms that restrict opinion and dissent, are now facts of life. As such, it is hardly conspiracy theory to suggest that vested interests are keen to see their further implementation. Future pandemics and the climate crisis could result in states of emergency, the use of emergency powers, and the activation of biosecurity infrastructure that has significant implications for social division and exclusion.

Freedom and Security

Perhaps most problematic are the forms of social division and exclusion that characterise the dialogue and rhetoric around vaccine status. Much like the divisions over Trump and Brexit, lockdown and face masks, vaccination status is another flash point that risks hardening into intolerance and intransigence. As this book has emphasised, the reasons for vaccine hesitancy are multiple and nuanced. This minority do not speak with one voice or hold a coherent or universal position. It is problematic to lump them together in one category. There is significant difference between someone with underlying health conditions balancing risk and judging it to be detrimental to their health, and someone who thinks the vaccines are part of a wider plan to move towards a biosecurity surveillance state. However, the mainstream argument that vaccine deniers are morally bankrupt, selfish, and a risk to others is reductive and misses many important distinctions. For some vaccinated people, their moral superiority becomes a marker of identity—'I'm a good person because I'm vaccinated'.

While recognising the important distinction between anti-vax and anti-vaccine mandate, it appears that some within this camp have also elevated their vaccination status to a marker of identity and superiority. Various media outlets across the globe such as France 24 (2023) recently reported that unvaccinated individuals on social media platforms have been referring to themselves as *"true bloods"* or *"pure bloods"* in reference to their refusal to take the vaccine, often suggesting that receiving blood from vaccinated people contaminates the body. As reports emerge of AEs associated with the Covid-19 vaccines, these people have their well-grounded fears confirmed, and are provided with 'proof' that they have made the right choice, preserved their freedom and bodily autonomy, are 'pure' and untainted by experimental drugs. Although situated at the extreme end of vaccine hesitancy, this also represents elevation of vaccine status to an external marker of identity. From what we can see, vaccination status provides a degree of belonging in a world increasingly rattled by crises and where the pressures of possessive individualism are both potent and socially corrosive. Perhaps this speaks to what Hall (2012) calls 'objectless anxiety' and the subject's need to anchor oneself to an external system of meaning making that provides both coherence and understanding. It also provides a marker that allows the subject to 'stand out', while also fitting in to the group.

This form of exclusion, along the lines of vaccination status, creates structural fault lines that may be difficult to cross. If those who believe Covid-19 to be a significant threat eject unvaccinated friends and neighbours from their social circle, while those who believe the vaccine impinges upon bodily autonomy and those individuals who succumb to the pressure are weak and somehow tainted, how do we bridge this hostile divide? As noted above, vaccination poses a set of ethical and moral questions about security, freedom, autonomy, and responsibility. These are complex questions that require understanding, nuance, and a willingness to hear alternative arguments. Unfortunately, for many reasons, that is not the structural climate in which we currently live (Raymen, 2022; Winlow & Hall, 2022). As technology reduces our online networks to echo chambers and people who think like us, and authoritarian politics seeks to identify problematic others, it is more likely that we will see both widening and hardening social divisions coupled with forms of cultural exclusion rather than productive attempts at closing the gap between us. Questions about security and freedom also return us to an earlier point about authority and the role of the state. Trust in authority has weakened significantly, particularly for some groups, and therefore the legitimacy of the state as a provider or facilitator of either security or freedom is damaged. Those who have lost faith in the state, in science, in experts, will increasingly find little common ground with those who continue to trust in those institutions. The social fabric is torn and the lasting legacy of the pandemic may well be greater social division.

Todd McGowan (2022) argues that the politics of the right is always particular while the politics of the left should always be universal. In his account, the universal is only possible through absence—showing each other what we all lack—rather than seeking universality through the accumulation of particulars. Any attempt at politics that seeks support from one group over another is ultimately the politics of the right and is unable to achieve any sought after universal. This is not to say that the politics of the right is doomed to failure. In fact, it is often more successful because it calls to people in a specific way—inclusion is defined in opposition to one another, political enjoyment is possible in being part of the in-group. As such, we can see that the politics of vaccination status is a politics of the right and is focused not on the universal but upon the particular, even when advocated for by those on the left. This divides and excludes people from different social groups and serves to harden their rhetoric, whether one is pro-vaccination or anti-vax. If McGowan is correct, we would need to identify the things we all lack rather than focus on the difference between these two groups if we are to bridge the divide between them.

When we look to the future, we know that new viral pandemics will emerge, and the environmental consequences of climate change may initiate various crises that require restrictive control measures on the activities of human populations. The stage is set for future states of emergency that will likely require individuals to, once again, make great and profound *sacrifices* to protect themselves and one another. The Covid-19 pandemic may be regarded as a litmus test for how much of our freedoms we are prepared to sacrifice in the name of protection and security. However, the onset of the virus and subsequent management also demonstrated how much some people are unwilling to quickly gift power, control, and surveillance to governments in the name of 'public health' or our 'own safety'.

It is imperative that we learn from the mistakes made during the Covid-19 pandemic. Across our body of work, we have, along with many other scholars, highlighted the myriad harms and inequalities experienced throughout this pandemic. Public inquiries such as the ongoing UK Covid-19 inquiry (2023) may recommend lessons learned about pandemic preparedness, government responses, scientific advice, and the differential impact of the virus on different social groups. Any future pandemic, though, will be experienced by us all through the lens of Covid-19. The entrenched divisions wrought by this pandemic will represent the starting point for future pandemics. The vaccine hesitant today will be no less hesitant at the outbreak of the next pandemic. Tools of digital surveillance will be more advanced and perhaps more invasive than current technologies. The tectonic shifts in political economy currently in the first phases of realignment may have solidified and present a different approach to neoliberal governance (Hall, 2022; Winlow & Hall, 2022). If we fail to learn the lessons from this pandemic including the forms of social division and exclusion wrought by what has happened, things will likely be worse next time round. If we do learn the lessons and understand what has happened and why, things may be significantly better, for all of us.

References

Bambra, C., Munford, L., Khavandi, S., & Bennett, N. (2023). *Northern exposure: COVID-19 and regional inequalities in health and wealth*. Policy Press.

Briggs, D., Telford, L., Lloyd, A., Ellis, A., & Kotze, J. (2021). *Lockdown: Social harm in the Covid-19 era*. Palgrave Macmillan.

Department of Health & Social Care. (2023). *JCVI statement on the COVID-19 vaccination programme for 2023*. HM Government. Accessed on 7 May 2023. https://www.gov.uk/government/publications/covid-19-vaccination-programme-for-2023-jcvi-interim-advice-8-november-2022/jcvi-statement-on-the-covid-19-vaccination-programme-for-2023-8-november-2022

France 24. (2023). Vaccine misinformation spawns 'pure blood' movement. *France 24*. Accessed on 7 May 2023. https://www.france24.com/en/live-news/20230125-vaccine-misinformation-spawns-pure-blood-movement

Green, T., & Fazi, T. (2023). *The Covid consensus: The global assault on democracy and the poor – A critique from the left*. Hurst & Company.

Hadas, D. (2022). After Covid: Pandemic restrictions stumble on like zombies. *City Journal*. Accessed on 1 May 2023. https://www.city-journal.org/article/after-covid

Hall, S. (2012). *Theorising crime and deviance*. Sage.

Hall, S. (2022). Neoliberalism and the opportunodemic: Covid-19, Furlough and why we missed the boat (again). *Journal of Extreme Anthropology, 6*(2), 44–62.

Kheriaty, A. (2022). *The new abnormal: The rise of the biomedical security state.* Regnery Publishing.

Kuldova, T. (2022). *Compliance-industrial complex: The operating system of a pre-crime society.* Palgrave Macmillan.

Lloyd, A. (2022). Covid-19 and the future of work: From emergency conditions to regimes of surveillance, governance and optimisation. *Journal of Extreme Anthropology, 6*(2), 1–20.

McGowan, T. (2022). *Enjoyment right and left.* Sublation Press.

Meier, B. (2020). *Pain killer: An empire of deceit and the origins of America's opioid epidemic.* Sceptre.

Pasquale, F. (2015). *The Black Box Society: The secret algorithms that control money and information.* Harvard University Press.

Raymen, T. (2022). *The enigma of social harm: The problem of liberalism.* Routledge.

Scott, B. (2022). *Cloudmoney: Cash, cards, crypto and the war for our wallets.* The Bodley Head.

Streeck, W. G. (2016). *How will capitalism end?* Verso.

Telford, L., Bushell, M., & Hodgkinson, O. (2022). Passport to neoliberal normality? A critical exploration of COVID-19 vaccine passports. *Journal of Contemporary Crime, Harm, Ethics, 2*(1), 42–61.

Tooze, A. (2022). Welcome to the world of the poly-crisis. *The Financial Times.* Accessed on 15 May 2023. https://www.ft.com/content/498398e7-11b1-494b-9cd3-6d669dc3de33

UK Covid Inquiry. (2023). *Terms of reference.* Accessed on 1 May 2023. https://covid19.public-inquiry.uk/terms-of-reference/

Wagner, A. (2022). *Emergency state: How we lost our freedoms in the pandemic and why it matters.* The Bodley Head.

Watson, O. J., Barnsley, G., Toor, J., Hogan, A., Winskill, P., & Ghani, A. (2022). Global impact of the first year of Covid-19 vaccination: A mathematical modelling study. *The Lancet Infectious Diseases, 22*(9), 1293–1302.

Woolhouse, M. (2022). *The year the world went mad: A scientific memoir.* Sandstone Press.

Winlow, S., & Hall, S. (2013). *Rethinking social exclusion: The end of the social?* SAGE.

Winlow, S., & Hall, S. (2022). *The death of the left: Why we must begin from the beginning again.* Policy Press.

Index

A

Abuse
  child/ren 4, 11, 20, 28, 32, 45
  domestic 45
  sexual 28
'Anti-vaxx' 12, 42, 57, 94, 107, 120, 123, 138, 141, 146, 151, 153, 154, 162, 165, 174, 184
Anxiety 11, 20, 29, 30, 38, 45, 112, 123
Australia 7, 22, 23, 93, 95, 120, 135, 137, 144, 151, 152, 170, 172, 174, 188
Authoritarian 2, 8, 10, 13, 21, 31, 34, 35, 42, 113, 140, 146, 154, 167, 169, 170, 174, 176, 185, 190

B

Big data 98, 102
'Big pharma' 12, 45, 56, 63, 65, 66, 69, 76, 146, 186
Bio-tech/nology 68

C

Canada 4, 23, 33, 43, 120, 129, 144, 146, 151, 159, 161, 166, 172
Capitalism
  disaster 101
  neoliberal 6, 7, 64, 80, 185
Censorship 107
China 8, 21, 22, 38, 68, 113, 114, 152, 170, 174–176, 188
Compliance 32
Conspiracy
  theorists 121, 172

theory 79, 94, 99, 101, 106, 113, 154, 188
Corruption 42, 70, 76, 100, 107
Covid-19
  cases 31, 128, 174
  deaths 24, 31, 72
  'deniers' 5, 189
  pandemic 3, 5, 8, 9, 11, 19, 23, 28, 32, 34, 39, 45, 58, 62, 66, 94, 96, 98, 101, 125, 137, 143, 158, 191
  restrictions 56, 76, 119, 136, 151, 152, 160, 166, 184
  test 158, 175
  vaccine 56, 69
  variant 8, 35

Debate
  alternative 104, 157
  critical 109
Digital
  apartheid 108
  censorship 105
  security 97, 98
  surveillance 192
  technology 12, 94–97, 101, 103, 106, 113, 114, 186
Digital capitalism 81, 98
Disease 5, 20, 22, 25, 32, 35, 36, 38, 39, 41, 45, 57–60, 68, 69, 79, 93, 119

European Union 109
'Event' 7, 8

Facebook 4, 34, 38, 41, 43, 97, 106, 122, 137, 155, 172

Germany 4, 7, 23, 27, 38, 44, 55, 63, 75, 135, 144, 151, 158, 159, 161
Global
  crisis 2, 6, 186
  economy 2, 102
Google 96, 106
Government/s
  UK 34, 35, 37, 61, 109, 163, 164
  USA 36, 38, 62, 65, 99, 162

Herd immunity 34, 145

Ideological messaging 135
Immunity 32, 33, 57–59, 74, 77, 80, 110, 129
Inequality 5–7, 11, 40, 59, 103
Information
  dis 154
  mis 154

Lockdown/s
  measures 1, 21, 22, 32, 38, 45, 107, 110, 120, 169, 175
  policies 1–3, 5, 8, 11, 19, 20, 23, 25, 26, 31–37, 41–45, 110, 162, 169

restrictions 22, 24, 114, 121, 124, 152, 158, 163, 173
strict 120, 131, 170, 172, 173

M

Mainstream media 26, 34, 38, 39, 57, 121, 124, 131, 146
Masks 22, 30, 37, 38, 124, 159, 175, 189
Mental health 11, 20, 30, 164, 171
Moderna 55, 56, 71, 74, 79, 80, 126, 127

N

Neoliberalism 6–11, 101, 102
New futures 10, 185
'Nudging' 20, 35, 76, 120, 141, 145

P

Pandemic
  global 9, 20–22, 121
  governance 2, 9, 35, 130, 192
Pfizer 2, 56, 63, 64, 66, 67, 74, 75, 79, 80, 185
Poverty 11, 20, 22, 25, 27, 30–32, 59, 73
Protest 7, 13, 59, 151, 152, 162, 163, 165, 166, 169, 173, 176
Public health 12, 22, 30, 32, 57, 58, 60, 62, 63, 65, 93, 94, 125, 127, 153, 166, 168, 172, 183, 185, 191

R

Resistance 12, 120, 121, 174, 176

Restrictions 38–40, 44, 93, 104, 126, 127, 154, 162, 173, 175, 187

S

Science
  established 57, 58
  one-sided 124
Security 13, 31, 96–98, 108, 109, 114, 185, 187, 188, 190
Self-harm 29
Side effects 67, 76, 77
Social
  control 10, 81, 172
  discontent 162
  division 3, 5, 6, 12, 20, 42, 45, 123, 127, 129, 152, 187, 189, 190, 192
  harm 3, 6, 66, 133
  inequality 185
  Protest 162, 173, 175
Social distancing 1, 5, 21, 22, 36, 41, 126, 152, 165, 170, 175
Social exclusion 3, 6, 11, 26, 111, 184, 188
Social media 21, 39, 105–107, 121, 145, 153, 155, 158, 184, 189
Suicide 29
Suppression
  political 7, 95
  social 45, 95

T

Twitter 29, 34, 106

U

Unemployed 30, 130, 139, 144, 156, 171
Unemployment 25, 30, 32, 45, 102
United Kingdom (UK) 2, 4, 7, 9, 10, 22–25, 29, 32–38, 61, 63, 73, 99, 104, 109, 111, 120, 129, 130, 134, 136, 140–143, 161, 183, 191
United States of America (USA) 6, 8, 10, 24, 29, 30, 32, 33, 43, 56, 60, 64, 69, 73, 75, 100, 111, 120, 124, 140, 155, 161
Unvaccinated 20, 56, 72, 111, 126–129, 133, 135, 137, 142, 144, 146, 153, 155, 156, 161, 162, 164, 166–168, 171, 189, 190

V

Vaccinated
  double 111, 127
  fully 72, 111, 131, 166, 167, 174
  The 12, 123, 126, 143, 144, 155, 184
  triple 55
Vaccine
  campaign/s 55, 72, 121, 127, 133, 152, 161, 163
  hesitant/ce 4, 77, 123, 133, 184, 186, 192
  history 12, 58, 63, 75, 165
  mandate 3, 4, 11, 13, 107, 110–112, 120, 127, 133, 135, 137, 145, 152, 154, 157, 159, 162, 168, 184
  opposition 168
  passport 3, 4, 6, 13, 20, 109–112, 127, 128, 146, 183, 187, 188
Violence 4, 12, 20, 28, 29, 40
Vulnerable
  adults 145
  children 11, 20
  elderly 74, 78
  patients 24

W

World Economic Forum (WEF) 8, 101
World health organization (WHO) 21, 23, 60, 67, 112, 119, 183

Y

Young people 77, 135, 175

GPSR Compliance

The European Union's (EU) General Product Safety Regulation (GPSR) is a set of rules that requires consumer products to be safe and our obligations to ensure this.

If you have any concerns about our products, you can contact us on

ProductSafety@springernature.com

In case Publisher is established outside the EU, the EU authorized representative is:

Springer Nature Customer Service Center GmbH
Europaplatz 3
69115 Heidelberg, Germany

www.ingramcontent.com/pod-product-compliance
Lightning Source LLC
LaVergne TN
LVHW020345260326
834688LV00045B/1536